William Henry Allen, Esq., DL, JP, (1844–1926). Founder of W H Allen, Sons, & Co. Ltd.

THE STORY OF QUEEN'S ENGINEERING WORKS BEDFORD

A History of W H Allen Sons & Co. Ltd

Michael R. Lane

UNICORN PRESS
LONDON

First published 1995 by Unicorn Press
21 Afghan Road
London SW11 2QD

ISBN 0 906 290 09 0

British Library Cataloguing
in Publication Data.
A catalogue record for this
book is available from the British Library.

Produced by Hugh Tempest-Radford *Book Producers*
Typeset by Goodfellow & Egan Ltd, Cambridge
Printed in Great Britain by St Edmundsbury Press

Foreword

by Sir Kenneth Allen, C Eng, FIMarE, MRINA

IT HAS been a pleasure to co-operate with Michael Lane in the compilation of this history of the Company founded by my Grandfather, William Henry Allen in London in 1880 and which he transferred to Bedford in 1894.

Mr Lane, commissioned by the present management, has had access to a considerable amount of documentation concerning the development of the Company. He has emphasised the policy of constant change to meet market requirements altering epoch by epoch. His account will be of considerable interest to a variety of readers – for example; there will be those who will recall the part they played in the past; those who have joined the Company recently or will do so in the future; those who have a desire to gain information about a firm founded at the turn of the century and which has played a major role in the growth of the industrial strength of British industry.

I am pleased Mr Lane has stressed my Grandfather's dedication to training and education, the importance he, and his successors attached to this and to good industrial relations. This approach, in due course, was emulated by many other industrialists.

It is unnecessary for me to highlight any particular area of the Company's activities because Mr Lane has provided a comprehensive account. However, it may be appropriate to mention a few thoughts and memories which come to mind when looking back over my career.

First; I am the proud possessor of the gold watch presented to my Grandfather by J E A Gwynne in 1877 (see Chapter I). I wonder if he would have received it had it been known he would be leaving Gwynnes in 1880 to set up his own business.

Second; when I worked at Deloitte, Plender and Griffith's office in London (see Chapter VI), in the late 1920s, one Saturday morning I was asked to sort out a pile of dusty papers on a corner table. Amongst them I found a copy of a report by W H Allen proposing alterations and improvements to increase efficiency in the Great Western Railway's Swindon locomotive engine works. Unfortunately I do not remember the date. It must have been a feather in his cap to have been invited to undertake this task. The poignance of course, was the

Sheila Hudson. I greatly appreciate their kind assistance and hospitality without which this book would never have been completed. In this connection I must also mention Mr John Kitchenman of the Diesel Engine Department who loaned me much valuable material and commented upon my draft; and Mr Bruno Dukic, the Ex-Works Photographer who produced most of the photographic material I have used.

My greatest pleasure has been the time spent with Sir Kenneth and Mr Norman Allen, grandsons of W H Allen and former Chairmen of the Company. They remained enthusiastic about the project and patient with me, reading and commenting at length upon each and every draft given them. I was constantly reminded of a painting hung in my school assembly hall of a boy sitting at the feet of the great Sir Walter Raleigh listening to stories of his great exploits. I felt privileged to have the benefit of their wisdom and first-hand experiences amongst the great and the good of the engineering and shipbuilding world.

I was fortunate in being put into contact with many former employees of the firm. Ron Alder, the former Financial Director; Henry Ayres and Jack Stennet, formerly of the Diesel Engine Department; Miss Sheila Chancellor, Mr Norman Allen's secretary; E F Clark, a former pupil and today President of the influential Newcomen Society; Alick Hutchinson, the great turbine expert; Gordon Mobbs, the Machine shop foreman; Paul Morgan, John Scivier and John Terry, all pump experts and Arthur Pope the gas turbine designer. To all these helpful people I say thank you. I apologise if any feel that I have not given their particular vested interest sufficient attention. I thank Lady Moser, Herman Oxlin's daughter and Mrs Verena Keable, Roman Strub's daughter for their co-operation and assistance.

I must thank also Mr Nigel Lutt of the Bedford County Archives and members of the Institution of Mechanical Engineers library for their assistance and access to their archives. Mrs Jane Burton has acted throughout as my assistant and secretary and done a splendid job preparing my manuscript on her word processor. My partner in the production of this book, Mr Hugh Tempest-Radford has been, as always, a joy to work with.

Grateful as I am to all those who have helped me, responsibility for the planning and writing of this book, and for any faults and errors, remains mine alone.

Michael R Lane

Street House
Boxted
Bury St Edmunds

Acknowledgments

It has been an enormous pleasure and a privilege to write this book. My first thanks are due to the management of Allen Power Engineering for having asked me to undertake this fascinating and at times obsessively interesting project.

I originally came into contact with Allens of Bedford during a search for archive material concerning William Foster & Co. Ltd of Lincoln whom Allen's acquired in 1960. I was asked to postpone my Foster project to concentrate upon the story of Queen's Engineering Works, who were about to celebrate their centenary. The amount of archive material available, especially their photographic collection, was most impressive and I was soon able to grasp something of the enormous ethos that W H Allen, the founder, and his sons and grandsons had built up in the years 1894–1968.

Clearly, this was a story not only about excellence in mechanical and electrical engineering, but of great foresight and humanity in affairs which lead to the evolution of a great industrial enterprise. Training, good industrial relations, the understanding that loyalty was a two-way process and the building up of an impressive network of friends amongst both customers and suppliers, all play a major part in the Allen story.

The Company's relationship with the Admiralty and the leading British shipyards over many years was almost unique and no less authorities than successive Engineers-in-Chief of the Fleet commented that in both world wars the Fleet would have had the greatest difficulty putting to sea without their Allen machinery.

I am most grateful for the great deal of time the present management devoted to interviews, to the provision of relevant documents and to reading and commenting upon successive drafts of this book. Some may feel I have not made as extensive use of the material provided as I might have done, but there were constraints upon the size of the book and I was anxious to cover as broad a spectrum as possible. A book of this kind may be likened to an iceberg: the information that is seen needs the support of a great deal that remains unseen.

I must make reference to Mr Tony Burton, General Manager; Mr Brian Wood, Business Development Manager; and especially Mrs

Contents

Grandson's discovery of his Grandfathers's *magnum opus*. I was not allowed to keep it.

Third; my brother Norman and I continued the policy of our forefathers by undertaking numerous overseas tours. Henry, Richard, Harold and Rupert Allen had done so as Mr Lane relates.

There is no doubt in my mind that despite visits by senior executives, customers appreciate personal contact with Chairmen and Vice-Chairmen and Directors. Of course, Allens had agents in many parts of the world. In due course it became clear that the volume of business in South Africa and Australia justified establishing subsidiary Companies to handle, on the spot, sales, service and eventually the manufacture of selected items.

I found it intensely interesting and satisfying to be involved in the selection of solicitors, accountants, chairmen and directors – the manager was always, in my time, a Queen's Engineering Works' trained engineer.

As a result of visits to customers, agents and overseas companies many lasting friendships were established and unusual events resulted. Of my recollections of the unexpected I will mention but two. One concerned an invitation by friends in Queensland, Australia, to attend an outdoor barbecue. It was a real trial to consume extremely hot food in great heat and high humidity; but it was part of the job even if one was homesick for normal British conditions. The converse of this happened when other Australian friends, from New South Wales, stayed with us in Bedfordshire. On a warm July afternoon my wife and I motored them through the Duke of Bedford's woodlands at Woburn. I asked what they thought of such an array of broadleaf and other beautiful trees. The Australian wife's answer was 'not bad, but I can't tell you what I would give at this moment for the sight of a gum tree'. She too was thinking of her native land and her normal lifestyle. Michael Lane's book is about more serious matters than these anecdotes.

I hope all who read it will enjoy it as much as I have.

Kenneth Allen

Kenneth Allen

A brief chronology

1844 W H Allen born Cardiff
1868 W H Allen joined John Gwynne
1880 Allen's York Street, Lambeth works established
1890 Richard Allen taken into partnership
1894 Queen's Engineering Works, Bedford established
1900 W H Allen & Son incorporated
1906 Manufacture of internal combustion engines commenced
1908 Percy Crowe appointed Director
1908 Manufacture of *Electra* turbine commenced
1912 Licence to manufacture French Harlé diesel engine
1913 Prototype Fullagar engine produced
1915 Biddenham Works built
1916 800 hp submarine diesel engine produced
1916 Le Rhone rotary aero engine manufactured
1916 Archibald Carmichael replaced James Reid as Works Manager
1918 HM King George and Queen Mary visited Works
1919 Crude oil engines introduced
1920 Company name changed to W H Allen, Sons & Co. Ltd
1920 H G & R S Allen appointed Managing Directors
1921 Burmeister & Wain air blast diesel engines introduced
1924 H E Boyd appointed Company Secretary
1925 Carmichael and Oxlin appointed Non-executive Directors
1926 W H Allen died: Richard Allen appointed Chairman
1927 William Foster, Lincoln acquired Gwynnes
1928 Airless injection diesel engines introduced
1928 Richard Allen, President Institution of Mechanical Engineers
1930 Company's Jubilee year: a year of depression
1931 The Hon Sir Charles Parsons died
1933 Percy Crowe died
1933 Airless injection diesel engines introduced for ship's propulsion and railway locomotives
1934 Licence granted to Jean Crepelle to manufacture diesel engines
1936 Archibald Carmichael retired. W G Poole appointed Works Manager
1937 Kenneth Allen appointed Director
1938 Hampton Pumping Station contract
1942 Richard Allen knighted
1943 Norman Allen appointed Director
1945 War time production exceeds £12 million
1947 Stoeckicht's epicyclic gearing introduced
1948 Gas turbine development work started
1951 Licence obtained for Burmeister & Wain 2-stroke diesels
1952 Company went public and obtained Stock Exchange quotation
1953 Denis Allen, Richard Allen's grandson joined Board
1954 W G Poole retired, succeeded by W A Train as Works Manager
1954 Company employed approximately 2,500 men
1955 Sir Richard Allen died; succeeded by Kenneth Allen
1956 T Golding, E H Hooke and K Rowell appointed Directors
1956 Prudential Assurance subscribed to whole of new £800,000 debenture stock
1956 Turbo-charging introduced on diesel engines
1957 Bedford foundry closed
1958 Ets Dujardin et Cie licensed to manufacture diesel engines
1959 New offices opened by HRH the Duke of Edinburgh
1959 Harold Allen retired
1960 Rupert Allen retired
1960 J W Boddy and P C Saltmarsh appointed Directors
1960 William Foster, Lincoln and Gwynnes acquired
1960 Important contract for Indian pipeline diesel engines
1961 Kenneth Allen knighted
1961 W A Train and E J Goodall appointed Directors
1962 Biddenham Pump Test House opened
1962 Intercooling introduced on diesel engines
1962 Allens acquired Nelson Engineering Ltd and J P Hall & Sons Ltd
1964 3,200 bhp V-form S37 diesel engine introduced
1964 Turbine agreement concluded with Kühnle, Kopp and Kausch
1965 Pump production consolidated at Bedford
1965 Norman Allen President of Institution of Mechanical Engineers
1966 Abortive pump merger talks with Mather & Platt and G & J Weir Holdings
1967 Allens Electrical Department closed
1968 Merger with Belliss & Morcom owners of Crossley Premier engines
1968 Amalgamated Power Engineering Ltd formed

CHAPTER 1

Origins of the Company 1880–1894

The Allen family crest.

EVENTS leading to the establishment of Queen's Engineering Works, Bedford may be traced to the day when young William Henry Allen (1844–1926) left his native Cardiff in search of fame and fortune. Unlike Dick Whittington, his decision to seek employment in London was not motivated by poverty for he came from a well-connected, middle class, Cardiff family. From an early age he had been keenly interested in engineering and saw London as the hub of the many technological advances taking place following the impetus provided by the Great Exhibition held in Hyde Park in 1851. He was not content with the slower pace of change in his native South Wales where the economy was dominated by coal and the manufacture of metals. He wanted to participate in the great debates taking place on wider issues at the leading engineering institutions and learned societies which were all based in the capital. He was no starry-eyed youth and the strength of his ambition will be understood when one considers that at this time he was already the owner of a small engineering company in Cardiff and had the responsibility of a young wife and two children.

W H Allen's descendants

The Allen family came originally from South Molton in Devonshire, the centre of the wool industry in the south west of England. Between 1617 and 1755 successive generations of the family were to provide mayors of the town on no less than ten occasions. In 1752, young William Henry's great-great-grandfather, William I (1726–74) moved to the little Somerset port of Bridgwater, where he acquired a fleet of sailing brigs plying between the north Somerset coast and South Wales. They carried grain and wool outwards and coal on the return journey. He prospered and soon his vessels sailed much further afield. William Henry's great grandfather, William II (1753–88) maintained the family interest in farming at Long Ashton on the outskirts of Bristol, although still retaining close ties with South Molton. His son, William III (1786–1847), after a period on the Long Ashton farm eventually moved to Cardiff where he represented the Nailsea Glassware Company, manufacturers of the then popular Bristol Blue glass, and acted as agent for the family shipping interests. Later he entered the catering business and built up an excellent reputation for his high class establishment catering for banquets, wedding breakfasts and similar functions. The business prospered and was carried on by his son, William George Allen (1816–46) and, after his death by his wife Ann (1810–87). William George was in the habit of making regular visits to London to keep abreast of the latest trends in gastronomy and during one such visit contracted pneumonia from which he died at the early age of thirty, leaving Ann to cope with a four year old daughter, a two year old son and the business.

W H Allen's parents

Ann, widowed after only six years of marriage, came from Llantwit Fardre, a village in Taff Vale, near Pontypridd. She had a strong, extrovert and ambitious character and devoted the remainder of her days to the well being of the children, sparing no expense to ensure that they had a good education and met the right people. Her brother left her valuable property in Barry which rapidly appreciated in value and this, combined with the profits of the successful catering business, were used primarily for the advancement of William Henry's career. Her social awareness was typified by the obvious delight she showed in telling her grandchildren of her earlier friendship with the Marquis of Bute, the ground Landlord of Cardiff and owner of 117,000 acres, and how she became involved with him in the development of Cardiff docks. She provided finance for building a new dock and new coal staithes for the transference of coal from rail to ship. At an early age young William Henry was sent to John Elwell's well known private school at Walliscote House, Weston-Super-Mare, the benefits of which he acknowledged for the remainder of his life. He then went on to Christ's College, Brecon to finish his studies, devoting most of his time to mathematics and mechanical drawing, gaining a Silver Medal awarded by the Department of Science and Art. At the age of 15½ years his mother decided that he should be apprenticed to Richard Neville & Company's Wern Foundry in Carmarthenshire for a period of seven years.

W H Allen's apprenticeship

The firm manufactured colliery machinery and winding gear at its Llanelli works and employed over 1000 hands. Work started at 6.30am which necessitated young William Henry rising at 5.00am and making a 4-mile trek across the bleak Brecon Hills six days a week. The work was heavy for the plant was very old fashioned and everything was done by hand. In later life he often commented, 'I learned my profession the hard way!'

One hundred years later, his grandson Norman recounted one of his grandfather's stories in his own Presidential Address before the Institution of Mechanical Engineers. 'When I joined the Llanelli Works I was interviewed by the master on my first day. He never spoke to me again until the day I left, when he gave me a little homily and a brown paper parcel containing a 3/6d edition of *Pilgrim's Progress*.' He vowed there and then that if ever he owned a company, he would put education and training at the forefront of his objectives. But it was during this period that his love for all things connected with mechanical engineering crystallised and while still a teenager he built his first working model steam engine which was said to have had a 3 in. diameter by 6 in. stroke cylinder. In later life he expressed great regret that unbeknown to him his wife had given the model away.

During his years in Llanelli he became a proficient organist, playing regularly in the little local church. It was there that he fell in love and eventually married a local girl, Ann Pemberton Howell (1847–86) from the nearby village of Felinfoel. The marriage took place in June 1865, and their first born son, Richard William, later Sir Richard Allen, was born in Cardiff in 1867.

Gwynne's Essex Street Works, established in 1849, shown during the construction of the Thames Embankment in 1868.

W H Allen's move to London

In the same year William Henry's elder sister Anne married a man named Nelson Fedden. Sometime before his mother had purchased for £5000 a small engineering works and foundry, Newbury & Company, in Mill Lane, Cardiff, employing about 120 men, for the future benefit of her children. Fedden was placed in charge pending William Henry's return to Cardiff, but he proved to be an inept manager and the business declined rapidly. William Henry returned home in the following year and found himself in the invidious position of being nothing more than a foreman in his own works.

The two men did not work well together and the partnership was soon dissolved. William Henry resolved to seek pastures new, believing that he could better himself elsewhere. In biographical notes written thirty years later he recalled an article in *The Engineer* describing a series of lectures held at The Royal Institution and he decided there and then to head for London. He recalled that at one of these meetings, shortly after he arrived in London, he approached Frederick Bramwell, later Sir Frederick, the famous engineer and President of the Institution of Mechanical Engineers in 1874, saying, 'Please Sir, I want to become a member of this Association'. He was politely advised 'to come back in 25 years time'. Fifteen years later it was Bramwell who proposed him for membership.

He wrote to three of the most important firms in London, John Penn & Son, marine engine builders, Merryweather & Company, fire engine builders and Gwynne & Company, centrifugal pump manufacturers, whose works were then in Essex Street, off the Strand. All replied that they had no suitable vacancy, but within a few days, following a crisis in the Gwynne family, Mr James Gwynne, the founder's eldest son, wrote to him requesting testimonials.

The highly respected firm of Gwynne & Company was founded in

1849 by John Gwynne (1800–55) on a site now occupied by the Temple Library. Although a Londoner by birth, John Gwynne spent much of his early life at Bushmills in County Antrim, where his family had interests in a small general engineering business. His brother George was an analytical chemist of some distinction who while employed in Pittsburg, U.S.A., became attracted by the potential of the centrifugal pump. Originally invented in France by de Demour in 1732, developments during the next hundred years appear to have been confined to the United States. The first recorded patent was filed by an American, W D Andrews, who supplied pumps for the new harbour works in New York in 1844.

George Gwynne was among the first to appreciate the merits of Andrews' patent and in the same year that Andrews obtained his patent he designed and built a double-entry balanced pump and secured an order for a '12 ft. diameter pump' (*sic*) for use in the Passaic Copper Mines. Soon afterwards he returned to London to become a chemical technician with Price's Patent Candle Company in Battersea. Immediately upon his return, he communicated his ideas about pumps to his brother John, who returned to London and devoted a year to the study of the mathematics of hydraulics and their application to his brother's new rotodynamic pump. In 1849, John took the plunge and founded Gwynne & Company with the financial assistance of his friend Twining, a merchant banker and well known figure in the tea trade. When the great scheme for stylishly embanking the north shore of the river Thames from Chelsea to Blackfriars was first proposed, Twining purchased most of the property in and around Essex Street, adjacent to his premises in the Strand, an event which was to prove most advantageous to Gwynne.

Gwynne & Company, London

In spite of early competition from the British engineers Appold, Bessemer and Whitelaw, the fledgling firm aroused considerable interest in the potential of centrifugal pumps which were first brought to the public's notice at the Great Exhibition in 1851. Their application at that time to Fen drainage, a subject then under close consideration, was immediately realised. During the same year, John Gwynne obtained a patent for his multistage centrifugal pump which today is in use throughout the world.

John Gwynne died in 1855 and control of his business was taken over by his eldest son James Eglington Anderson Gwynne (1831–1915). James was a man of strong character and acknowledged as a very good businessman. In middle life he developed new and varied interests which included gas blowers and boosters, electric lighting plants and sheep-shearing machines. The business constantly expanded under his leadership and this, combined with problems associated with work on the Thames Embankment, necessitated a move to new, larger premises in 1868. He purchased a site in Brook Street, Holborn, today the home of the Prudential Assurance Company and sold the Essex Street Works to J J Astor, the proprietor of *The Times* newspaper.

Sadly, at this time, domestic problems arose in the Gwynne family. After John's death the business had passed to James who kept it almost entirely in his own hands and this was resented by his two younger brothers, John (1838–1912) and Henry (1840–89), who held only relatively minor positions in the firm. The younger brothers were supported by their mother, Agnes Gwynne, daughter of Sir James Anderson, a leading Harley Street physician, who encouraged their claim for greater recognition in the business. The break came in April

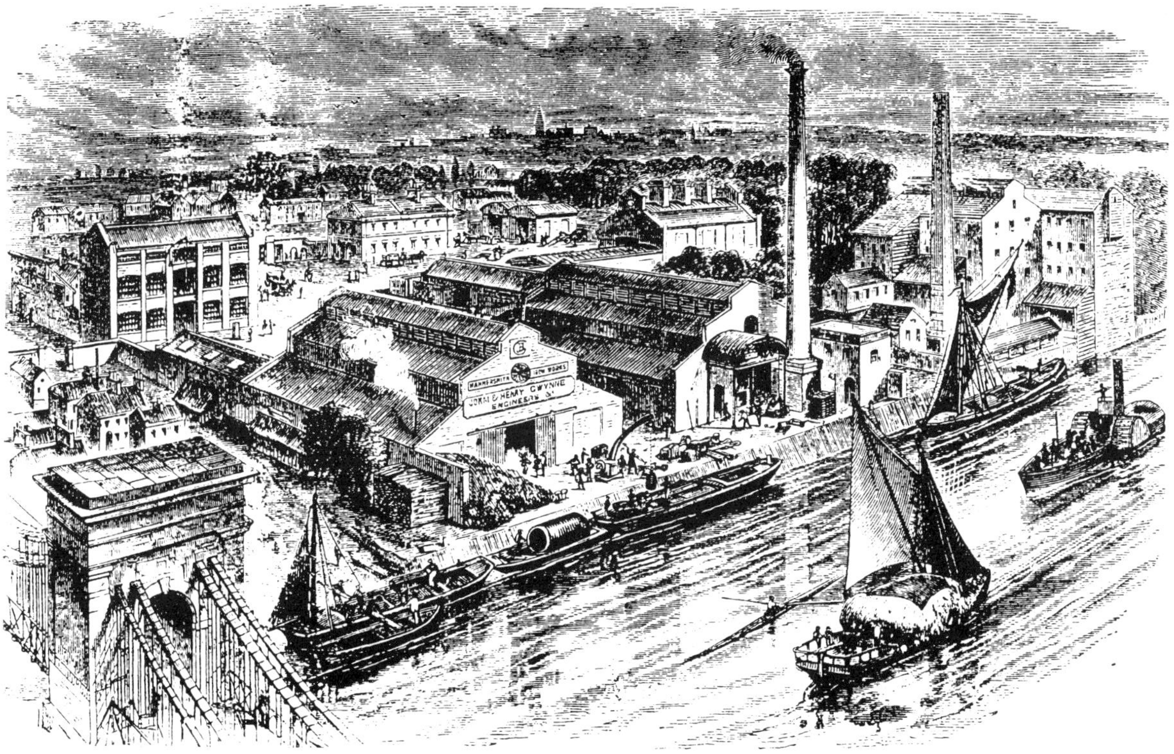

John & Henry Gwynne's Hammersmith Works. Sir Joseph Bazalgette's Suspension Bridge completed in 1887 in the left foreground.

1868 when James moved the works to Brook Street. The boys' mother loaned John and Henry £7000 and they set up a new company on the banks of the Thames adjacent to Hammersmith Bridge, trading as J & H Gwynne & Company and competing with their elder brother. They prospered greatly and in 1898 became a limited liability company.

It was during this family crisis that William Henry Allen was invited to submit testimonials. Years later he wrote,

> 'Naturally at that young age I hadn't any, but having faith in myself and relying upon my personal appearance I determined to go to London. It was a poor journey in those days taking eight hours. My future employer seemed to be impressed with my personality and after we had discussed the economics of workmanship he engaged me there and then, hardly allowing me to go home to fetch my bag. This part of my life was nothing short of romantic. I remained with Mr Gwynne for eleven years and during the last few years the whole of the business was carried out by myself. I was not only the manager, but chief clerk, cashier, cost clerk, chief draughtsman, mathematician and general foreman of the whole establishment where we turned out £50,000 worth of work a year. My work there at the beginning was carried out under very difficult circumstances. The education I had had scarcely fitted me for that class of work and there was a great deal to be learnt. In two years, however, I gained the complete confidence of my employer.'

When William Henry joined the firm a wide variety of types and sizes of centrifugal pump and their associated steam engines were the mainstay of the business. Later electric-light generating sets, using

W H Allen's original York Street, Lambeth Works now forming part of Waterloo Station.

early Gramme Dynamos manufactured by Patterson and Cooper, were introduced as another application for their steam engines. Soon Mr Gwynne realised the true worth of his manager and increasingly left the management of the business entirely to him for long periods of time. It was during these periods that William Henry Allen acquired the priceless experience of not only handling men, but ensuring the weekly wages bill was met, liaising with and satisfying both customers and suppliers and retaining the confidence of the firm's financial backers while having overall responsibility for production, design and quality. In 1877 Gwynne presented William Henry with a gold watch simply inscribed 'Presented to William Henry Allen by J E A Gwynne for his general ability.'

Amongst Gwynne's customers with whom William Henry dealt personally were many of the leading engineers and shipbuilders of the day. Several lifelong friendships were established and by the end of the decade it was suggested to him that he should become his own master. Naturally Gwynne resented this and although he tried very hard to dissuade his employee, a break became inevitable and in 1880 William Henry resigned on some undisclosed matter of principle.

He was fortunate in quickly finding suitable premises in York Street, Lambeth, in which he established his new enterprise. This site now forms part of Waterloo Station. The works and an adjoining owner's house had been built originally by Reynolds, founder of the early mass circulation newspaper *Reynolds Weekly News*. Later, it had been acquired by Merryweather & Sons, the famous fire engine manufacturers since 1690, who had recently moved to Greenwich under threat of compulsory purchase of the York Street Works by the London & South Western Railway.

The premises were in a very run-down condition and it took some courage to take on the £400 a year lease, but in William Henry's own words, 'I made no difficulty about it and in two days the property was mine.' The task of obtaining some basic machinery and tools and furnishing the office took only an afternoon and he finally left Gwynne & Company on 26th October, 1880.

York Street Works established

The York Street Works opened for business the following morning. Mrs Allen and the children bade their father godspeed as he left their Westminster home, and threw a white silk slipper after him for good luck. Little could they have realised that they were witnessing the birth of a remarkable industrial enterprise and the profound effect it was to have on all their lives. Within a few weeks the works were providing employment for 100 skilled men, many of whom had left Gwynnes. Undoubtedly William Henry had been very popular with the men at Essex Street and on the day he left Gwynne's employment they presented him with a handsome clock inscribed, 'Presented to W H Allen as a mark of esteem and regard in which he was held by the employees of Messrs Gwynne & Co. 26th October 1880.' The clock is still a proud possession in the Allen family. He never forgot the loyalty of these men and treated them as friends for the remainder of his life. Many references were made to them in Queen's Engineering Works Magazine published annually by the firm in the years 1904–39.

A stationary steam engine driving the overhead shafting was installed and running within a month, and by the end of 1880 the Company's first order was despatched. This was for an 8 in. centrifugal pump ordered by the confirming house John Mathieson & Co. of Leadenhall Street in the City of London for an Egyptian customer, valued at £50. A few weeks later a second order was received for a similar, but larger 15 in. pump. This was sold using the trade mark *Conqueror* a name which rapidly became known worldwide and remained in constant demand until well into the twentieth century. Initially centrifugal pumps were used mainly in waterworks for pumping water and sewage, in land drainage and irrigation schemes, in mines and quarries, and in large industrial plants. Soon this use was broadened to include marine applications and dock-pumping schemes. Literally thousands of *Conqueror* pumps were manufactured by the firm during the next eighty years for an ever widening variety of applications in competition with Gwynne's established *Invincible* range. During 1881, in competition with Gwynnes, he started to manufacture a range of direct-coupled reciprocating steam engines to drive his pumps.

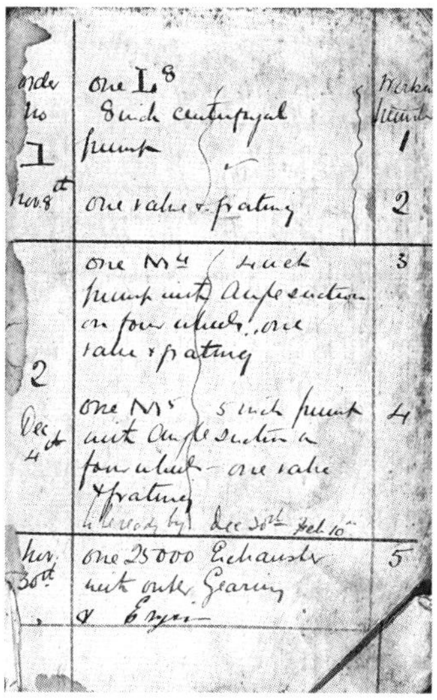
Order No 1 Nov 8th — One L8 8 inch centrifugal pump — 1; One valve & grating — 2
2 Dec 4th — One No 4 inch pump with angle suction on four wheels, one valve & grating — 3; One No 5 inch pump with angle suction on four wheels — one valve & grating — 4
Nov 30th — One 25000 Exhauster with outer Gearing & Engine — 5

An extract from W H Allen's first order book dated 8th November 1880 calling for an 8 in. centrifugal pump for an Egyptian customer.

Immediately prior to establishing the York Street Works, William Henry took a former colleague into partnership. Little is known about Richard Wright other than that he had a good brain and was a gifted draughtsman. Wright was a quiet somewhat introverted character whom William Henry trusted implicitly and who was content to remain in the background as a thoroughly reliable second in command to the driving force in the business. The partnership worked satisfactorily for thirteen years when changes became necessary and he retired from the business.

We have already seen that John Gwynne devoted much of his time to the development of electric lighting machinery in the second half of the 1870s. It is therefore not surprising to learn that within two years of the establishment of Allen's York Street Works he was continuing this work and negotiated an order for a pair of small electric light engines. These were designed to run at 1,100 rpm and had output of 15 amps at 350 volt to supply arc lamps connected in series. Clearly, he fully appreciated the great possibilities for the development of

An early 30 hp steam engine-driven condenser circulating pump – circa 1881.

interrelated mechanical and electrical engineering equipment and it was this foresight which laid the foundations for the firm's future remarkable success.

Development of the dynamo

The 1880s were an exciting period in the development of electrical machines. Every schoolboy knows that it was Michael Faraday, the famous physicist, who invented the primitive electric motor as early as 1821. A decade later, in his famous paper before the Royal Society, he gave an account of his experiments which led to the invention of the dynamo laying the foundations of the present gigantic world-wide electrical power industry.

Most subsequent development work during the next forty years was carried out on the continent of Europe and the first really practical ancestor of the modern dynamo was produced in 1870 by a Belgian engineer, Theophile Gramme, working in Paris, the home of so many major technological advances in the nineteenth century. Nicholas Cugnot built his first steam carriage there in 1770; Joseph Montgolfier invented the hot air engine in 1810; Marc Seguin patented a forced-draught multi-tubular locomotive boiler in 1827, two years before Stephenson's *Rocket* won the Rainhill trials; Jean Joseph Etienne Lenoir built the first practical gas explosion engine in 1860; Dr Rudolf Diesel was born in Paris in 1858 where he lived until his family fled to London during the Franco-Prussian War in 1870. After the war he returned to Paris for a further five years. It was his regular visits to the technical museums in Paris which aroused his intense desire to became an engineer. Frenchmen Panhard & Levassor, living in Paris, became licensees for Otto's 4-stroke engine in 1886 and in 1891 they produced the first really practical motor car.

Colonel Rookes Evelyn Crompton C.B., R.E.

The Gramme dynamo was a series wound direct current generator with a commutator consisting of insulated copper segments which, it was found, could work equally well as a motor. Improvements were soon made jointly by Emil Burgin, a Swiss engineer and by Colonel Rookes Evelyn Crompton, a descendant of Samuel Crompton, the inventor of the spinning mule. Following a distinguished career in India as an aide to the Viceroy, where he pioneered the use of steam traction on the Indian trunk roads, Crompton decided to devote his time to the new and promising field of electric light generation. He founded the renowned firm Crompton & Company, Arc Works, Chelmsford, to manufacture and instal generating and lighting equipment. In 1878 this became Crompton Parkinson Ltd.

Originally carbon arc lamps known as Jablochkoff candles, named after their Russian inventor, were employed for providing illumination. The first British installation to use the Gramme dynamo and Jablochkoff candles was at London's West India Docks. This was followed by an installation at the Stanton Iron Works new pipe foundry in Derbyshire, then owned by Crompton's cousins. Concurrently, James Gwynne completed installations at the Gaiety Theatre, Billingsgate Fish Market and Holborn Viaduct in London. William Henry Allen had been closely associated with all three projects during 1878.

It soon became obvious that carbon arc lamps would never be suitable for domestic lighting purposes. During 1879, in response to an urgent request from his friend Joseph Swan, Crompton visited Swan's laboratory in Newcastle-upon-Tyne where he saw a row of twenty small incandescent lights burning brightly without flicker. These were the result of a great deal of experimentation during which Swan had perfected a satisfactory lamp filament which also overcame the difficulty of exhausting the lamp's glass globe. He used cotton thread partially converted to cellulose by immersion in sulphuric acid and then carbonized. Crompton realised immediately that Swan's invention made possible the introduction of the public supply and distribution of electric lighting similar to that well established by the gas producers using coal gas, and urged his friend to start manufacturing his lamps as quickly as possible.

Colonel R E Crompton

Unknown to Swan, the American inventor, Thomas Alva Edison, had been working along similar lines and had arrived at much the same conclusions as Swan in 1881. Both men secured some measure of patent protection and after embarking on legal arguments decided that they each had something to offer the other. The formation of the famous Edison & Swan Electric Light Co. Ltd followed in 1883. In subsequent years many millions of their electric light bulbs were produced on both sides of the Atlantic.

Crompton received a number of prestigious contracts for his

electric light generators in Germany, Austria, Sweden, Switzerland and France, quickly winning a decisive lead over his Continental rivals, but he failed to secure the necessary financial backing from British bankers. Like so many of his contemporaries throughout the 'Golden Age' of the British manufacturing industry, he found himself unable to compete with the new state-subsidised concerns emerging on the Continent. This compelled him to confine his activities to England and in 1886 he founded the Kensington & Knightsbridge Electric Supply Company to supply illumination to homes in the area. His generators supplied direct current at 100 volt to storage batteries which overcame the inevitable problems associated with the early mechanical and electrical equipment at his disposal.

Sebastian Ziani de Ferranti, the father of modern electrical engineering and pioneer of alternating current, from a sketch made by his sister in 1882.

Sebastian Ziana de Ferranti

It was at this time that a brilliant young engineer, Sebastian Ziani de Ferranti appeared on the scene. Fascinated by Crompton's work while still a student at University College in London, he decided to concentrate his enormous energies upon the problems of electricity generation and distribution. Upon graduation he secured employment with Crompton's great rivals Siemen Brothers. Within a very short time he developed a greatly improved a.c. generator or 'Alternator' employing Lord Kelvin's zig-zag windings. This was followed by a meter for measuring electrical current consumption, and in 1883 he began manufacturing on his own account.

Ferranti meters were installed at the Grosvenor Gallery Company's generating station in Bond Street operated by Coutts Lindsay & Co, and from small beginnings grew rapidly into a public supply company with an output of 1,000 kW. Unlike Crompton's generating stations it produced alternating current at 1,200 volts using transformers connected in series. Storage batteries could not of course be used with a.c. current and mechanical failures were frequent. Although there were numerous complaints from customers, the Company was so impressed with young Ferranti's suggestions that they appointed him as their Chief Engineer. Ferranti lost no time in consulting W H Allen who had undertaken several machining jobs for him in the previous year and orders for 5.5 kW, 350 volt series wound dynamos running at 900 rpm were placed. These were employed to provide power for arc lamps in the generating station and excitation to the main alternators.

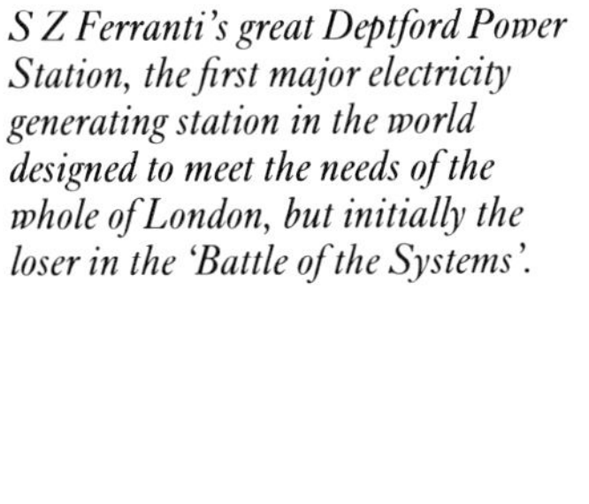

S Z Ferranti's great Deptford Power Station, the first major electricity generating station in the world designed to meet the needs of the whole of London, but initially the loser in the 'Battle of the Systems'.

Ferranti was undoubtedly a visionary and within four years he formulated plans for a £1¼ million scheme to distribute alternating current over a wide area from a single large power generating station at mains pressures higher than anything that had been previously contemplated in Europe or the United States. He chose a site on the Thames at Deptford because of its convenient access to boiler feed, cooling water and ship-borne supplies of coal. Named the London Electric Supply Corporation, the station was designed to be large enough to meet the needs of the whole of London at that time and ultimately was to have a capacity of 120,000 hp. He planned that overhead mains cables running alongside the tracks of the London, Brighton and South Coast Railway, would supply current of 10,000 volt to a series of substations where transformers would supply street mains at 2,400 volt. The supply to individual premises would then be further reduced to 100 volt.

By the end of October 1889, two 1,000 kW alternators, each driven by a 1,500 hp vertical tandem compound steam engine built by Hick, Hargreaves & Company of Bolton, were in use. Allen supplied three 17.5 kW 300 amp 55 volt shunt-wound direct acting exciting

Allen compound steam engine direct coupled to a 17.5 kW 55 volt d.c. exciter dynamo set supplied to the London Electrical Supply Corporation for S Z Ferranti's Deptford Power Station 1888.

dynamos direct-coupled to tandem compound engines working at 200 psi, each priced at £675. But even larger 5,000 hp engines were planned. 'The Battle of the Systems' as it became known had begun with Ferranti's advanced system for the distribution of high-voltage a.c. current on the one hand and the advocates of low-voltage d.c. supplies from a series of small local generating stations on the other. Undoubtedly, public prejudice against high-voltage electricity was strong at the time and later that year the Board of Trade intervened. The resultant Electric Lighting Act of 1888 not only drastically reduced the area which Ferranti intended to supply but permitted competition from the low-power generators with small initial expenses, which temporarily made Ferranti's great power station something of a white elephant. For the next thirty years or so the d.c. system held the ascendancy before most of the world adopted the a.c. system.

'Battle of the systems'

A similar struggle ensued in the United States. George Westinghouse, famous for his world-wide railway air-braking and signalling systems, advocated the high-voltage alternating current and Thomas Edison championed the low-voltage direct current alternative.

W H Allen decided to remain on the fringe of this great struggle and to concentrate his efforts on the design and manufacture of smaller engines to drive his pumps, fans and d.c. generators. He appreciated that whichever of the protagonists ultimately won the day, the new public generating stations planned would require large powerful engines necessitating capital expenditure beyond his means. Furthermore, he quickly understood the significance of the Hon. Charles Parsons' steam turbine patents of 1884. He was among the first to compare them in importance with James Watts' beam engine and separate condenser patented in 1760. Allen was convinced that his Company's future lay in the development of auxiliary machinery, especially for marine applications and in meeting the special needs of the Royal Navy with whom he had already established a close working relationship. His judgement was sound because within a few years Parson's turbines dominated electricity generation on land. In the early years of the twentieth century great ships like *Carmania, Lusitania, Mauretania* and *Transylvania* were fitted with Parson's turbines as prime movers, but all had Allen's auxiliary machinery. It was not until World War II, when the Royal Navy installed alternating current generators in naval vessels that Queen's Engineering Works commenced the manufacture of a.c. machinery.

Dr Gisbert Kapp (1852–1922). Co-patentee Allen-Kapp dynamos.

In 1875, while still General Manager at Gwynnes, W H Allen interviewed a well known lady, Luisa Cappiani, who was seeking suitable employment for her son, Gisbert Kapp. She was of Scottish parentage but had been born and brought up in Linz. She married an Austrian national in charge of the administration of Trieste docks, but unfortunately he died when Gisbert was only five years old. She then embarked upon a successful singing career, travelling widely, visiting most European capitals, using the name Cappiani, an Italianisation of the family name.

Gisbert was born in Mauer, near Vienna, in 1852 and received a good education firstly in Vienna, then in Prague and afterwards he studied mechanical engineering at the Federal Polytechnic in Zurich from which he graduated at the age of nineteen. He spent a year at sea as a ship's engineer, a year in an engineering factory in Augsburg and two years in the Austrian Navy.

Dr Gisbert Kapp

Undoubtedly W H Allen was charmed by Cappiani and young Gisbert was engaged. The 1870s were still in the period when many budding young continental engineers sought employment and experience in English factories. Gisbert soon proved his worth and in a very short time was appointed Gwynne's Chief Draughtsman. He became closely involved with James Gwynne's project for generating electricity for lighting purposes.

In 1879, for reasons now unknown, he left Gwynne & Co. and joined Richard Hornsby & Sons, agricultural engineers and steam engine builders of Grantham. He probably wished to further broaden his experience and better himself and put to greater use his considerable knowledge of languages. He travelled widely in Russia, Switzerland, Italy and North Africa for Hornsby and it was during a visit to the Paris Exhibition in 1881 that he began to appreciate the possibilities and vast potential of electrical engineering.

He made contact with R E Crompton and was appointed General Manager of the Arc Works and laboratory at Chelmsford in 1882. This marked the start of Kapp's creative period and within a short time he was responsible for five important patents which he patented jointly with Crompton. He also became a prolific writer of technical papers, demonstrating the scientifically-based quantitative methods he was applying to his designs. However, he was obviously not entirely happy in Crompton's employment and in 1884 he put up his plate as a consulting electrical engineer in London. One suspects there had existed a clash of personalities between these two remarkably talented men which is largely confirmed in Crompton's autobiography published forty-six years later.

Concurrently with these events, W H Allen decided to embark upon the manufacture of electrical machinery. Within a short time a working arrangement developed between the two men and Kapp was invited to supervise Allen's new electrical department. However, he retained his independence as a consulting engineer. The first task undertaken was the design of the dynamos for S Z Ferranti's Grosvenor Gallery generating station.

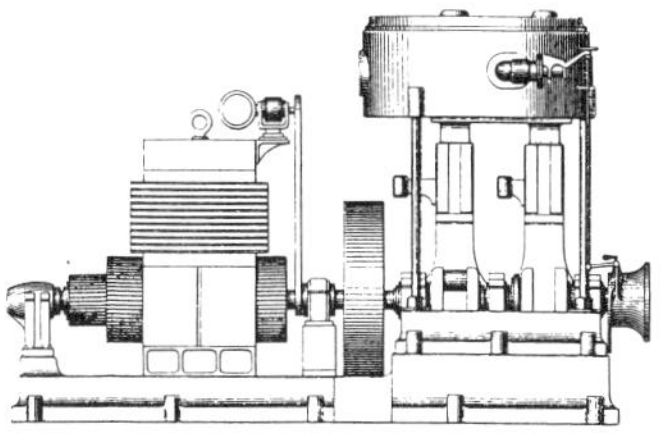

The Admiralty pattern direct-coupled twin-cylinder steam engine and Allen-Kapp dynamo installed in HM ships 1885.

Kapp had patented the compound-wound dynamo in 1882 and in 1885 jointly patented with W H Allen the self-regulating series wound dynamo which overcame many of the problems of voltage regulation associated with the earlier machines. Early dynamos had been designed for high-speed running and when used with reciprocating steam engines had to be belt driven. The belts absorbed a lot of the engine power, were frequently troublesome and reduced the overall efficiency of the plant. He showed that it was possible to make an efficient slow-speed dynamo which could be directly coupled to Allen's steam engines thereby enabling the firm to offer a compact generating plant which contributed greatly to their successes in the marine electrical market. A further patent filed jointly by the two men in 1885 related to improvements in the mechanical construction and ventilation of electrical machines by the provision of air ducts in the armature core.

Admiralty connection established

Since W H Allen's days with James Gwynne in the 1870s his relations with the Admiralty had been excellent and the part these played in the introduction of electricity on board ship was very considerable. The first Allen electrical machinery supplied for use in warships consisted of six twin-cylinder steam engines each direct coupled to 200-light, 12 kW dynamos running at 300 rpm. These were ordered in August 1885 for HMS *Thunderer* and *Devastation*, three sets being installed in each vessel for ship's lighting. By the end of that year they had supplied 21 sets of steam engines and direct coupled dynamos to the Royal Navy for electric lighting. The capacity of dynamos in those early days was expressed in terms of the number of lamps they would illuminate, the wattage of a 16 candle-power lamp being approximately 60. The dynamos were of the 2-pole type, compound-wound with smooth-core armatures. The brushes were made from copper gauze. The magnets were of forged steel machined all over and magnetically isolated from the cast iron base by gunmetal brackets. These were followed by a further order for *Dreadnought* in December 1885, these vessels being the forerunners of a long and unbroken line of naval ships fitted with Allen generating sets.

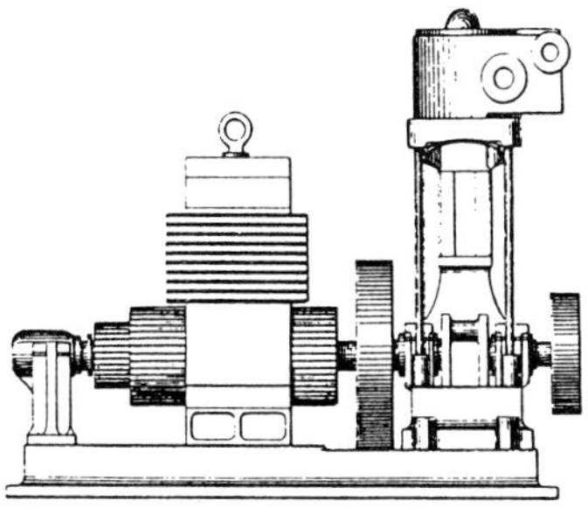

An early direct coupled steam engine and dynamo for ship's electric lighting.

The earliest orders for mercantile marine installations were for 60-light machines ordered by Cammell Laird & Co. Ltd in November 1885. These were 3.6 kW, 60 volt dynamos with direct-coupled steam engines and the order stipulated that the supplier should also be responsible for the supply of the lamps, switchboard cables and switches, in fact everything for lighting the ship.

The Electrical Installation Department of the Company was established in June 1886 and from small beginnings in completing the electrical installation in *Orizaba*, the Company wired on average twenty vessels per annum for the next twenty-five years. Branches were established at Glasgow, Newcastle, Belfast, Liverpool, Southampton and London, but in due course the shipbuilders mastered the

Twin-cylinder steam engine and direct coupled Allen-Kapp 200-light dynamo as supplied to HM ships Devastation, Thunderer *and* Dreadnought. *in 1885.*

art of wiring and tended to set up their own departments, in consequence it was deemed advisable in the circumstances to discontinue this service and maintain one branch only as a stores at Tidal Basin in London's dockland.

Early electrical machinery

Coincidental with marine developments, Allen electrical generating machinery was supplied for lighting commercial premises and private houses. One of the earliest dynamo sets designed by Gisbert Kapp was supplied to Allen's friend Sir Alfred Yarrow, the celebrated marine engineer and shipbuilder for his new house which was being built in the wilds of Hampstead Heath, now the fashionable Fitzjohns Avenue. It proved an immediate success and Yarrow & Co. Ltd remained exceedingly important Allen customers throughout the great shipbuilding years of this century. William Henry Allen fully appreciated the importance of his network of friends, associates and customers and to no small degree this network has been responsible for the Allen success story.

In 1888, Rashleigh Phipps & Danson of Grays Inn Road were responsible for the installation of Allen generators in Marshall and Snelgrove's Oxford Street Stores, and at Carlton House Terrace in London, and Rougham Hall in Suffolk. Later Richard Crittall & Co. installed 540 amp, 105 volt sets at the Grosvenor Hotel, Victoria, which were quickly followed by other leading hotels. Inevitably with the emergence and rapid growth of electrical power companies this class of work was limited and not capable of expansion.

Kapp's dynamos were built and tested in the cellars under Allen's York Street Works under conditions of great secrecy. He was a man of fine character, most interesting to work with and liked by everybody with whom he came in contact. However, his fertile brain meant that his ideas followed in such rapid succession that alterations and modifications were frequently called for before the project could be finalised and put into production. This is a frustrating characteristic often found in men with brilliant minds and required the qualities of a man like W H Allen to say, 'Enough is enough, get on with the job.' Essentially the two men worked well together and it was a great disappointment when Kapp was persuaded to take a new appointment elsewhere.

Charles C Hawkins, MA, Head of the Electrical Department 1890–1908.

In 1889 W H Allen appointed Charles C Hawkins, MA as assistant to Gisbert Kapp. He was essentially an academic educated at Eton and Magdalen College, Oxford, where he obtained a double first in natural sciences, and at the Hanover Square School of Electrical Engineering, followed by a short period on the staff of Johnson & Phillips, manufacturers of electrical machinery since 1875. In 1890 Hawkins was confirmed as head of Allen's Electrical Department, a position he held with great distinction until his retirement in 1908. He wrote *The Dynamo* a standard text-book for both students and designers and was the author of many technical papers.

Whether Kapp left Allen's business altogether at this time, or whether he maintained a consulting connection is not known, but personal relationships between the two men remained excellent and Kapp acted as a private tutor to Allen's son Richard.

In April 1891 Kapp joined W H Preece, later Sir William Preece, as designer of the new electric lighting station and distribution system at Bristol. Preece had been Engineer-in-Chief of the Post Office and played a major role in developing tele-communications. His comment to the Lord Mayor of Dublin when making the first direct phone call from London to Dublin, 'I can smell your cigar!' was long remembered. Preece also played a prominent part in the Board of Trade's investigation during the Battle of the Systems. He was a personal friend of W H Allen and presented the prizes at the annual distribution of prizes to pupils and apprentices in 1905.

Space precludes going further into the details of these two mens' fascinating careers, but suffice it to say that the Bristol generating station was opened in 1893 and was the largest provincial undertaking in the United Kingdom at the time. In 1894 Kapp was appointed General Secretary of the newly-formed Association of German Electrical Engineers, a post he held for ten years. His responsibilities extended far beyond merely running the Association; he prepared the rules and standards covering all aspects of materials, plant, installation and distribution applicable to the German Empire. He was allowed to continue his private practice and undertook work in Germany, Russia, Norway, Switzerland and Italy. He never abandoned his British nationality, and in 1905, when his children had grown up, he decided to return to England, accepting the newly created Chair of Electrical Engineering at the University of Birmingham, a post he held with great distinction. Upon his return to England his old friends and colleagues entertained him to a celebration dinner at Oddenino's Restaurant in London. This says a great deal for the man, who after a decade's absence, was not forgotten. The guest list reads like a *Who's Who* of electrical engineering and names like W H Allen, Sir William Preece and Colonel R E

Dr Kapp's later career

An early 60-light 155 volt Allen-Kapp dynamo (1887).

Crompton were prominently to the fore. He died on 10th August, 1922.

His son, Professor R O Kapp, carried on in his father's footsteps. Educated in Germany, he graduated in Electrical Engineering at Birmingham University in 1909. He then spent five years in Switzerland with the great Swiss company Brown Boveri & Co. working on electric traction projects. After the war, and for many years thereafter, he was connected with the construction of the National Grid for electricity distribution in this country; and then shortly before World War II he became Pender Professor of Electrical Engineering at University College, London.

Developments in marine engineering

By 1880 the days of sailing ships were almost over and the demands for mechanical propulsion for all types of vessel were growing rapidly. In 1881 a steamship with engine power totalling 120,000 ihp was launched. Improved designs of boilers and condensers led to improved feedwater conditions and the adoption of higher working pressures. To take advantage of these improvements, expansion of the steam had to be spread over more than one stage leading first to compound engines, then very shortly to the classic triple expansion engine in 1871. Within five years quadruple expansion engines had been built.

All this sophistication meant that more and more auxiliary power was required in the ship's engine room, and it was this market that W H Allen sought to capture. Main propulsion units were the forte of a few very large, capital intensive, specialised companies and Allen concentrated upon their needs for high quality, absolutely reliable auxiliary machinery such as pumps, electric generators, boiler room forced-draught fans and engine room ventilation fans.

Among the earliest recorded examples are direct-coupled steam-

An early steam engine driven forced-draught fan for ship's boiler rooms (1884).

engine driven 20 in. diameter circulating pumps running at 110 rpm for the Cunarders *Umbria* and *Etruria* built by John Elder & Co. in 1884. The engine cylinders were 15 in. diameter x 12 in. stroke working at 110 psi. The first order was received from the Royal Navy in 1883 calling for a similar pump for installation in *Racer* and from that moment the firm's close association with the Navy has continued uninterrupted to the present day. The first engine driven fan was delivered in 1884. That year the number of pumping sets delivered rapidly increased, the largest of which were two 20 in. centrifugal pumps, each driven by a separate single-cylinder vertical steam engine mounted on a common bed-plate, for the Isle of Man Steamship Company's new vessel *Mona Queen*. In 1885 tandem compound engines were introduced having the high pressure and low-pressure pistons linked by a common piston rod. These were used for driving fans. That year also saw W H Allen fulfilling a long held ambition, for he was elected a Member of the Institution of Mechanical Engineers. Regular meetings at their Westminster headquarters provided one of the most important forums for the leading mechanical engineers of the day and were undoubtedly a source of great pleasure to him.

Early marine auxiliaries

The first order received from a foreign navy, the precursor of many, came from the Italian Navy in 1887 for two steam driven fans. Ties between Britain and the Italian Navy had been close since 1858 when the Consulting Civil Engineer, James Meadows Rendel, designed the great Italian Naval Base at La Spezia. Rendel's great friend, Sir William Armstrong, later Lord Armstrong, supplied big guns to the Italian Navy, and his son, George Wightwick Rendel, one of our most distinguished Naval Architects and a director of Armstrong's great company at Elswick on the Tyne, accepted an invitation to take charge of a new Italian shipyard being built at Pozzuoli, near Naples, in 1885. One suspects that both Armstrong and George Rendel would have been part of W H Allen's network of friends and associates at this time.

The business progressed satisfactorily. In 1880 Allen made a profit of £700 on a turnover of £10,000. The following year the turnover trebled and continued to rise each successive year such that by 1890 he was employing 450 men. Profits were re-invested in the business

An early steam driven forced-draught boiler room fan as developed by Richard Allen at the York Street Works in the 1880s.

and additional plant and machinery were acquired and several enlargements were made to the premises. In the first ten years trading on his own account Allen secured valuable overseas orders from Australia, Japan, South Africa and Egypt to supplement his sheet anchor activities of pumps, electric generators and marine auxiliary machinery for U.K. customers. Several surviving documents of the period make reference to his friend and mentor, Archibald Douglas Bryce Douglas, head of the Fairfield Shipbuilding and Engineering Company. Obviously Douglas was of great assistance in helping W H Allen establish himself on Clydeside and other shipbuilding centres and their friendship lasted for many years. Another name frequently mentioned was that of Lord Pirrie, Chairman of the great Harland & Wolff shipyard in Belfast and engine works in Glasgow.

Export markets established

During these formative years Allen set the seal on the technical excellence of his designs and the high quality of his products. He fully appreciated the importance of keeping abreast of the latest scientific research and continued his practice of regularly attending meetings of the scientific and engineering institutions in London and elsewhere. He understood the great benefits which Bismark's Germany had derived from the introduction of technical education in the 1870s and from the very beginning instituted training schemes in his works. He was regarded by many contemporary engineers as not 'doing quite the right thing' and the expense and effort involved was perceived as unnecessary. However, Allen insisted that technical education was the absolute foundation of good engineering.

Richard Wright's retirement in 1893 was the point at which Allen decided to bring his son, Richard, then aged 26 into the partnership. Richard had received his engineering training with the Naval Construction & Armaments Company of Barrow-in-Furness, originally

The famous explorer Sir Henry Morton Stanley on the steps of the York Street Works with W H Allen and his eldest son Richard during an election campaign. Circa 1890.

Richard Allen enters partnership

the Barrow Shipbuilding Company. Founded in 1871 by Sir James Ramsden, this Company had been an important constructor of naval vessels since 1877 and in Richard's time employed over 800 men on its 200-acre sheltered site at Barrow-in-Furness. The Company was subsequently purchased by Vickers Ltd, enabling them for the first time to supply warships complete with engines, guns and machinery. Richard then spent some time at John Elder's yard on Clydeside and joined his father at the York Street Works in 1888.

In January 1886, William Henry's beloved wife Anne died at their home 1, Deans Yard, Westminster. Fifteen months later he married Madeline Fedden of Bristol, thirteen years his junior. They had first met at his sister's wedding to Nelson Fedden, Madeline's uncle, twenty years earlier and the two families remained great friends for many years. In 1890 Richard Allen married Geraldine Fedden, Madeline's younger sister, and their first born, Muriel, arrived the same year that Richard entered the partnership. At that point the name of the Company was changed to W H Allen, Son & Company. Sadly, W H Allen's second marriage was not a success and within a few years he and Madeline decided to part.

Merryweathers, the former occupiers of the York Street Works, retained the premises for many years longer than they had wished in the belief that the site would be required by the London & South

Western Railway for its new enlarged Waterloo Station and therefore become valuable. But railway finances south of the Thames were precarious at the time and the expected development was long delayed, which accounts for the dilapidated state of the works when finally, in 1880, William Henry acquired a lease on the property.

After only a few months possession the railway company began to move and purchased a 6 in. strip of Allen's land for which the charge was £200. Two years later they required a further three or four feet for which they paid £1,500. In 1884 they took another slightly larger strip and paid £14,000. This process continued for several years and each time the price per square foot was increased. In 1885 when enlargements were made to the north side of the station it became necessary to build a new 220-lever signal box adjacent to Allen's foundry. Whenever casting took place smoke and fumes caused problems in the elevated signal box. The railway company decided that Allen must be 'got rid of' and demanded to know how much he required to vacate the whole site. Off the top of his head he quoted a figure of £40,000 and after two months haggling they accepted his price. A telegram dated 22nd September 1893 from Allen's architect a Mr F W Hunt, remains extant cryptically stating 'Settled for 40,000, Hunt'.

The search for a new site

Immediately, Allen began to search for a site for a new works. He and Richard travelled extensively throughout Essex and North Surrey without finding anything suitable and eventually, at the suggestion of an employee, headed for Bedford on 12th November 1893. He found Bedford to be a pleasant small county town with an established engineering tradition as the home of James and Frederick Howards' famous Britannia Iron Foundry. Howards had been prominent manufacturers of agricultural machinery but were still suffering the after-effects of the Great Agricultural Depression (1875–1884) and there appeared to be an adequate pool of skilled labour available. The local Auctioneers could not offer anything suitable, but Allen had noticed an ideal site adjoining the Midland Railway. Legend has it that he recruited the aid of a small boy to locate the owners. The land formed part of the extensive Queen's Park Estate on the west side of Bedford owned by the Whitbread family. After only two hours negotiations a purchase price was agreed and, there and then, Allen paid over a ten per cent deposit thus securing the site which now forms part of our industrial heritage.

CHAPTER II

The Formative Years, 1894–1914

THAT William Henry Allen was a man of considerable foresight and courage is nowhere better illustrated than by the action he took that foggy November afternoon in Bedford. The legal formalities were completed in five weeks and the purchase was concluded. An old photograph remains extant showing him cutting the first turf, on 20th January, 1894, preparatory to excavating for the foundations. The architect responsible for the new buildings was his old friend F W Hunt, architect and surveyor to the Portman Estate. The contract for the steel work was placed with Lysaght of Bristol and Samuel Foster of nearby Kempston was awarded the building contract. The first machine tools were transferred from York Street and installed in the new factory in September, 1894.

The 20-acre site Allen purchased was on the west side of the Midland Railway's main line from St Pancras to the north, between Ford End Road in the south and Bromham Road in the north. The western side of the site ran alongside the as yet undeveloped Hurst Grove. Sixteen acres were designated for factory development and the Hurst Grove frontage for new residential property.

W H Allen cutting the first turf on the 'Green Field' site of Queen's Engineering Works, Bedford. 20th January, 1894.

The first stage of the development comprised a substantial detached brick-built office building which fronted Ford End Road and a 20,000 sq.ft. factory building in the rear. Behind this were separate foundry, smithy and pattern store buildings, in total about 40,000 sq.ft., or twice the area the firm had occupied in York Street. A new siding connected the factory with the railway's main line, enabling coal, iron and other raw materials to be delivered right into the works and finished products to be despatched with a minimum of fuss. It is believed that in excess of 100 of the York Street employees opted to stay with the firm and moved to Bedford, many rising to senior positions as the Company grew. Allen never forgot to recognise the loyalty of these men, without which the benefits of the move would have been much slower to materialise.

By the end of 1900 the area of the factory buildings was doubled, a separate dynamo shop and brassfoundry were added and a new drawing office was built on the end of the office block. Unfortunately details of sales and profits during this period have not survived, but we know from Allen's subsequent writings that sales rose from

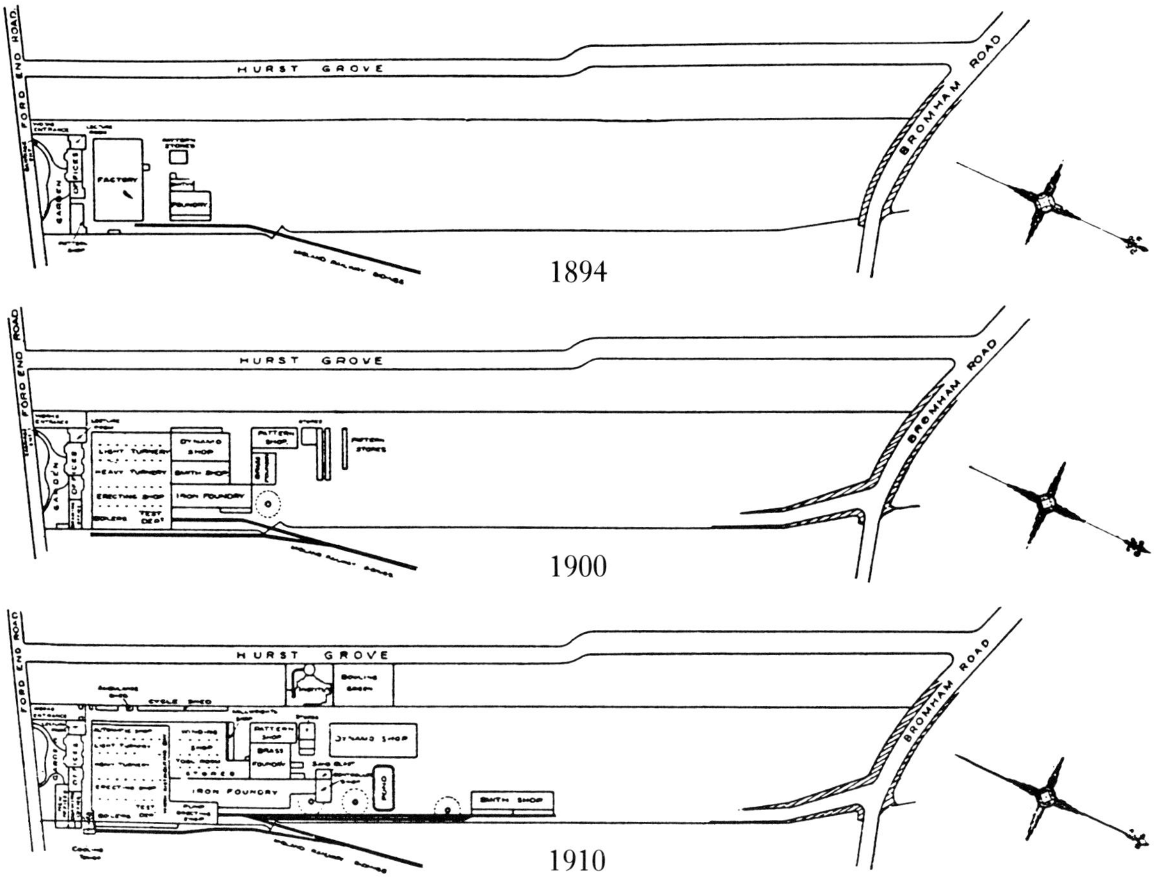

The rapid development of Queen's Engineering Works site during the years 1894 to 1910.

£45,000 in 1894 to £128,000 in 1900, with an unexplained downturn in 1897. During 1898 Allen was taken seriously ill and was absent from the works for several weeks leaving Richard in charge of the Company, no doubt providing him with valuable management experience.

Emphasis on training

From the very beginnings of Queen's Engineering Works Allen continued to demonstrate his almost passionate belief in the importance of proper scientifically-based theoretical and practical training. He engaged G H Starr as the first Bedford apprentice a month before the new works actually opened. Thirty years later Starr, then an Engineer Commander in the Royal Navy and Chief Engineer in the battle cruiser *Repulse*, returned to propose the toast to 'The Chairman of W H Allen, Sons & Company' at the 12th Annual Dinner of Past and Present Students Association. He recalled how he had been interviewed by Mr Allen who explained to him that although he had spent two full years at a Technical College, his market value as an engineer without practical training was precisely nothing. Starr started his apprenticeship on the very day the first lathes were delivered to the new works and for several months he gained valuable experience millwrighting.

At this time concerns were being expressed both in Parliament and at meetings of the great technical institutions about the training of engineers. It became widely accepted that engineers in this country were lagging behind other professions in matters of education. The problem was originally debated by the Institution of Naval Architects and subsequently at both the Institution of Mechanical Engineers and at a special conference organised by the Institution of Civil Engineers. W H Allen's friend Sir Alfred Yarrow was the great advocate of the 'Sandwich' system whereby a student undertook periods of practical work during his academic training. This was supported by the Professors. Allen favoured a proper full time college education followed by a period of continuous work in a workshop. Lord Rosebery, the great Scottish educationalist and head of the Herriot Watt College in Edinburgh, favoured 'Day Release' schemes thereby prolonging the period of academic training. It is interesting to note that a few years later Sir Alfred sent his son Norman to Queen's Engineering Works as a pupil.

Professor Ernest H Lamb, the Pupil's Demonstrator at Queen's Engineering Works 1903–13.

At the time of the move from Lambeth W H Pretty was the Demonstrator responsible for all pupils' and apprentices' training. In 1903 he resigned to take up an important appointment in Canada. He was succeeded by Ernest H Lamb, son of the distinguished mathematician, Dr Horace Lamb, with the added title of Scientific Adviser to the firm. He rendered ten years valuable service both as a tutor and an adviser at the princely salary of £285 per annum – how times have changed! In 1913 he was appointed to the Chair of Civil Engineering at the University of London College in Mile End Road. His departure from Bedford was marked by a presentation in the works at which his qualities and character were praised by both management and many of his pupils, both past and present. During his period of office over 100 pupils and apprentices passed through his hands.

One of the first innovations to be proposed by Lamb and enthusiastically endorsed by W H Allen was the introduction of the Allen Prize. This was to be awarded annually to the former pupil of the Company who, in the opinion of the directors, had shown the most marked progress in engineering ability during the year. It carried with it a premium of 25 guineas. The Prize Giving became one of the most important events in the firm's calendar and in the following years many distinguished visitors such as Sir William Preece; Sir William White, Chief Adviser to the Admiralty; T Harry Riches, the locomotive engineer and old school friend of W H Allen's at Brecon College; and Gisbert Kapp, performed this pleasant task.

Another notable event at the turn of the century was the formation of Queen's Works Cricket Club. Although having no direct bearing on the commercial success of the enterprise, Allen always understood the great value of sporting and social activities in improving the character and cohesion of the workforce. No doubt Richard played a major role in this activity for in later life he became Captain of the Bedfordshire Cricket Club; Chairman of the Bedford & District Cricket League; and a member of the M.C.C.

But returning to affairs of the Company affecting its *raison d'etre*, little information has survived about orders fulfilled in the period 1894 to 1900 although it would appear that centrifugal pumps accounted for a major share of the turnover. Clearly Egypt was an important market for *Conqueror* pumps for irrigation schemes and in 1900 W H Allen visited the country. At the time there was the promise of major contracts to provide Cairo with a proper water supply and sewage disposal scheme. During his visit he had a long interview with Lord Cromer, the famous British statesman who played an important role in Egyptian affairs for many years.

The Conqueror *pump*

Rotodyne pumps generically termed centrifugal pumps, since they were historically the earliest, quickly gained in popularity when in competition with reciprocating types. Pumps should be categorised by the direction in which the fluid discharges through and out of the pump. The earliest centrifugal pumps developed by Gwynne and others had a radial flow impeller and were therefore correctly termed centrifugal. When the flow was discharged without alteration to the direction they became axial flow pumps, but of necessity there are many variations between these two basic types. Mixed- and conical-flow pumps soon featured prominently in Allen's manufacturing programme, and by the end of the century the majority produced at Queen's Engineering Works were the mixed-flow type. However, pure axial flow pumps were not produced in any quantity until well into the 20th century. It is also necessary to distinguish between single- and double-suction pumps, between single- and multi-stage pumps; and between vertical- and horizontal-spindle designs.

In general the more closely pumps produced an axial-flow, the lower the head generated, but they could more easily pass large flows. Conversely pure centrifugal pumps have a lower throughput but are capable of generating higher heads. They require volutes on the discharge to convert velocity energy to pressure. For clarity some of the many options offered by Allens are shown in the accompanying margin diagrams.

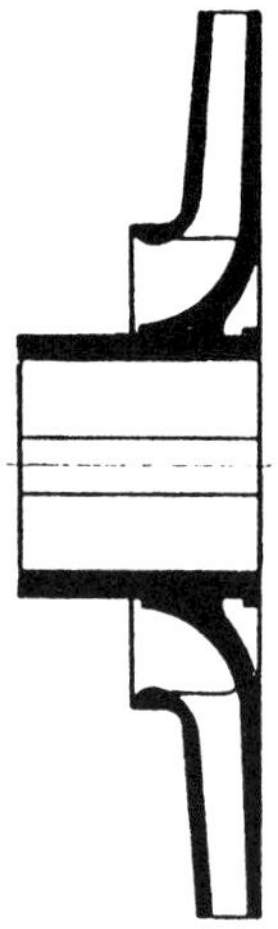

Centrifugal

By the turn of the century the Allen 'L' type centrifugal pump was available from stock in nineteen sizes with discharges varying from 100 gallons of water per minute to 28,000 gallons. These pumps were especially applicable to irrigation schemes. Generally both impellers and casings were produced from cast iron, although for marine applications gunmetal was often used for the impellers.

It was only a matter of time before pumps were produced for dealing with sand and gravel in applications such as quarrying and dredging. These were followed by unchokable single-stage pumps capable of pumping solids such as stones and bricks. The cast-iron casings were supported on the bearing bracket and the spindles could be horizontal or vertical. The impellers arranged with either one or two blades were of special construction.

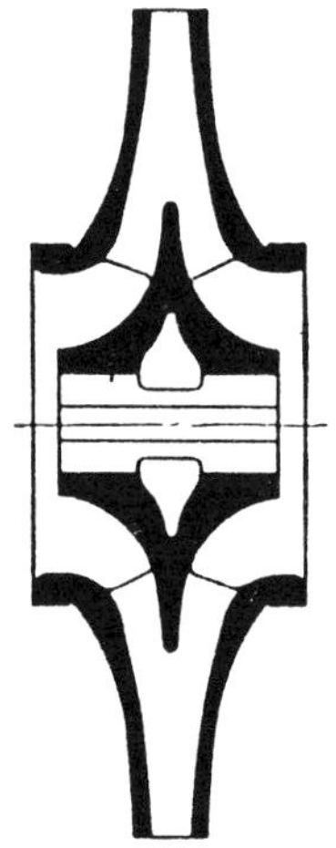

Double entry

Typical examples of larger installations completed in the 1890s were an electrically driven installation comprising a 400 bhp motor driving a 27 in. impeller dealing with 13,000 gallons of water per minute with a 50 ft. head, and a 350 bhp compound steam engine driven installation with a similar pump pumping 12,500 gallons per minute. As one might expect, Holland was an important market for pumps for many land drainage schemes. In 1897 Allens supplied four massive pumps to the Prince Orange Foundry Co. for installation at Medemblik, a small town on the Zuider Zee, 30 miles from Amsterdam. Each pump with 54 in. impellers was capable of lifting 16,500 gallons per minute against a head of 8.2 ft. at a speed of 125 rpm. Although originally supplied with coupled steam engines, some years ago they were converted to belt-driven electric motors and are today preserved as an industrial museum.

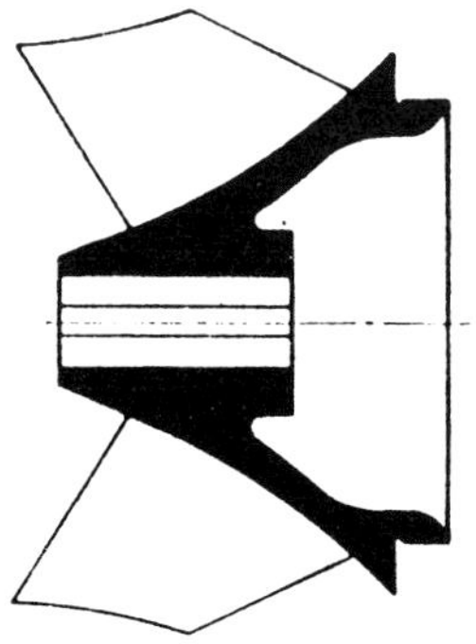

Mixed flow

By the end of Queen Victoria's reign Allen pumps were being extensively used by waterworks for pumping water and sewage disposal; in electricity generating stations for pumping cooling water; in ships for dealing with condensate and feed water; in graving and floating docks; and for irrigation and land drainage schemes. Increasingly special pumps were being called for by the oil and chemical industries for dealing with highly viscous materials.

In 1898 Allens were responsible for the pumping machinery installed to service the dock complex at Barry in South Wales, comprising two impounded wet basins and a graving dock. The steam-engine driven pumps consisted of four 40 in. and one 32 in.

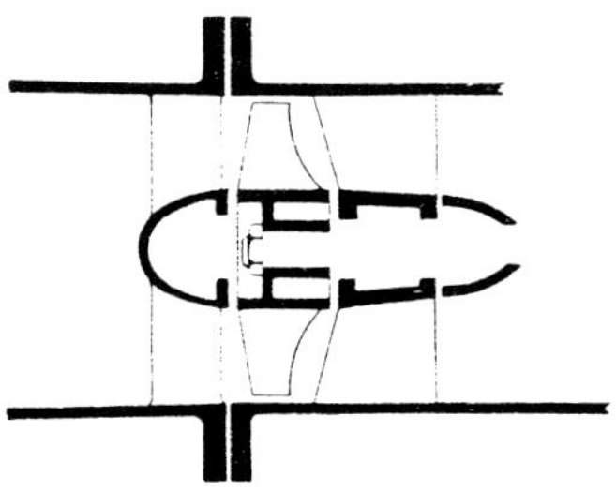

Axial flow

Four Allen centrifugal pumps supplied to the Dutch Prince Orange Foundry Company in 1897 for drainage duties at Medemblik on the Zuider Zee. Originally steam driven, each pump was capable of handling 16,500 gallons per minute against a head of 8.2 ft.

split casing pumps arranged in such a way that by means of a system of culverts they could be used for impounding the basins or dewatering the dry dock as necessary. After forty years continuous service the steam engines were replaced by a.c. electric motors and are still in regular use.

But it was in the realms of reciprocating steam engines that Allen probably made the greatest advances in the ten years 1894–1904. Earlier, in 1891, he presented a fascinating paper before the Institution of Civil Engineers in which he traced the evolution of steam-engine driven auxiliary machinery for marine applications. He stressed the great benefits derived from direct coupling the engine to the machinery whether it be a pump, fan or electric generator, both as a means of saving space in the ship's engine room and improving the overall efficiency of the plant. Until the mid-1880s most of the engines were inverted open-type single cylinder reciprocating engines working at boiler pressures of about 110 psi belt driving their load.

Reciprocating steam engine developments

Within a short time boiler pressures were increased to 150 psi for use in triple-expansion main propulsion engines and compounding was introduced on auxiliary machinery for greater economy. The first large vessels so fitted were three fine ships built for the North German Lloyd line with compound cylinders measuring 8 in. diameter x 16 in. diameter x 10 in. stroke running at 120 rpm for driving the condensate and bilge pumps. More power was required to drive the bilge pumps than the circulating pumps and the next development was to take steam from the main engine's high-pressure steam chest and having done its work in the auxiliary engine, exhaust it into the low-pressure steam chest of the main engines. This was probably the first example of a back pressure engine which the firm developed and became renowned for in the next decade. The underlying trend was for speeds to increase and short-stroke engines became the norm, but simplicity, accessibility and economy combined with durability and absolute reliability received the greatest attention.

Twin cylinders and compound cylinders increasingly replaced single cylinders having the advantage of working with considerably less vibration. Arthur Maginnis in his paper before the Institution of Mechanical Engineers in 1909 quoted that, on average, boiler pressures had increased from 77.4 psi in 1881 to 195 psi by 1909 and that engine piston speeds had increased from 447 ft./min. to 654 ft./min. in the same period.

Many different types of high speed engine were devised in this period. Originally the way forward had been demonstrated by Peter Brotherhood, who as early as 1874 built a novel 3-cylinder radial engine running at 2,500 rpm at a pressure of 450 psi. Later versions using compressed air were used for propelling the Whitehead naval torpedo developed at Woolwich Arsenal. Probably the best known steam engine was that of Peter W Willans who had set up a factory at Thames Ditton to manufacture small launch engines. He became a great friend of Crompton, who persuaded him to move to Rugby in order to develop larger engines expressly for electric power generation. The Willans' engine comprised two sets of triple-expansion cylinders arranged vertically like the tiers of a wedding cake. They were single acting, the steam passing from one cylinder to another by means of piston valves working within the hollow piston rods. He built engines in sizes up to 500 hp running at 500 rpm. It is on record that so impressed was Willans with Allen's new office building at Bedford that he persuaded Allen to allow him to copy it at his new Rugby factory.

The Willans engine

Allen continued to develop his conventional open-type engines and by 1896 was able to claim that 4,000 sets of engines and dynamos had been built during the past twelve years. Marine work, especially naval construction had been in the doldrums for several years and the great *Dreadnought* building programme was still on the drawing board. Probably the most prestigious orders received from the Royal Navy during this period were 600 amp sets with two-cylinder engines for *Terrible, Powerful* and *Magnificent*.

One of the chief features of Allen engines built at this time was the patented arrangement by which the governor could be regulated manually while the engine was running. Mounted directly on the crankshaft it retained the advantages of the flywheel governor, which of course could not be regulated while the engine was in motion. It was also found to be advantageous when the engine, normally connected to the condenser at sea, could be made non-condensing when in port.

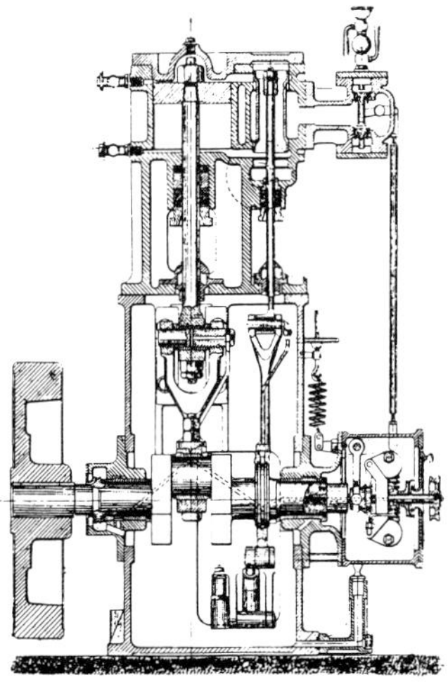

Section through a single cylinder totally enclosed high-speed steam engine showing the crankshaft mounted centrifugal governor.

All Allen-built steam engines up to about 1897 were constructed with drip lubrication and the disadvantages of this at high rates of revolution soon became apparent. The mess caused by oil being splashed about was a cause of great annoyance to ships' engineers and although efforts were made to enclose the motion, the problem was not entirely solved until the advent of forced lubrication.

In 1882 the Institution of Mechanical Engineers Research Committee arranged for a series of very important experiments to be carried out on the friction of bearings by Mr Beauchamp Tower. This work was done at the Edgware Road Works of the Metropolitan Railway using a machine specially developed by the famous Victorian engineers Easton & Anderson of Erith. The resultant report laid the foundations for a rational theory of lubrication. During a discussion at the Institution twenty-six years later on a paper given by Allen's friend T Harry Riches, on the subject of the forced lubrication of axles-boxes, W H Allen, then a member of the Council, quoted the following interesting anecdote:

> 'Sebastian Z de Ferranti, when he was a boy in 1881, had asked me to make a little force-pump, which he believed was the first time forced lubrication was used in any practical way. Ferranti's employer, Lord Wantage (of the Grosvenor Gallery), had asked him to put 3,000 hp of generating plant into a cellar in New Bond Street, London. There were about fifteen engines in the cellar and everything worked well except the outside bearing of an alternator. No doubt the bearing was too small, or it was not round, or set up, and it caused trouble, and Ferranti proposed a forced lubrication arrangement which worked perfectly. As an instance of how blind fashion was, after that time the outside bearing of nearly every alternator in the kingdom was made with forced lubrication, but to no other bearing was it applied. But why should it be limited to this outside bearing? Messrs. Belliss then took the system up, and adapted it for their connecting rods; but why should it be limited to connecting rods? In the end it went all through the engine and since that date all sorts of machinery has been fitted with forced lubrication.'

Forced lubrication

Allen added that the advantages of forced lubrication were manifest. First of all, the machinery could run very much faster; practically no oil was splashed about or wasted; it was filtered regularly; and there was hardly any wear. As evidence of this he said that he had in his Bedford works a crankshaft that had been put in an engine made for Harland & Wolff seven years earlier. The shaft was 6 in. diameter and had made over 340 million revolutions, and so far as could be measured by a micrometer there was absolutely no wear.

In other words, the great man was saying to his peers 'you can't tell me anything about forced lubrication'. However, mention of the name Belliss opens a new chapter in our story. It is perhaps ironic that after neck-and-neck competition for nearly a century the two companies merged their interests in 1968.

Origins of Belliss & Morcom

In December 1866, George Edward Belliss, a native of Birmingham, in partnership with another young engineer name Joseph Seekings, acquired the business of Bach & Co., where Belliss had served his apprenticeship. The business had originally been established in Broad Street, Birmingham by two brothers in 1852. They manufactured steam engines, pumps and agricultural machinery and were credited with building the first conventional portable steam engine which became the work-horse of the agriculturist worldwide until over-taken by the traction engine.

About 1863 Belliss became associated with the boat-builder J Samuel White of Cowes in the Isle of Wight, building steam launches. Belliss conceived the idea of increasing the power-to-weight ratio of the vessels by increasing the engine revolutions which enabled White to build launches about half the weight of those previously used. Naturally this attracted the attention of the Admiralty. But, this development was not in accord with Seeking's Quaker beliefs and the partnership was dissolved in 1865, leaving Belliss as sole proprietor.

The next twenty years saw tremendous developments in the construction of naval vessels and Belliss's higher speed main propulsion engines became widely adopted. Naval torpedo boats, using fire-tube boilers and light-weight engines became formidable

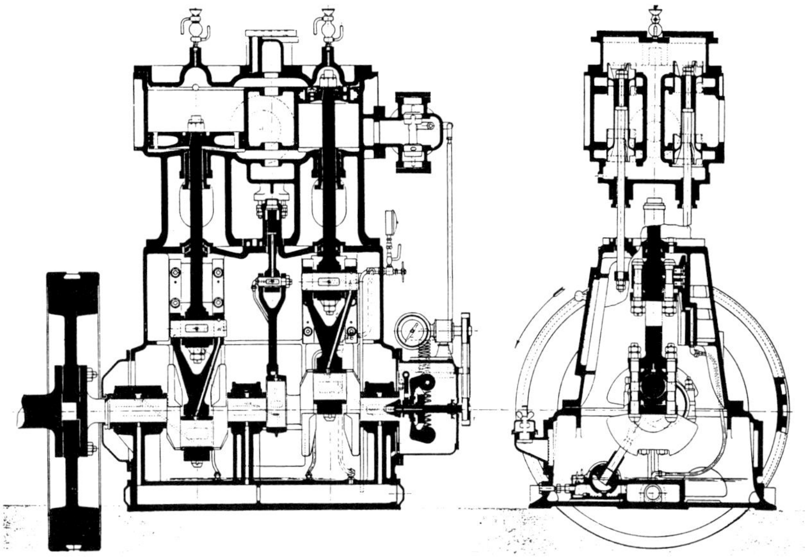

An Allen two-crank compound cylinder totally enclosed forced lubrication reciprocating steam engine produced in sizes from 50 bhp to 650 bhp.

weapons of war. Mr J Edward Belliss in his fascinating paper given before the Newcomen Society in 1965 recounts the extraordinary story that Belliss and White were never able to get on good terms in their face-to-face encounters and met only twice during their long association, all negotiations between them being conducted by correspondence.

Belliss high-speed totally enclosed engine

Over the years Belliss acquired many friends in the Royal Navy and was a regular visitor to H M Dockyards. He became especially friendly with Alfred Morcom, who had been appointed Chief Engineer of Portsmouth Dockyard at the early age of 35 after a brilliant career as assistant to the Engineer-in-Chief of the Navy and a lecturer on marine engine design at the Royal Naval College, Greenwich. In 1884 Belliss formed a partnership with Morcom, although they continued to trade as G E Belliss & Co. Shortly afterwards Morcom introduced Belliss to a young engineer, Albert Charles Pain, whom he had known at Portsmouth. Pain was appointed Chief Draughtsman in 1886 and in 1891 he designed and patented his totally enclosed force-lubricated engine. Apart from the total enclosure of the crankcase and the forced lubrication of all moving parts, the other outstanding feature of the engine was the valveless oil pump, driven by an eccentric in the well of the baseplate discharging at a pressure of about 10 psi. After a few years the patent was allowed to lapse and several other British manufacturers quickly took up the design. The original Pain engine, after thirty years continuous service, was presented to the Science Museum, South Kensington, where it is exhibited as an outstanding example of motive power development.

This development coincided with the introduction of a new steel-hulled torpedo-boat destroyer. Belliss & Co. supplied the two 4-cylinder triple expansion main propulsion engines each of 2,000 ihp. They had cylinders measuring 18¾ in. diameter x 27¼ in. diameter and two of 28 in. diameter x 18 in. stroke running at 175 rpm. The Yarrow type water-tube boiler produced steam at 200 psi and the engines exhausted to a vacuum of 26 in. of mercury, giving

An Allen 3-crank triple expansion totally enclosed forced lubrication steam engine direct-coupled to a d.c. dynamo.

the vessel a speed of 21 knots. In this instance Belliss supplied most of the auxiliary machinery which included air compressors, forced-draught fans and a compound-engine driven dynamo set for electric lighting.

The real competition between W H Allen and Belliss & Co. had commenced. Belliss & Co. started manufacturing electric generating sets in 1889, and in order to secure their financial position became incorporated in 1893. Within a few years they had a range of totally enclosed forced-lubrication engines ranging from 5 bhp to 2,500 bhp running at speeds up to 1,500 rpm and suitable for use with superheated steam up to 350 psi.

The back-pressure system of making use of the latent heat of steam by letting the engine exhaust against a positive pressure into a process main was introduced in 1899. That year in order to raise additional capital they obtained a quotation on the Birmingham Stock Exchange and became a Public Company trading as Belliss & Morcom & Co. Ltd. The story of the development of Pain's high-speed forced lubrication steam engine is told in an erudite paper given by Alfred Morcom before the Institution of Mechanical Engineers in July 1897.

Development of Allen reciprocating engines

Allen's first totally enclosed forced-lubrication engine built in 1897 was a compound engine having 6½ in. diameter x 13 in. diameter x 6 in. stroke cylinders for driving a d.c. dynamo. Soon many other orders followed mainly for land installations for driving dynamos and pumps. D.c. motors were introduced at this time together with electrical control gear. Several important orders were received in 1898/99 for back pressure engines, but these seem to have presented the firm with some unexpected technical problems. W H Allen in his annual report for the year 1900 stated 'We were not altogether prepared for the difficulties encountered in new design engines and the carrying out of specification obligations', which undoubtedly contributed to the poor results that year. Allen realised the need to concentrate upon the design and manufacture of bigger engines and the Engine Test Bay was enlarged to accommodate engines up to 1,500 bhp. In 1904 a big 1,080 bhp high speed totally enclosed three crank triple expansion engine with cylinders measuring 18 in., 27 in., and 44 in. diameter x 16 in. stroke was supplied to Crompton for driving a 750 kW alternator. This was shipped to Australia.

No review of the Company's activities in the last decades of the 19th Century would be complete without reference to forced-draught fans, ventilation fans and condensers. Together with the engines and boilers these items formed a cornerstone in the development of modern ships, both mercantile and naval. The demand for higher speeds made it necessary to employ forced-draught in order to provide sufficient air to burn the necessary quantity of coal. In addition it was necessary to reduce the temperature in the stoke-hold. It was soon realised that the centrifugal fan provided the best means of achieving the necessary air pressure.

Forced draught fans

The first application of forced draught was made by Thorneycroft in his early experiments with fast-running boats for the Royal Navy. Allen supplied his first engine and fan to the navy in 1883. During the next decade he made in excess of 700 sets and they continued as an important product and development activity at Queen's Engineering Works for many years. The early development work was started at York Street concurrently with Kapp's work on the dynamo. Later, Richard took a special interest in this work because anything to do with ships and the Navy retained a special place in his affections. For some time he was assisted by a young naval officer who became Admiral Goodwin, Engineer-in-Chief of the Fleet.

Mention has already been made of the Isle of Man ship *Mona's Isle*. She provides a typical example of the sort of forced-draught installation being incorporated in merchant vessels. She had eight sets of 7 ft. diameter direct-coupled fans each of which were capable of delivering 40,000 cub. ft. of air per minute. Holt's China Line vessels which ran from Liverpool to China without stopping had 6 ft. 6 in. diameter fans direct-coupled in pairs to a single cylinder engine delivering 20,000 cub. ft. of air per minute. This company has remained an extremely important Allen customer until the present day.

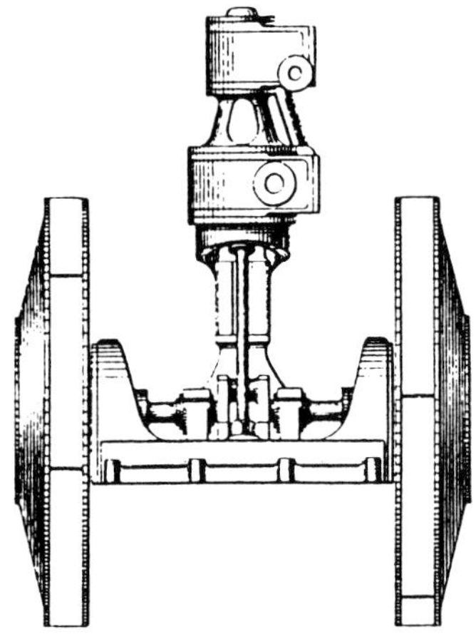

Early direct coupled forced-draught boiler room fans. Installed in Holt's China Line vessels.

A Mr White, the Chief Constructor of the Navy, in a paper given before the Institution of Naval Architects, gave the results of tests carried out by the Admiralty in *Howe*. Whereas, with natural draught the engine gave 8,200 ihp and a speed of 15.9 knots; with forced draught the power output was increased to 11,600 ihp and the speed to 16.9 knots; an increase of 40 per cent in power and 6 per cent in the speed.

It was James Watt who discovered the effects of the law of latent heat on the efficiency of a steam engine, which resulted in his use of the separate condenser. With the advent of high pressure steam engines in the 19th century, where economy was an all important consideration in marine applications and large land installations, the condenser was used in order to obtain the lowest possible exhaust pressure by condensing the steam after it left the cylinder. In this way the overall efficiency of the engine was increased. The achievement of the highest vacuum possible from the exhaust steam became every designer's aim. Initially a fine spray of water was used. Later, the surface condenser was developed in which the cooling water and the condensate were kept separate. An air pump was then employed to remove the air in the steam in order to maintain the vacuum. The condensate was then returned to the boiler reducing the amount of make-up water required for the boiler feed. Early marine boilers fed with sea water suffered from serious corrosion and accumulations of

Surface condensers

A condensing plant complete with steam driven air pumps.

salt, which had to be blown-down at frequent intervals. The great importance of a closed circuit feeding the boilers with distilled condensate had been fully appreciated as early as 1860.

By the time W H Allen started his own business the laws of thermodynamics as they affected the steam engine were well understood, although the problems of heat balance involved ever increasing and complicated mathematical calculations. Allen's policy of employing well qualified and highly trained assistants paid off.

The first surface condensing plant for an electric light generating station working in conjunction with Willans' engines was built in 1885. From that date onwards Allen regularly supplied surface condensers and pumps for both land and marine applications. The works produced a great many centrifugal condensate extraction and boiler-feed pumps and the Edward's type reciprocating air pump. Later, with the advent of the steam turbine, the kinetic rotary air pump was produced to which reference will be made later.

In 1904 Richard Allen undertook an investigation into the problems of obtaining the highest vacuum with low capital expenditure and running costs. This remains one of the most comprehensive investigations ever carried out on the subject. The following year he was awarded the coveted Telford Prize, awarded by the Institution of Civil Engineers, for his paper entitled 'Surface Condensing Plant'. During this period he was personally responsible for several patents describing air supply equipment for ships and became recognised as an expert on the design of forced-draught machinery and self-acting shutters. He published a book entitled 'The Air Supply to Boiler Rooms in Modern Ships of War' which ran into three editions.

Incorporation 1900

The year 1900 provides us with the first real glimpse of the Company's financial structure for in that year it became incorporated as a Limited Liability Company under the terms of the Companies Act. It remained a Private Company but the directors liability was limited by shares. The Issued Capital was £150,000 divided into £1 ordinary shares plus a Debenture of £40,000 guaranteed by The Law Guarantee & Trust Society. This Company survived for sixty-eight years until the formation of Amalgamated Power Engineering in 1968, when it continued to trade as A P E – Allen Ltd.

W H Allen was appointed Chairman and Managing Director at a salary of £3,000 per annum, and his son Richard was appointed Joint Managing Director at £1,000 per annum. Richard's agreement specified W H Allen as the senior Managing Director and that Richard 'notwithstanding his appointment as Joint Managing Director, should at all times, be under the control of the said W H Allen'. The Company Secretary was George Robert Henley, who had been with Allen since the York Street days. The Company's bankers were the London & County Bank (Bedford branch) and the London & Westminster Bank (Lambeth branch).

The £1 ordinary shares were allocated as follows:

W H Allen – Founder of the business	134,743
R W Allen – Eldest son of the founder	15,000
H G Allen – Third son of the founder	50
P B Crowe – Founder's son-in-law	50
J W Kempster – Manager & Chief Electrician	50
C C Hawkins – Head of the Electrical Dept.	50
G R Henley – Company Secretary	50
	149,993

The Board agreed at its first meeting on 5th July, 1900 that the cash raised by the Debenture should be allocated in the following manner:

£14,000 Repayment of bank loan
£16,000 Working capital for prompt payment of creditors
£10,000 Capital expenditure upon new plant and machinery.

The trading results for 1900 were disappointing. Turnover was down from £128,000 to £120,000 and costs were higher than expected. The Chairman in his Annual Report gave the following reasons for this down-turn. He and Richard had devoted much of their time to planning and supervising the extensions to Queen's Engineering Works and this had necessitated his spending three months in London. He spent also some weeks in Egypt and Richard spent three months in the United States studying American methods and inspecting new American machine tools. To use W H Allen's own words, 'this took away a great deal of their leading power'. Further, the works had been quite seriously affected by the Boer War and over fifty employees had been called to the Colours. But he added, 'prospects for 1901 are very much better'. The order book stood at the reasonably satisfactory value of £91,000.

The years 1901/2 were years of consolidation and by the end of the period profits had reached £15,776 and a dividend of 8 per cent was declared for the year. Nevertheless in 1901 it was deemed necessary to raise another Debenture for £20,000 at 5 per cent redeemable in five years; and in 1902 a further Debenture for £20,000 at 4¾ per cent redeemable in 1910 was sanctioned. The successful growth of the enterprise and the constant need for additional working capital and capital expenditure was making the Company extremely thirsty for cash. Allen, in spite of approaching his 60th year retained all his foresight and energy and remained supremely confident about the future.

George R Henley, Company Secretary 1900–19.

Richard made a second visit to the United States and was greatly impressed by the utility and performance of American machine tools, especially the comparatively recently introduced milling machine and grinding machine. He ordered one of the first Brown & Sharpe 'Universal' type milling machines to be employed in Britain. He saw also the great benefits of the new high-speed tool steels coming into use in America. He commented very favourably upon the 'comforts' provided for employees in the American engineering factories, such as the provision of proper well-ventilated lavatories and wash rooms and the provision of clothes lockers, facilities virtually unknown in this country at the time.

In 1902 John W Kempster, the Manager and Chief Electrician resigned after fifteen years service to take up a new appointment with Harland & Wolff in Belfast. Although disappointed, W H Allen took this set-back philosophically, for his foresight had produced a pool of highly-trained bright young men ready to fill such gaps. In 1912 Kempster had the great distinction of being appointed Chairman of Harland & Wolff, which speaks well of his earlier training and experience at Queen's Engineering Works and no doubt produced beneficial side-effects for Allen.

John W Kempster

Initially, after moving his business to Bedford, W H Allen took lodgings in the town retaining his house in Dean's Yard, Westminster. He then acquired Kimbolton Lodge in the Kimbolton Road district of Bedford. In 1900 he decided to acquire 190 acres at Bromham, on the west side of Bedford. He borrowed £14,000 from the Company and his architect son, George Pemberton Allen, working with the famous ecclesiastical architect Arthur Bloomfield, to whom he had been articled, designed a quite magnificent residence for him which became known as Bromham House. Splendid gardens and a park were created and a farm was established. The house was frequently used for entertaining visiting overseas customers, among the first of whom was the Imperial Japanese Naval Commission which had become an extremely important customer. On his death the house was sold and became a hospital. Shortly after completion of the house W H Allen transferred 1,000 of his shares to George Allen in appreciation of his excellent work.

Bromham House

It was suggested to Allen that, in addition to the Allen Prize, steps should be taken to keep former pupils in touch with the Company. Many by this time were scattered far and wide fulfilling important posts both at home and abroad. It was agreed that a Queen's Engineering Works Magazine should be introduced with the object of presenting to its readers the present state of the business and reviewing its growth and the nature of work being undertaken. It was to be instructive and well-illustrated as well as interesting. The first issue was launched in April 1904 and this excellent publication continued to be issued annually until the 1960s.

Sir Hubert von Herkomer's portrait of William Henry Allen.

In 1904 W H Allen, who was already a Justice of the Peace, had the honour of being appointed High Sheriff of Bedfordshire. During the year a well-known portrait painter, Sir Hubert von Herkomer, CVO, was commissioned to paint his portrait. The story survives that upon some suitable occasion von Herkomer asked W H Allen how much he would charge to take his son as a pupil in the works. Allen is reputed to have replied that pupillage was expensive and that he thought the cost would be about equal to the figure quoted for the portrait. There is no evidence that von Herkomer junior saw service with the Company, but figures survive indicating that at this time the Company received an income of about £3,000 a year from its premium pupils.

1905 was a milestone in the Company's history and at 9 o'clock on the morning of 27th October W H Allen called together members of the staff in the Pupils' Lecture Hall to mark the occasion of the firm's 25th Anniversary. In a speech he recalled the remarkable growth of the enterprise not forgetting the difficult times encountered in 1887, 1894 and 1900, and recalled his promise of 1897 to build an Institute for the benefit of all employees, now numbering about 1,000. He proposed that this promise should now be fulfilled and he told the assembled company that he had purchased three-quarters of an acre from the Queen's Park Estate adjoining the works in Hurst Grove as a site for the new building. Following this meeting the still considerable number of employees who came to Bedford with Allen from York Street in 1894 presented him with a silver ink stand. George Allen was instructed to proceed with the preparation of drawings, which were to include a new library and Fosters of Kempston were again awarded the Building Contract.

The Allen Institute

The building was opened on 3rd August, 1907. The Hurst Grove side of the Institute comprised a smoke-room, library, games room and billiard room. The works side comprised a large dining hall and kitchen. The idea was that during the working day the men could have their food prepared in the kitchen and served in the comfort of the dining hall, and in the evenings the whole building would be placed at their disposal for recreational and entertainment purposes.

The Allen Institute in Hurst Grove, opened in August 1907. The fulfilment of a promise made by W H Allen in 1897 to provide a building for the benefit of all employees.

In his address at the opening ceremony W H Allen recounted that recently he had been showing a rather important gentleman round the works, who commented, 'You are pandering to the working classes'. Allen had replied, 'Yes, I have found it very successful, if giving them some of the fruits of their labours is pandering.'

In the same address he referred to one John Burns and his two brothers, who had worked for him at York Street for some years. Burns became a well-known socialist orator and regularly spent his Sunday afternoons speaking in Trafalgar Square. He became a member of the newly formed London County Council and eventually he was elected to Parliament, becoming the first socialist to hold Cabinet rank. Allen surmised, much to the amusement of his audience, that when the King sent for him, 'the interview must have been one of historical importance!' W H Allen went on to say, 'nature had given him the gift of love and respect for all whom he had to work with' and that it was a very long time since he had had to discharge a man. Such declarations of paternalism are frowned upon today and seem quite out of place in the modern bureaucratic world, but perhaps we have lost something rather precious in the process of social change.

John Burns

1905 was a good year for George Allen because in addition to the Institute, he was instructed to proceed with a £6,000 extension to the offices and make further important additions to the works. In all these projects he worked very closely with James Reid, the rather severe looking Aberdonian who had been with W H Allen since the very first day he established his York Street business. Reid retired in 1915 and it is interesting to note that during its eighty-eight years of independent existence the Company had only four Works Managers.

Another of the great strengths of the Company was the stability of the Board. Three younger members of the family were appointed Directors during the period under review, otherwise the Executive

Board remained unchanged until W H Allen's death in 1926. Allen's third son, Harold Gwynne Allen was appointed to the Board in August 1906. He was born in Kensington in March 1874 and it is interesting to note that such were his father's relations with his employer, James Gwynne, the child was christened Harold Gwynne. He was educated at Westminster School and Trinity College, Cambridge. Throughout his business career he concerned himself primarily with the Company's commercial affairs. He became head of the Tendering and Contracts Department and for many years served on the Council of several important trade associations. In 1903 he married Hilda Langley, the daughter of the second master at Bedford Modern School. She subsequently bore him two sons, about whom we shall learn a great deal in due course, and three daughters, one of whom died in infancy. He became a J P and in 1925 was appointed High Sheriff of the county. He retired from the business in 1959 after over sixty years continuous service and died in 1960 in his 86th year.

Harold Gwynne Allen

A London office was established in 1904 at Queen Anne's Chambers close to the Admiralty and the centre of London's engineering district around Victoria Street. W H Allen's son-in-law, Percy Barby Crowe, second son of Sir Joseph Crowe, was appointed Manager in charge. He had served his time with the old Barrow Shipbuilding Company and married Allen's eldest daughter, Annie, after her brief marriage to Francis Fedden, Richard's wife's uncle, who died suddenly in India. Crowe was for many years a colonel in the Territorial Army, commanding the 1st Battalion of the Royal Fusiliers. He was a popular sportsman and an accomplished linguist. He was elected to the Board in July 1908, served until 1932 and died a year later. His particular interest was in dock-pumping plant and he played a major role in negotiating important contracts for the graving dock machinery installed at Colombo in Ceylon (Sri Lanka) and at the Naval Dockyard in Chatham. Two sets of unique horizontal compound engines and pumps were supplied to the former, each capable of emptying the dock in four hours which involved the discharge of some 68,000 tons of water. In 1907, because of his linguistic abilities, he was sent to Karlsrühe in Germany to negotiate a licence for manufacturing steam turbines from the Gesellschaft für Electrische Industrie who then owned Dr Kolb's patents.

Colonel Percy Crowe, VD. Director W H Allen, Sons & Co. Ltd from 1908–32.

The third member of the family to join the Board was W H Allen's fifth son, Rupert Stanley Allen. His fourth son Glendower, was never employed in the Company. After service in the Boer War with the Compton Horse Regiment he emigrated to Canada and spent the remainder of his life in Vancouver. Rupert was born in Marylebone in December 1879. He was educated at Repton School and the City & Guilds College in London, spending most of his adult life in the works concerned with production and welfare matters. Following the retirement of C C Hawkins, Rupert was for a time head of the Electrical Department becoming a Director in 1911. He served on the board of the Engineering Employers' Federation for many years. He married Gladys Hill, daughter of Dr Eustace Hill, who was knighted for his services as Medical Officer of Health for County Durham. Later, his daughter, Joscelyne, married Dr Henry Nash who for many years acted as part-time medical adviser to Queen's Engineering Works. Rupert gave the Company over sixty years continuous service. He retired in 1960 and died at his home, Turvey Abbey, in 1972.

Rupert Stanley Allen

Fairly consistently during the period to 1914, home sales

accounted for 60 per cent of turnover and export sales for 40 per cent. 1908 was a particularly bad year, industry generally was in the doldrums and the recession was felt worldwide. The situation was made worse for Allens by penal tariff restrictions imposed by the Australian Government seriously affecting the Company's growing trade with the Antipodes. W H Allen had always appreciated the value of personal contact with overseas customers and agents who by now existed in most developing countries. He was concerned also that his heir-apparent, Richard, should broaden his horizons as much as possible. One suspects from the many articles both wrote in the Queen's Engineering Works Magazine that they enjoyed their overseas experiences enormously.

Intrepid travellers

W H Allen visited Egypt in 1903, 1906 and 1909, a clear indication of the importance he attached to this market. Such was the demand for pumps for irrigation purposes that a special model was introduced named the *Nile Conqueror*. By 1909 there were indications that Allen's health was beginning to fail. He was often incapacitated with arthritis and that year he took Harold with him. In 1912 he made a long tour of India, but this was to be his last extended overseas visit.

By 1904 it had become clear to the directors that the Japanese market held considerable potential for the Company's products and agents were appointed. In August 1906 Richard embarked upon a four months world tour, travelling through Canada to Japan, then on to China, Straits Settlements (Malaysia), Ceylon (Sri Lanka), Aden, Egypt and home via Marseilles. He was especially impressed by the great strides being made by the Japanese engineering and shipbuilding industries. In 1911 he returned to Canada and then in 1914 made another visit to Japan. This time he went by the recently-completed Trans-Siberian Railway, which in those days must have been somewhat of an epic journey without the comfort and pleasures of an ocean liner.

The Company annually participated in major engineering, electrical and marine exhibitions. Examples were the Electrical Exhibition at Olympia in 1905; the Marine Exhibition in Newcastle-upon-Tyne in 1906; Dublin Exhibition in 1907; and the Franco-British Exhibition in Paris in 1908. Upon that occasion the works were closed for a day and a special excursion was arranged from Bedford for the benefit of employees wishing to visit and sample the delights of Paris.

Space precludes mention of the many actions W H Allen continued to take in the fulfilment of his very genuine concern for the physical and moral well-being of his employees. The Annual Prize Day together with the Past and Present Pupils Annual Dinner had become very popular events. The Allen Institute had proved to be a great success and an ever-widening range of sporting and social activities were regularly held. To mark the King's Coronation in 1910, he donated some of his own shares in the Company to establish an Annuity Fund and a new contributory pension fund was established way ahead of its time. He established a Maternity Fund and was ever ready to quietly assist those in need or distress. Reading between the lines of comment in the Queen's Engineering Works Magazine one realises just what a generous and civilised man he was.

Generous and civilised employers

A small, but nevertheless typical example of Allen's generosity concerns a Mr Nicholls, the Midland Railway Stationmaster. When Allen heard that he was retiring he sent him a gift of 10 guineas in recognition of his courteous service.

CHAPTER III

Technological Milestones 1906–1914

THE years 1906 to 1913 were technologically milestones in the Company's history. Several very important and prestigious contracts were received from the leading British shipyards for auxiliary machinery for a new generation of fast ocean going liners. The naval building programme was greatly expanded and accelerated and the formidable *Superb* class *Dreadnought* type battleships were introduced. New *Minotaur* class cruisers and fast torpedo boat destroyers were built concurrently. During this period the Company introduced steam turbines, and as an entirely new departure preliminary work was done on internal combustion engines. These included petrol/paraffin oil engines, air-blast diesel engines and the Fullagar gas engine. The Admiralty placed several large contracts all requiring Allen pumps and generators for new graving and floating docks and land installations for servicing the big ships coming into service. In the second half of this period the Works were fully stretched giving employment to over 1,300 men. So great was the electrical load on the works, the Company began to take current from the town's mains for the first time.

The first of the important marine orders was for large pumps for the 38,000 ton liners *Lusitania* and *Mauretania* together with electrically-driven forced-draught and ventilating fans for entirely new designs of water tube boiler. The circulating pumps were the largest of their kind in the marine service and comprised eight 32 in. centrifugal pumps driven by 8 in. x 10 in. single-cylinder totally-enclosed steam engines arranged in pairs. They developed 350 bhp at 300 rpm. The casings and impellers of the pumps were cast in gunmetal. Thirty-two forced-draught fans were supplied to each vessel, the fan impellers being 66 in. diameter. Similar types of machinery were supplied to the Cunard 'Atlantic Greyhounds' *Umbria* and *Etruria* and later *Campania* and *Lucania*.

A pair of forced-draught fans and 50 bhp d.c. motor as installed in the Mauretania *and* Lusitania.

The most important marine orders executed in 1909 were eight 400 kW generating sets comprising 3-cylinder totally-enclosed compound engines driving Allen dynamos for the new White Star liners, *Olympic* and *Titanic*. They were built to a strict specification both as to consumption and output although the final written confirmation of the order was a hand-written note from Lord Pirrie, then Chairman

HMS Superb, *a* Dreadnought *class battleship commissioned in 1906 and fitted with Parsons steam turbines.*

The Cruiser HMS Indefatigable *built in 1908 having 43,000 hp engines and 31 Babcock & Wilcox boilers.*

Pride of the Atlantic run, the 38,000 ton Mauretania *about to leave on her maiden voyage. Allen supplied the principal auxiliary machinery including main pumping engines and electrically driven forced-draught and ventilating fans.*

of Harland & Wolff. This simply stated, 'Please proceed with the manufacture, Pirrie'. Such were W H Allen's relationships and goodwill with the leaders of the British Shipbuilding industry! In 1910, shortly before his retirement, Lord Pirrie paid his old friend the compliment of visiting Bedford and touring the Works with him.

Titanic *disaster*

Richard Allen was prevented at the last moment by unforeseen circumstances from sailing on the maiden voyage of *Titanic.* Everybody knows the appalling fate of this huge ship, but perhaps it is not so well-known that a survivor reported that the last thing he remembered as he left the stricken vessel was the sound of the Allen generators continuing to function as if nothing had happened.

In 1908 the Company was so involved with Admiralty new construction work that the Board was called upon to read The Official Secrets Act. That year contracts were placed for electric light machinery, main circulating pumps and air compressors for the battleships *St Vincent, Collingwood* and *Vanguard.* The generating machinery comprised three 200 kW enclosed-engine driven dynamo sets for each ship. In 1905 Allen had obtained a licence from Albert Daw to manufacture his patent air compressors which were specified by the Admiralty for providing compressed air for torpedoes.

The largest and most powerful pumps so far supplied to the Royal Navy were installed in a new cruiser *Indefatigable.* The pumps installed in *Bristol* achieved the unprecedentedly high efficiency of 82 per cent. Machinery was supplied also for the Royal Australian Navy's new fast torpedo boat destroyers.

The Japanese Navy

The Imperial Japanese Navy became very important customers in this period resulting from contacts Richard had made, although initially the machinery supplied was not for ships but for what became recognised as the finest dockyard installation in the Far East at Sasebo. Allen supplied electrically-driven 42 in. main dewatering pumps, 12 in. drainage pumps and 9 ft. x 9 ft. cast iron penstocks or sluices together with all the associated hydraulic equipment for the graving dock.

Clearly, W H Allen greatly admired and knew personally the Hon Charles Parsons. Even when the steam turbine was very much in its

Triple expansion steam engines and 400 kW electric lighting sets supplied to the S.S. Olympic *and* Titanic *representing a milestone in the Company's history.*

infancy, Allen realised that it would eventually replace the reciprocating engine in performance and economy. He understood also, that as important as it was, the multi-stage reaction turbine was only a part of Parsons' brilliant achievements, and that his work on gearing, governors, electric rotor design and high voltage generation would have an equally lasting place in the history of engineering.

The Hon. Sir Charles Parsons

Charles Algernon Parsons (1854–1931) was the sixth and youngest son of the Earl of Rosse, an Irish nobleman and a distinguished engineer and astronomer, who became President of the Royal Society. Charles' education at Trinity College, Dublin and at St John's College, Cambridge followed by a period of training at Sir William Armstrong's Elswick Works on the Tyne are well documented elsewhere. Our immediate interest in this most remarkable man starts when, after a period with Kitson's of Leeds where he developed his epicyclic engine, followed by an extended honeymoon in America, he became a Junior Partner in Clarke, Chapman & Co. of Gateshead, in January 1884. The firm specialised in the manufacture of marine auxiliary machinery very much as W H Allen, including pumping machinery and electric light generators, and Parsons was placed in charge of the Electrical Department. He was immediately faced with the same problems as Allen and Kapp concerning the design of dynamos and the coupling together of the prime mover and the generator at a compatible operating speed.

In the incredibly short space of four months Parsons filed two patents in April 1884 describing an electric generator and its steam turbine drive. Having the successful parallel flow water turbine in mind he realised that in order to obtain good efficiency it was necessary that the steam should pass through a large number of successive stages with only a small pressure difference across each. In that manner the velocity of the steam bore a correct relationship to the velocity of the turbine blade. In developing his design he had to solve a number of complex engineering problems, which were quite outside the scope of ordinary engineering practice. A suitable form of blading had to be developed and methods of manufacture devised. He realised that exceptionally high rotational speeds would be necessary and this involved extensive and unique tests on shafts and bearings. Eventually he opted for a shaft speed of 18,000 rpm, which was fifty times that of contemporary reciprocating engines, using

A large Allen d.c compound wound multi-polar 400 kW dynamo as installed in the SS Titanic. *Electrically driven commutator grinders were supplied with these machines enabling commutator to be ground with armature in situ.*

The Hon Sir Charles A Parsons (1854–1931). The pioneer of the steam turbine, large electricity generators and high precision reduction gearing.

steam at 80 psi exhausting to atmosphere. A means of lubricating the bearing at those high speeds had to be found and he devised a direct-driven screw pump of novel design. He arranged for the steam to be admitted half way along the rotor discharging at both ends in order to minimise the end thrust. He developed a very efficient direct-acting centrifugal governor and later perfected and patented an oil pressure relay system of governing. His d.c. generator was of equally bold and novel design. Never before had dynamos been run at such high speeds. One suspects that W H Allen must have often wished that he had been in the right place at the right time to recruit this brilliant young engineer for his own organisation.

During Parson's partnership with Clarke Chapman, about 360 turbine generators with outputs up to 75 kW were constructed. In 1888 he supplied a 75 kW set to the Forth Banks Power Station in Newcastle, the first time turbines had been used for a public power supply. That year he decided to dissolve his partnership and established his own works at Heaton in Newcastle. Unfortunately, his earlier patents remained the property of Clarke, Chapman, which precluded him from building axial flow type turbines. He lost no time in designing a new machine in which the flow of the steam was radial and by 1891 he constructed a very efficient 100 kW condensing turbine. This was followed two years later by a large 150 kW turbo-generator for Portsmouth Electric Power Station. In 1895 he purchased his original patents which enabled him to resume development of the axial flow turbine which he preferred. From that moment progress was rapid and by 1900 his turbine had outstripped the reciprocating steam engine in both size and economy. The following table charts his progress.

Year	1884	1892	1900	1913	1923
Power kW	7.5	100	1,250	25,000	50,000
Steam consumption lbs/kW hour	129.0	27.0	18.2	10.4	8.2

Turbinia

In 1899 Parsons turned his attention to marine propulsion and at his own expense he built the 100 ton experimental vessel *Turbinia*, fitted with 2,100 hp turbines driving three propeller shafts. On test this little ship attained a record speed of 34½ knots. Later, much to the consternation of the 'Top-brass' at the Admiralty, he unofficially demonstrated the vessel at the great 1897 Naval Review at Spithead although it has been suggested that Vice-Admiral Sir John Durston, the Engineer-in-Chief of the Fleet was aware of Parsons' intentions. The little ship raced between the assembled ranks of the 35 miles of flag-bedecked warships at a great speed with practically nothing but the funnel visible. The fleet's fastest destroyers were ordered to intercept the intruder, but in vain and *Turbinia* showed them a clean pair of heels.

The first steam turbine driven vessel Turbinia *attained 34.5 knots at the Naval Review Spithead 1897.*

W H Allen was present at the Spithead Review and a decade later he wrote,

> 'It was a wonderful sight, and the Admiralty took him (Parsons) up. He did not sell the boat to them; I think he had sentimental reasons for not doing so, and in my opinion he was right. The Admiralty ordered a larger 30 knot destroyer from him named *Viper*, which seemed to be a great success, and resulted in the ordering of a second named *Cobra*. During manoeuvres *Viper* got on the rocks off the Channel Islands and was lost. *Cobra*, coming south shortly after collapsed in two off the East Coast. No-one knew how this came about, but it was believed to be

> due to the unequal pressure exerted on the hull when the boat was suspended on two waves. In spite of this, the Admiralty stayed with Mr Parsons and the outcome was that they ordered a larger vessel, a third-class cruiser, *The Amethyst*, which proved a great success. Later, the Admiralty authorised the *Dreadnought* class, which marked the beginning of great things in ship design. Now we have the *St Vincent* class building.'

In 1905 the Admiralty decided that in future turbine machinery should be used exclusively in all classes of warships. *Dreadnought* was commissioned in 1906. In the same article Allen wrote,

> 'I first came into contact with Mr Parsons in Portsmouth Dockyard in 1882 and was shown a turbine driven dynamo which had disintegrated on test. They tried the Parsons' turbine before the world knew anything about it. The one in question ran at 15,000 rpm and with the little commutator going at that speed came to pieces by centrifugal force. Naturally, that was the end of the Parsons' turbine for the time being; but he was not finished by any means and stuck to his work and went on with his experiments.'

This experience prompted Allen to add,

> 'The Admiralty are pioneers of science and are really a great Technical School. Although they are often spoken against, yet they have probably done more to advance the cause of science than any other body in England.'

Parsons' Marine Company

Following up his success at Spithead, Parsons established the Parsons Marine Steam Turbine Company with a capital of £500,000 and proceeded to build the Turbinia Works at Wallsend for the manufacture of marine main propulsion steam turbines. In 1901 the first turbine driven passenger vessel, *King Edward* was built for service on the Clyde and others followed quickly. In 1907 the 38,000 ton Atlantic liner *Mauretania* went into service. Her 70,000 hp turbines enabled the ship to attain a speed of 26.04 knots and the vessel remained in continuous service until 1935. All these ships were fitted with a direct-coupled drive from the turbines to multiple propellers, as on *Turbinia*. Parsons realised that if further progress was to be made the only solution would be reduction gearing between the turbine and the propeller shaft. Speed was less important than operating economy. He realised that it was important that the gear teeth should be extremely accurate both in form and pitch and it was in this area that Parsons did some of his most brilliant work. In 1912 he devised what is known as the Parsons' Creep Mechanism. The work table of the gear cutting machine rotated slightly faster than the master wheel, with the result that any errors existing in the latter were distributed spirally round the wheel being cut instead of being concentrated at one part of the circumference. The method of 'creep cutting' created an entirely new standard of accuracy for mechanical gearing and facilitated the use of steam turbines in ships ranging from slow cargo boats to the fastest warships and liners. The first large liner to be fitted with a geared power unit was *Transylvania*, which was torpedoed and lost in the Gulf of Genoa during the First War. In later years this technology played a very major role in the development of many diverse products produced at Queen's Engineering Works and later still at the Company's Atlas Works at Pershore.

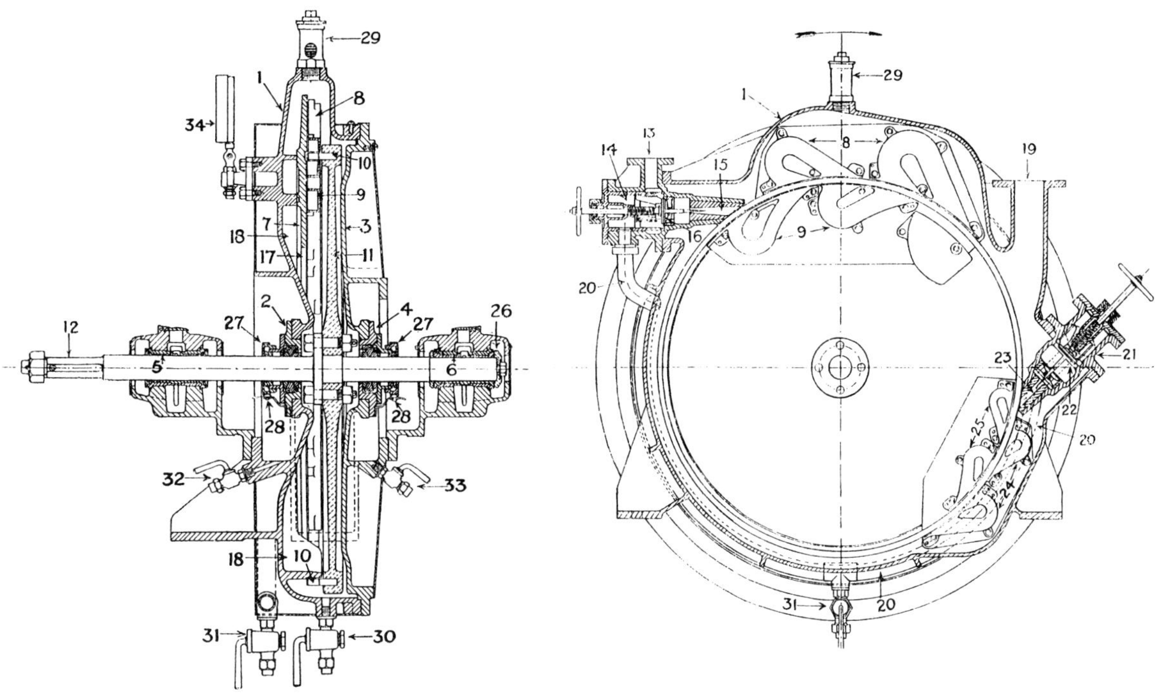

Sectional elevations of the Allen Electra *single stage velocity compounded impulse turbine introduced in 1907.*

In January 1906 the Allen Board confirmed the signing of an agreement with the Hon Charles Parsons. Unfortunately details of this agreement have not survived, but it is believed that it was more a design consultation agreement than an actual licence to manufacture, for the original Parsons' patents had expired in 1903. In fact no Parsons' type turbines were built at Queen's Engineering Works until 1913. This agreement with modifications, was renewed every five years until the Second World War. It has been said that such was Allen's regard for Parsons' work, he was content to pay royalties long after the relevant patents had expired.

The Electra *turbine*

On 21st October 1907 the Board confirmed an agreement reached between Richard Allen and Percy Crowe on the one hand and a Herr Kraus and the Gesellschaft für Electrische Industrie of Karlsrühe on the other, for the manufacture under licence at Bedford of the *Electra* radial flow impulse turbine. This was in accordance with the designs of a Herr Kolb. Richard Allen and Percy Crowe had travelled to Karlsrühe together, Crowe being well-qualified to undertake such negotiations both as a fluent linguist and because of his practical experience with turbines.

Before joining Allen, Crowe had been in charge of the Metropolitan Electric Light Company's Manchester Square generating station in London. Originally the station operated eight Willans 300 hp single-acting reciprocating engines, but the vibration they caused, transmitted through the water mains, caused so much annoyance to Lord Portman's tenants a quarter of a mile away that an injunction was obtained to stop the engines. These were replaced by eight 300 hp Parsons' turbines whose performance contributed greatly to his future success. W H Allen personally had been involved in this controversy and the incident helped to cement the friendship between the two men.

The Electra turbine was a single-pressure stage velocity compounded type. The one piece casing had a concentric cover bolted on one side to allow the rotor to be inserted. Both casing and cover were

250 bhp Allen Electra *2-stage velocity compounded steam turbine direct coupled to an Allen d.c. generator (1911).*

dished inwards to carry the shaft glands. Ring lubrication bearings were supported clear of the casing from the bottom half of the casing and cover respectively. Bolted to a facing inside the casing a ring carried two sets of redirecting channels. Two sets of nozzles were fitted, a L.P. set above the centreline and a H.P set (used when exhausting to back pressure) below. The moving blades and their distance pieces were individually caulked into a groove cut in the side of the steel rotor disc. The turbine illustrated was used for driving auxiliaries such as forced-draught fans, ventilating fans, circulating pumps and air pumps, either direct-coupled or through reduction gearing and could be exhausted to a condenser or against a back pressure of 25 psi. The initial steam pressure required was 180 psi and the turbine ran at 700 rpm.

When run in the condensing mode the steam was admitted to the L.P. steam chest and admitted to the nozzle through a control valve whence it was discharged into the wheel blading and passed in succession through the re-directing channels. The steam traversed the blade ring five times so that the combination constituted a five-velocity compounded stage before exhausting to the condenser. The steam was also led to the second or H.P. steam chest and similarly fed to the second nozzle through a control valve. After passing through the ring of blading and the lower re-directing channels it was exhausted against the back pressure in the exhaust main.

Neither a speed nor an emergency governor were necessary in most applications. The speed was controlled by a throttle valve and the fan resistance obviated the need for an emergency governor. A pressure relief valve, drain cock and pressure gauge were fitted to the casing.

Within a short time single-stage machines were in production at Queen's Engineering Works for driving marine auxiliaries such as forced-draught and ventilating fans, kinetic air pumps and circulating pumps, and these could be arranged horizontally or vertically, direct coupled or through reduction gearing. It was said the fleet would have had the greatest difficulty putting to sea without its Allen machinery.

They also manufactured two-stage pressure velocity compound turbines of a similar design for direct driving electricity generators. The casing was divided into two compartments by a central diaphragm which carried the H.P. re-directing channels on one side and the L.P. nozzles and re-directing channels on the other side. The shaft was provided with two wheels. The H.P. casing was fitted with several nozzles with hand-operated valves which could be used to 'cut out' nozzles for greater economy on light loads. Steam exhausted from the H.P. stage flowed through an opening in the diaphragm into the L.P. nozzles.

These machines required a centrifugal governor which was driven through a worm drive from the end of the shaft. The governor operated a throttle valve in the supply pipe next to the control valve. An emergency governor was also fitted to shut the stop valve in the event of an undue increase of speed. Many years later Alick Hutchinson, then chief turbine designer at Allens, developed a 'leverless' oil pressure operated governing system which largely overcame earlier problems. Today the system is controlled electronically.

Development work proceeded at such a pace that by 1909 the Company was able to conclude an agreement with the French firm Piccard Pictet for the manufacture of turbines in France. The following year *Electra* turbines for driving 250 psi boiler feed pumps, and 250 bhp two-stage turbines direct coupled to dynamos were in production.

Surface condensing plant with steam turbine driven circulating pump and kinetic rotary air pump.

Reference was made earlier to the kinetic air pump for which the Company obtained a licence to manufacture from the Controflo Condenser & Kinetic Air Pump Company. Early on it had been realised that the efficient working of a steam turbine was largely dependent on a high vacuum in order to make effective use of the energy in the steam represented by the lower part of the entropy-temperature chart. On test it had been found that an increase in vacuum from 28 in. to 29 in. had reduced steam consumption by 15 per cent. The idea was not new, it having been patented by Christian Schicle of Oldham as early as 1862, but it was ahead of its time. It was not until the advent of the turbine that speeds sufficiently high to drive rotary air pumps became available, causing a revolution in the design of condensing plants.

All this technical activity was further proof of the foresight and wisdom of W H Allen in continuing to build his business on solid scientific and technological foundations. By 1910, a score or more of highly competent engineers were employed by the Company in all branches of its business. It had acquired an ethos all of its own and worldwide had become acknowledged as experts in its fields of specialised activity. But there could be no room for complacency since the Company had no monopoly of technical competence and very fine competing products were being produced in Germany, Switzerland and the United States. Nationally we were increasingly slipping behind our competitors in technical education in the applied sciences.

In 1910 the Board approved the construction of a new laboratory adjoining the Allen Institute. It comprised three rooms; the first was an analytical laboratory; the second contained the furnaces and apparatus required for metallurgical work; and the third contained the balances and measuring apparatus and Zeiss photo-micrographic equipment. The whole was placed in the charge of

G A M Cunningham, recently recruited from the National Physical Laboratory, Teddington.

In 1913 the Institution of Mechanical Engineers paid the firm the compliment of visiting Queen's Engineering Works during its Summer Meeting held in Cambridge. Many eminent engineers, including Sir Frederick Donaldson, the President, were among the 150 guests. In his speech of welcome W H Allen returned to his pet theme of the importance of education and learning. He commented,

I.Mech.E. visit to Bedford

> 'The Institution is really a school and we are the scholars. We should do all that we can individually and collectively to promote its interests to the benefit of ourselves and the world at large. In our researches we have found out many great things and the Institution has been of immense use to us as practitioners.'

Sir Frederick then took the opportunity of thanking W H Allen for his generous gift which had enabled the Institution to establish a Benevolent Fund – 'For relieving the necessity of those who had fallen upon evil times or the families of those who died before being able to make adequate provision.'

Each year a dozen or so young men were admitted to the works to complete their training, swelling the now impressive list of former graduate pupils, students and craft apprentices, many of whom later secured important posts worldwide. In January 1912 Melville Allen, Richard's eldest son started work at Queen's Engineering Works. Born in 1891, he had been educated at Harrow and Trinity College, Cambridge. So delighted was his grandfather with this development that he wrote to the Company Secretary and it was resolved by the Board that the letter should be minuted.

Melville Allen

> 'The coming of a grandson in a business is so unusual and rare an occurrence that some observations are due from me. Melville will commence his apprenticeship at the works at an age only eighteen months younger than when his father became my partner. There was no question in his case. It was mine and his mother's wish to see him launched in life to make his own name along with his father. It is to be hoped Melville will do the same. Every opportunity is to be given to him to find some footing for himself. All the foremen have expressed the wish to be of use and help in Melville's training and with a high sense of duty Melville has the chance of making a name and place in the world for himself by following in his father's and grandfather's footsteps. I pray he may succeed.'
>
> (SIGNED) – W H Allen

In the decade following Etienne Lenoir's successful development of the gas engine in his little Paris workshop in 1865, many engineers mistakenly thought that the future of prime movers lay in the further development of the gas engine. Although the introduction of the totally enclosed forced-lubrication high-speed steam engine and Parsons' turbine undoubtedly retarded developments in the United Kingdom, a number of French and German engineers and George Brayton (1834–92) in the United States persevered with developments of the gas exploding engine. Nicholas Otto (1835–95) and Rudolf Diesel (1858–1913), both German nationals, are probably the most famous, and their work formed the basis for the development of the millions of internal combustion engines in daily use throughout the world today. Stated simply, in the Otto cycle the heat is taken in at a constant volume and ejected at another constant volume, the compression curve being adiabatic; whilst in the Diesel cycle the heat was taken in at a constant pressure and rejected at a constant volume.

The heat cycle expounded by the French physicist Nicholas Sadi Carnot (1796–1832), consisting of two isothermal and two adiabatic curves, formed the basis of Diesel's work and his heat engine was the first to be derived entirely from theory. He proved mathematically to his satisfaction that the engine would work before a single piece of metal was touched. By the end of the 19th century Continental engineers were ahead of their British counterparts in the design of internal combustion engines.

Origins of internal combustion engine

In the United Kingdom four distinguished names come to the fore when considering the development of the internal combustion engine. Firstly, the brothers Crossley, Francis (1839–97) and William (1844–1911). They obtained a licence from Otto as early as 1866, and produced the first internal combustion engine to be manufactured in the United Kingdom in their Manchester factory. They remained market leaders for big engines in this country for many years. Secondly, the name Herbert Akroyd Stuart (1864–1927) must be mentioned. Throughout the 1890s his smaller engines were the most popular in use in England and many have incorrectly credited him with pre-dating Diesel's patents, but the two were fundamentally different. Whereas Diesel sought improved thermal efficiency, Ackroyd Stuart concentrated his endeavours upon making the gas engine run on liquid fuel. Although a brilliant engineer, Akroyd Stuart lacked commercial acumen and he sold his patents to Richard Hornsby of Grantham for little benefit to himself. Hornsby continued to manufacture the Ackroyd Stuart engines for a number of years winning many prizes at the great agricultural shows and establishing an important export trade.

Thirdly, the Quaker William Dent Priestman (1847–1936) founded his small engine works in Hull in 1870 and he was the first to supply internal combustion engines for marine applications as early as 1891. Fourthly, there was Sir Dugald Clerk, a practical engineer who developed and patented the 2-stroke cycle in 1881 and became one of the world's leading patent advocates. Academically he was regarded by many as the doyen of British internal combustion engine designers.

Diesel licensed Mirrlees, Watson and Yaryan & Co. Ltd to manufacture the first British-built diesel engine in 1897. By the time his patents had expired he had licensed 81 firms to use his patents worldwide. Thus, by the turn of the century there were five classifications of internal combustion engine available, the one common feature distinguishing them from other heat engines was that the heat which was converted into work was generated within the cylinder.

1. Diesel engines – Air only compressed. The temperature due to compression sufficient to ignite the oil fuel which is injected and sprayed into the cylinder by high pressure air at the end of the compression stroke. With the later advent of the airless or solid injection engine, this system became known as the air-blast diesel.
2. Semi-diesel engines – Air only compressed, but compression was lower than in the diesel engine and the temperature due to compression was insufficient to ignite the fuel. The fuel was injected into a

vaporiser on the cylinder head. Part of the vaporiser called the Hot-bulb was unjacketed and its temperature raised before starting by means of a blow-lamp. After starting its temperature was maintained by the heat of combustion of the fuel. The mixture of air and fuel vapour was ignited by the hot-bulb. The combustion took place mainly at constant volume, but partly as in the diesel engine.

3. Explosion engines – The fuel oil was vaporised by heat in a vaporiser before entering the cylinder, and this vapour was drawn in and mixed with air during the suction stroke as in a gas engine. The vaporiser was heated before starting by a blow-lamp and its temperature was afterwards maintained by the heat of combustion of the fuel. The mixture of air and vaporised fuel was compressed and then ignited by a hot-tube which was kept hot by the combustion of the fuel.

4. Explosion engines – The vaporiser was heated by the exhaust gases or hot water from the cylinder jacket surrounding the vaporiser. Combustion did not take place in the vaporiser. The vaporised fuel and air mixed during the suction stroke, was compressed and then ignited by an electric spark as in the gas engine.

5. Explosion engines – Using unheated vaporizers or carburettors, the mixture of air and fuel produced in the carburettor was compressed and then ignited. This classification covered the original petrol engine which was extensively developed for use in motor-cars.

All the above were available working on either the 4-stroke cycle advocated by Otto or the 2-stroke cycle developed by Clerk.

By 1905 Allen recognised the value of the internal combustion engine for driving small pumps where portability was important and the liquid fuel readily available. In that year he supplied the Imperial Japanese Navy with four paraffin oil engines direct-coupled to centrifugal salvage pumps, which were used for raising the Russian Ironclads sunk in the recent conflict between Japan and Russia. We do not know if these engines were manufactured at Queen's Engineering Works. They may well have been supplied by Richard Hornsby, for we learn shortly afterwards that Hornsby was in contact with Allen concerning the possibility of his son becoming a pupil at Queen's Engineering Works.

However, an article in the Company's magazine in 1906 confirmed that experimental work on internal combustion engines was in progress and an indicator card taken from the experimental engine was reproduced. That year W H Allen made an extended visit to Egypt and secured an order for a 12 hp single-cylinder paraffin oil engine direct-coupled to an irrigation pump. At the end of 1907 the Board authorised putting in hand as a speculation four hot-oil bulb paraffin engines direct coupled to d.c. dynamos; three had 2-cylinder engines with cylinders measuring 4 in. stroke x 5¼ in. stroke; the fourth was a single cylinder unit of the same cylinder size. They further agreed to participate in the forthcoming Franco-British exhibition to be held in Paris in October 1908. One of the oil engine generating sets was employed to illuminate the stand, and this ran successfully for 12 hours a day for several months and was awarded the coveted Grand Prix prize by the exhibition organisers.

An Allen 6 bhp single cylinder paraffin oil engine and 4 in. Conqueror *pump used extensively by the British and Japanese Navies.*

In June 1908 the Chairman commented in his Annual Report to Shareholders that, 'For the past three years the Directors have been giving close attention to the design and construction of oil engines, the first large and several smaller ones showing promising results.' In his review of events published in the Company's magazine he added,

An Allen 4-cylinder paraffin oil engine and 20 kW dynamo for ships' emergency lighting.

'We have also supplied a number of petrol engines and pumps for salvage purposes, this type of machinery having proved very successful.' This confirms that both hot-bulb paraffin oil engines and spark ignition petrol engines were in production by this date.

From other snippets of information to survive one gathers that the guiding hand of the Royal Navy was providing Allen with encouragement to proceed with this line of development. Belliss & Morcom had recently purchased Wade & Jones Ltd, together with their patents and manufacturing rights for high-speed oil engines and paraffin carburettors. They had already submitted an Admiralty design prototype oil engine and dynamo for shipboard lighting. It needs little imagination to guess that Allen would not have been content to be left behind in this race. Belliss & Morcom were also successfully supplying small paraffin oil engine dynamo sets complete with batteries for farm houses and country estates where gas was not available.

Allen paraffin oil engines

The Allen oil engine business grew steadily and by 1914 1, 2 and 3-cylinder paraffin oil engines were in regular production at Queen's Engineering Works. The engines were all 4-stroke, spark ignition type engines with an overhead exhaust valve and a side air inlet valve operated directly from the camshaft. They were produced in sizes ranging from 2.5 bhp at 800 rpm single-cylinder engines to 75 bhp at 300 rpm 3-cylinder engines. Later the design was modified to incorporate side by side valves and to work equally well on paraffin, petrol, alcohol or town or producer gas. A 4-cylinder version was also added to the range which developed 46 bhp at 750 rpm. The adjacent illustration shows this type of engine direct-coupled to a 35 kVa 220 volt 50 cycle alternator. Most engines were supplied direct coupled to pumps and electric generators. The Royal Navy did not sanction their use in H M ships until about 1913, but important orders were received from India, Egypt and from many water undertakings and drainage authorities in the United Kingdom.

Negotiations with Dr Diesel

In April 1911 the Board confirmed that it had been in negotiation with Dr Rudolf Diesel regarding the granting of a licence for the manufacture of diesel engines. In May it was minuted that the Board considered the asking price to be too high and Percy Crowe was

The prototype 550 bhp 2-stroke, opposed-piston Fullagar gas engine and dynamo installed in the Gateshead Power Station.

instructed to seek an interview with the Diesel Oil Engine Company, which had established an office in London. In June each Director was provided with a copy of a revised draft agreement which was considered by the Board at its July meeting. Nothing more is mentioned in the Company's archives and the matter appears to have died a natural death. This may have been occasioned by an unfortunate fatal accident involving a diesel engine which occurred in the London Docks.

Later that year it was announced that the Company had successfully negotiated a sub-licence for the manufacture of diesel engines from the French company Shutter Harlé et Cie of Paris. They had obtained a licence from Dr Diesel in 1907 and are perhaps best remembered as the maufacturers of the first French submarine diesel engines. In September 1913, Dr Diesel mysteriously disappeared from a cross-channel ferry on a calm moonlit night approaching Harwich, and was presumed drowned. About the same time Allens supplied a diesel engine and dynamo to Bedford Corporation Electricity department, but further progress was retarded by Admiralty commitments and the outbreak of war in August 1914.

In May 1911 the Board discussed an approach from Hugh F Fullagar, a Cambridge graduate and former Parsons' employee, who had patented an entirely new design of gas engine. It was claimed the engine developed greater power that any other internal combustion engine of comparable cylinder size. He had established a company in Gateshead, The Fullagar Gas Engine Company, to exploit his invention, but lacked manufacturing facilities and expertise. The

Hugh Francis Fullagar, (1872–1916), a Cambridge graduate and former Parsons employee became a consultant and patentee establishing his own business. Later Belliss & Morcom built a similar 2,000 bhp engine to the Allen prototype.

engine had four cylinders each measuring 12 in. bore x 18 in. stroke and worked on Clerk's 2-stroke cycle. It was said to be capable of developing 550 bhp at 250 rpm, the piston speed being 750 ft. per second. The total weight was 21½ tons. Allens agreed to quote but pointed out the difficulties of testing such an engine and made it a condition that Fullagar should take it off their hands upon completion untested.

Fullagar presented a paper before the Cleveland Institute of Engineers in which he stated his engine was primarily intended to utilise waste gases to drive air-blowers for furnace blast and for driving electric generators. He claimed that the engine was much more efficient than a steam turbine of comparable size.

Harold Allen gave a very concise description of the engine in the 1915 edition of the Queen's Engineering Works magazine. The mechanical simplification of the engine permitted the size, weight and number of parts of the ordinary multi-cylinder internal combustion engine to be reduced by half, whilst the high temperature and pressure stresses in the cylinder and engine frame and the imperfect balance encountered in large gas engines were entirely avoided. The conditions of running were, it is claimed, actually easier than in an ordinary steam engine of equal power. The other advantages claimed were perfect balance, uniform turning effort, a lack of valves, reversibility and accessability.

The prototype was built at Bedford and then installed in Fullagar's Gateshead works coupled to an Allen 335 kW d.c. dynamo running at 250 rpm. It successfully supplied current to the County of Durham Electrical Power Distribution Company for a number of years. It was realised that the design was equally applicable to gas engines, heavy oil engines and diesel engines. Although Allens appear to have manufactured only the prototype, Belliss & Morcom built a similar 2,000 hp engine for the Weardale Waste Heat Power Station. The design was later taken up by the English Electric Co. Ltd at their Rugby Works producing main propulsion air-blast diesel engines incorporating improvements in patents filed by Cammell Laird, the Birkenhead shipbuilders. Engines based on Fullagar's design were built as late as 1941.

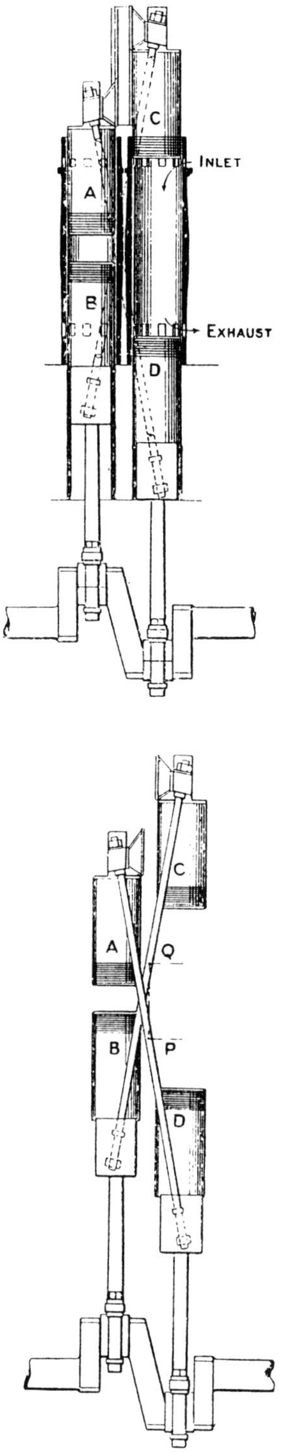

Diagrammatic layout of opposed pistons in Fullagar's prototype 550 bhp gas engine showing exhaust porting and attachment of oblique rods.

The working of the engine is shown diagrammatically in FIGS A & B. The open-ended cylinders arranged side-by-side each with two pistons were rigidly interconnected in pairs by oblique rods, external to the cylinders as shown in FIG B. The pistons at the end of their stroke uncovered inlet and exhaust ports in the walls of the cylinder which were without valves.

The action of the engine was as follows – An explosion between pistons A & B drove A up and B down drawing pistons C down and D up by the attachment of the oblique rods, giving equal and opposite impulses to the two cranks. The side thrust produced by the oblique pull was taken by the crossheads of A & D which were provided with suitable guides. The obliquity of the rods is small, less than the maximum obliquity of the connecting rods, so that the friction was actually less than would be the case if each piston had its own crank and connecting rod. At the end of the explosion stroke, as soon as pistons A & B had uncovered the inlet and exhaust ports a fresh charge entered the cylinder under pressure at the same time expelling the products of combustion through the exhaust port.

During the next half revolution of the crankshaft, compression of the fresh charge took place between pistons A & B simultaneously

Queen's Engineering Works during the early part of the 20th Century.

The iron foundry.

The heavy machine shop.

The tool room.

High speed engines on test.

The pump erecting shop.

The milling machine bay.

The dynamo winding shop.

The pattern shop.

Belt driven Conqueror *sand pump.*

with an explosion between pistons C & D. The cycle of operations in each cylinder was thus completed once in every revolution. Air and gas were supplied to the cylinders by auxiliaries, the air pressure being about 3 psi from low-pressure engine-driven air pumps. On test the indicated efficiency achieved was 37.6 per cent, whilst the mechanical efficiency of the engine itself reached 90 per cent.

Concurrently with work upon the Fullagar engine Allens were invited to manufacture a petrol engine designed by the British Anzani Company. The work was to be undertaken at a fixed price and this they wisely declined, insisting upon retaining a free hand in costing the work.

Frequently, the Chairman reminded shareholders at the Annual General Meetings that the business had been created originally for the manufacture of centrifugal pumps, mainly for drainage purposes in Holland and irrigation in Egypt. However, it should not be thought that with recent technical developments associated with totally-enclosed steam engines, steam turbines, internal combustion engines and electrical machinery, that the pump side of the business had been allowed to assume a secondary role.

In 1908 a young Swiss engineer, Herman Oxlin (Öchslin), joined the staff of Queen's Engineering Works and quickly assumed responsibility for the development of multi-stage turbine pumps. He was educated at Schaffhausen in Switzerland where he was born in 1881, and graduated at Zurich University becoming personal assistant to Professor Stodola. This was followed by a couple of years in the Swiss Locomotive and Machine Company's works at Winterthur. Although leading manufacturers of railway locomotives, the firm is perhaps best remembered by many as the manufacturers of the Abt rack railway counter-pressure locomotives for mountain railways being built at that time. Surviving examples of this system may still be seen toiling up Snowdon in North Wales during the summer months.

Paraffin oil engine driven pump with mud cutter.

So successful was Oxlin that the Chairman wrote in the works magazine, 'We have greatly improved our knowledge of the construction of turbine pumps, for which we are now doing regular business. Several pumping plants have been supplied for dock purposes in Japan. We have two sets of pumps for the Kings Bastion Dock, Gibraltar under construction and we have obtained very successful results with these pumps in the Sudan.' One wonders if these successes had anything to do with the sudden resignation of H R Stirlin the former head of the department.

Multi-stage turbine pumps were but a small part of the huge amount of Allen machinery and equipment supplied to Japan at this time. Richard Allen's visits combined with the excellent work of the Company's agents, James Morrison & Co., appointed in 1904, certainly reaped a rich harvest. Major contracts were received for pumps, steam engines, generators and large condensing plants for Kobie, Takata, Osaka, Harima and Sasebo docks and the Sasebo Arsenal. New Japanese battleships were fitted with Allen forced-draught fans and blowers and *Electra* turbines were introduced in 1912. Many single-cylinder and 3-cylinder paraffin oil engines coupled to salvage pumps were supplied during this period, together with single-cylinder, compound and triple-expansion steam engines direct-coupled to pumps, electric generators and fans. More than a dozen large condensing plants were supplied. The Imperial Steel Works and Japanese Railways, as well as many private Japanese industrial concerns purchased Allen machinery. One suspects that in

Turbine pump suitable to 1,500 ft. head.

Conqueror *high-lift 5-stage turbine pump: 1,800 gallons per minute, 250 ft. head.*

terms of value, Japan was the Company's most valuable export market at this time. In spite of penal import restrictions, the Australian market, handled by Fyvie & Steward, came second and Egypt was third.

Throughout the 19th Century Great Britain 'ruled the waves'. *Collingwood*, the first of the *Admiral* class ships was one of fourteen first-line battleships built in the 1880s. The much larger and more expensive *Magnificent* class launched in 1895 made all other existing vessels obsolete. It has been said that if she had been set to fight a fleet comprising every ironclad launched in Great Britain up to 1881, she would have sunk them all and emerged from the contest an easy winner. But Germany responded in 1898, and the race for naval supremacy commenced.

Dreadnought and her cruiser class counterpart *Invincible* were completed in 1906. *Dreadnought* weighed 17,900 tons and carried eight 12 in. guns which could be fired broadside simultaneously. Soon designs were put in hand for *Super Dreadnoughts* weighing 25,000 tons having ten 13.5 in. guns. *Dreadnought* and *Invincible* were the first capital ships built for the navy to be driven by Parsons' turbines. *Dreadnought* developed 23,000 hp and her *Super Dreadnought* successor 33,000 hp; such was the rapid rate of progress in the design of ships, guns and propulsion machinery.

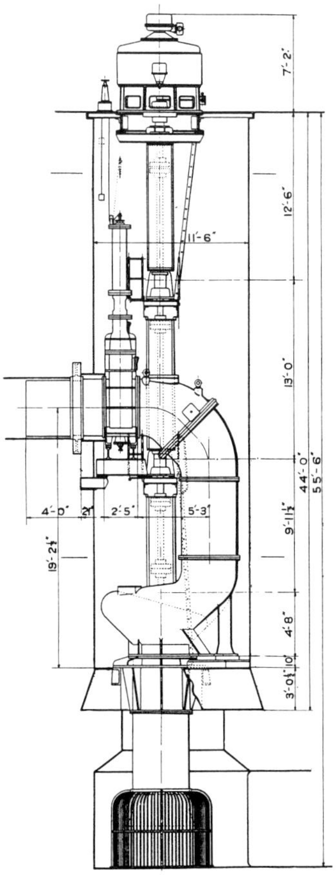

General arrangement of a 720 hp dock pump for one of HM Dockyards.

Queen Elizabeth, the first of the *Super Dreadnought* class battleships was launched in Portsmouth Dockyard on 16th October 1913. It soon became clear that the accelerated naval building programme would necessitate additional floating dock capacity and a giant 680 ft. long x 150 ft. wide dock was completed by Cammell Laird in 1912 and towed round to Portsmouth.

Allen supplied the 16 in. centrifugal pumps for raising the dock, which were driven by two horizontal steam engines complete with the necessary condensing plant. They also supplied two 200 kW electric lighting sets with shunt-wound d.c. dynamos driven by totally enclosed steam engines. Richard Allen attended the Portsmouth trials during which the battleship *Monarch* was successfully raised.

This class of work highlighted the need to increase the capacity of the Works Pump Test House and the Board approved expenditure to increase this to 4,000 gallons per minute. About the same time a new Babcock & Wilcox 300 psi water tube boiler and superheater were installed enabling the Steam Test Bay to improve its procedures when testing large engines using superheated steam at the higher temperatures and pressures being called for. Pump production also greatly benefited from the introduction of new American moulding machinery in the iron foundry for castings up to 2 tons weight; and the brassfoundry was enlarged and modernised for the casting of gunmetal casings and impellers. The Electrical Department also received attention; a new dynamo shop and test bay was built, allowing the old dynamo shop to become the winding department, thus considerably increasing the output of dynamos and associated equipment.

The giant floating dock built by Cammell Laird in 1912 for the Admiralty, fitted with Allen pumping machinery and capable of lifting 32,000 ton vessels.

Concurrently with the Portsmouth floating dock contract Allens undertook other important land work for the Admiralty at Chatham and Gosport. The Priddy's Hard, Gosport contract, valued at £14,833 was interesting in that they executed the job in its entirety, supplying and erecting on site the engines, dynamos, boilers, condensing plant, pumps and fans. Most H M Dockyards placed important orders for paraffin oil engines direct-coupled to salvage pumps at this time.

An interesting overseas dry dock contract was the new dock at the Spanish Arsenal located in the fine natural harbour at El Ferrol in north-west Spain. British engineers had been involved with construction work at the Arsenal since a Newcomen beam engine had been installed for pumping duties in 1796. The pumping plant for the new dock, which was built on the site of the original 1770 dock, was supplied and erected by Allens. They supplied the engines, pumps, Babcock & Wilcox boilers, steam and water piping and a travelling crane. Two 225 bhp totally enclosed engines and 36 in. pumps capable of removing 14 million gallons of water in 5 hours were installed. Upon completion the dock was handed over to a consortium of British shipbuilders, Vickers Ltd, Armstrong Ltd and John Brown Ltd, for the construction of three 15,000 ton displacement cruisers commissioned by the Spanish Government.

Dock and harbour work

Many commercial ports were also undergoing enlargement and modernisation in the years immediately prior to the World War, and Allens secured a substantial share of this work. Interesting dock pumping machinery was supplied to the Port of London, Leith Docks in Scotland, Smith's Dock at South Shields, the new Port of Immingham on the Humber, and at Hull. The three pumps supplied to the Port of London were capable of discharging 7 tons of water per second, putting them in a class all of their own. The new graving dock at Immingham, owned by the Great Central Railway, was officially opened by H M King George V in June 1912 and aptly named King's Dock. The Allen dewatering machinery comprised three 40 in. centrifugal pumps driven by 330 bhp Westinghouse a.c. motors each capable of delivering 30,000 gallons per minute. Alternating current was generated at the power station on the dock and the use of electrical power for driving the pumps was entirely logical. The Chairman commented in his Review of Events in 1912, 'Although we do not like to dispense with our old friend the steam engine, it is clear that where electric current can be easily obtained it is the proper system to adopt for this class of duty.'

2,200 bhp 3-crank totally-enclosed triple expansion high-speed steam engine and alternator.

Electricity was also used at Hull for the pumping machinery supplied for the large new dock jointly owned by the North Eastern and Hull & Barnsley Railways. At this time the port handled the third largest tonnage of any port in the United Kingdom. This was opened almost exactly two years after Immingham by H M King George V, in June 1914. Allen supplied two 42 in. pumps each capable of delivering 36,000 gallons per minute against a head of 40 ft. when running at 375 rpm. The 390 bhp d.c. electric motors were designed and built by Allens.

Fen drainage work

Several Fen drainage schemes were undertaken at this time and many new pumping stations were established throughout the Eastern Counties from the Humber to the Thames. Some of the earliest applications of Allens' internal combustion engine were for driving small drainage pumps. The advent of the multi-stage turbine pump was of considerable interest to local drainage commissioners. One worthy of special mention was that at Lakenheath in the Fen District. The old 40 ft. diameter water wheel which had been in constant use for over fifty years was replaced by a multi-stage pump only 40 in. diameter. The commissioners found great difficulty in comprehending how such a small machine could discharge so much water on the high side of the river.

Although all these great schemes mentioned above have been described in a few words, the reader must not forget the immense amount of design, calculation, drawing office time and project co-ordination involved in each. There were no computers to aid the designer and the slide rule and logarithm tables were his main tools, combined with years of training and experience which only firms like Allens could provide. These projects were handled from conception to completion by small teams of dedicated engineers with none of the bureaucratic committee structures so often encountered today. The satisfaction of a job well done must have been enormous.

Throughout this interesting period in the Company's history the bread and butter activities continued. There was a constant flow of orders for small centrifugal pumps, and small electric dynamos and their associated prime movers. Unfortunately figures giving the relative importance of the various activities have not survived and it is sometimes difficult to obtain a clear perspective. But by 1914 the name of W H Allen, Sons & Co. Ltd had become a household name in most branches of mechanical and electrical engineering.

Industrial relations

Considered from a business standpoint, the years just before World War I were a period of prosperity, but they were not without their difficulties. In 1912 there was a serious coal strike, there were strikes on the railways, and although Queen's Engineering Works was not directly affected, there were many damaging disputes throughout the engineering and shipbuilding industries. The Trade Unions everywhere were becoming more militant and in June 1914 the 32 engineering unions lodged a claim for a 48 hour working week, which the Board viewed sympathetically. Allens experienced some difficulties in obtaining its necessary raw materials, but thanks to the importance the Chairman had always attached to good human relations within the organisation, the Company remained free from damaging industrial disputes. It did however decline a formal request from the Amalgamated Union of Enginemen, Firemen, Mechanical & Electrical Workers to finance a new banner. Later that year the Company had its first recorded face-to-face meeting with representatives of the Toolmaker's Union and the Iron Founder's Union. The Directors took this opportunity of meeting the workers' representatives very seriously and the meeting was both constructive and cordial.

CHAPTER IV

The Great War Years 1914–1919

THE declaration of war on 4th August 1914 came suddenly and unexpectedly for the majority of the British people. Had they been told earlier in the summer that within a few weeks tens of thousands of our young men would be rushing to join the colours, they would have thought such prophecies the ravings of a madman. Even more improbable would have been any suggestion that a large number of them would not survive the next four years. Indeed, for many weeks after the declaration, most people remained convinced that it would all be over by Christmas.

Outbreak of War August 1914

Many Members of Parliament, professional men, academics and businessmen were uncertain about the need to go to war until the moment Germany actually invaded Belgium. Initially, as trouble loomed, the majority believed that Britain should keep out of a war precipitated by the assassination of a little known Eastern European Prince in Sarajevo, unless we were directly attacked. Perhaps the strongest opposition to these *laissez-faire* arguments came from the Admiralty who, for some years, had been acutely aware of the dangerous potential of the huge new battle fleet being assembled in German shipyards and they fully understood that without continued mastery of the seas the British Empire was threatened.

Since 1908 British shipyards had been fully employed and many superb new, technically advanced vessels of all kinds were on the stocks. Parliament had been persuaded of the urgent need to safeguard our maritime supremacy, but preparations for land warfare remained minimal. The attitudes of the cavalry dominated at the War Office and few steps were taken to modernise the army. Consequently, it was a comparatively small number of firms such as W H Allen, Sons & Co. who were kept fully employed on Naval work. By the outbreak of hostilities over 50 per cent of the Company's output went to Admiralty contracts. At this time some 1,300 men were employed in the works, but within a week or two over 300 had rushed to join the colours.

By November 1914 trench warfare had become established across Northern France and thousands of men perished daily fighting for a few yards of muddy, shell infested, no-man's land. Horrifying lists of casualties began to appear in the press and on civic notice boards.

The Allen family did not escape these tragic events. On 4th November, 1914 Captain John Francis Allen, W H Allen's sixth and youngest surviving son, was killed at Ypres. He was born in 1881, educated at Repton, and became a career soldier, holding a commission in the 1st Battalion Royal North Lancashire Regiment. He went to France in August 1914 and received his fatal wounds while rescuing two men who had been buried by a bursting shell. Following his death his father produced a beautifully bound book as a tribute to his life and presented a copy to each member of the family.

The firm made generous allowances to employees who had joined the armed services and those who were staff members were placed on half pay. Provision was made also for the widows of men killed in action. In the works, staff members were paid sickness benefits in full after one year's service.

As well as the heavy programme of naval work for the Admiralty, several important orders for merchant ships under construction had to be completed as a matter of urgency. These included four 400 kW steam-engine driven generating sets for the White Star steamships *Olympic* and *Britannic* as well as eight 300 kW sets for the Holland America Line vessels. For the first time several types of marine auxiliary machinery, including pumps, fans and generating sets were supplied driven by diesel engines.

Due to unusually low water in the Nile in the early part of 1914, there was a large backlog of orders outstanding for pumps for use with artesian wells. These were urgently required for raising the water that lay below the desert so as not to interfere with the Nile itself. This situation might have been very much worse had it not been for British initiative in building the recently completed Aswan dam.

Cairo main drainage

The important Cairo main drainage contract was also nearing completion. Up to that time there was no means, other than evaporation, of getting rid of rain water and in the rainy season this teeming city was often brought to a standstill. The project had been on the drawing board since 1885 and was not finally sanctioned by the Government until 1908. W H Allen had begun discussions in Egypt with Lord Cromer about this scheme as early as 1900 and one suspects that he was extremely disappointed at not being awarded the contract for the pumping machinery. Simpsons of Newark secured the order for the four main pumping engines which were located at Kafr el Gamous, 15 km north east of Cairo. Each comprised triple-plunger type pumps driven by a vertical open type 200 hp steam engine capable of pumping 660,000 gallons per hour against a head of 250 ft. Almost as a consolation prize, Allen secured the order for three compound electric light engines exhausting to a surface condenser. The Allen dynamos supplied the lighting to the pump house and power to drive the auxiliary machinery. In Cairo itself, Allens were awarded a further order for two compound electric light engines installed at the air compressing station. This station supplied the compressed air produced by large Hughes and Lancaster compressors for raising the sewage from some sixty ejector stations in the city to the main collector. The sewage then flowed by gravity to Kafr el Gamous, intercepting sewage from some of the suburbs en route. It was then pumped to the purification works and an adjoining farm, where a large area was under cultivation growing fruit and vegetables. The social benefits of this scheme were enormous for the huge population of Cairo.

200 kW steam turbine and gearing with cover removed.

The activity of greatest interest at Queen's Engineering Works during the early days of the war was the building of several Parsons'-type turbines. By 1913 the Board had realised the limitations of the *Electra* turbine in spite of the existing strong demand for these machines. They had proved to be extremely economical and reliable and four machines driving boiler feed pumps and fans had given excellent continuous service in the works over a long period. It seems probable that the Admiralty had exerted some pressure upon Allens to conclude a new agreement whereby they could develop Parsons' designs for application to ships auxiliary machinery. No doubt this suited Parsons whose capacity was fully employed manufacturing large main propulsion engines and ever-bigger electricity generators and a new licence agreement was concluded in December 1913.

Allens produce Parsons' type turbines

Immediately, the Admiralty confirmed a contract for two Parsons'-type turbines driving 200 kW dynamos complete with their own surface condensers and kinetic pumps for new warships under construction. A new turbine shop was established in the works by partitioning off a section of the iron foundry which had recently been extended to 400 ft. in length. Prototypes were also put in hand for new turbines for driving circulating pumps.

The Chairman commented in his Annual Report for 1914, 'We have considerably improved our ideas of the manufacture of steam turbines and are taking these up with the determination of making a great success of this branch of the Company's manufactures.' In 1914 a licence agreement was concluded with A G M Mitchell for the manufacture of greatly improved thrust bearings which were equally applicable to both turbines and pumps.

The new 200 kW turbine was of the impulse-reaction type. The first two rows of blades formed the impulse section; the steam being directed onto the first through nozzles and the second through a portion of a row of guide blades fixed in the turbine cover opposite the nozzles. After passing through these, the steam passed through the blades of the shrouded reaction type and then through the ordinary reaction blades.

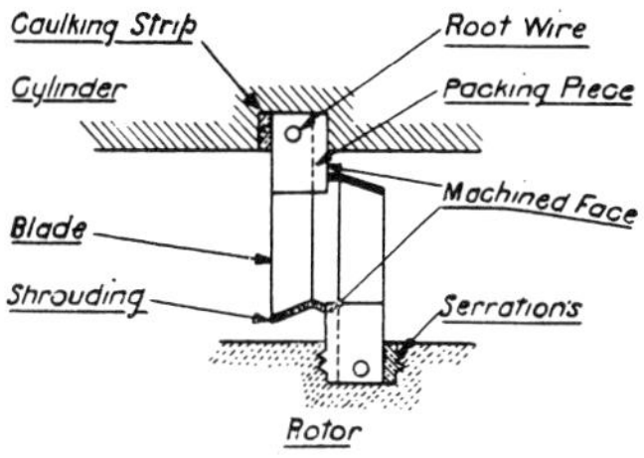

Shrouded Reaction Blades

For the more technically minded reader the construction and assembly of the blades in these early turbines will be of some interest. The blades of the impulse wheel had packing pieces half the depth of the groove to allow proper caulking. The shrouding strip was punched to suit the pitch of the blades and riveted on.

The reaction and shrouded blades were built up in segments in a former with a groove having the same radius as the rotor or cylinder. They were firstly threaded on a wire alternately with the packing pieces and then caulked. The binding strip or shrouding was then brazed onto the tips of the blading. There were generally four or six segments in each row, care being taken to ensure that the joints in one row were not opposite those in the next row. The segments were then caulked in, the only addition being blade stops which were fitted flush with the face of the dovetailed slot at the end of each cylinder groove.

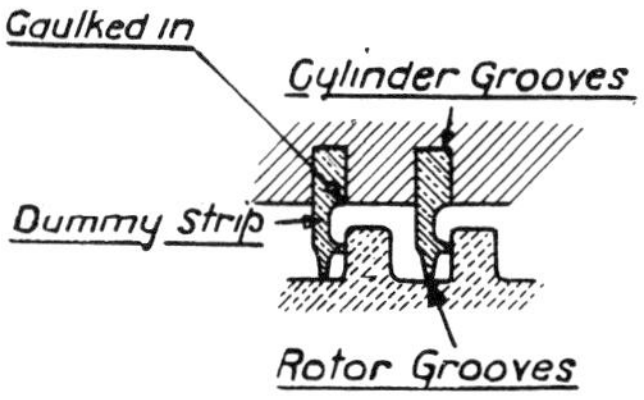

The shrouded reaction blades had a special type of packing piece which projected some distance above the groove and was wider than the blade, all as shown in the accompanying sketch. The rotor segments were serrated to let them sink into the side of the groove which was made sufficiently wide to allow a separate strip to be caulked in on the opposite side. After all the blades had been caulked in, the reaction blades were skimmed in a lathe to give the correct tip clearances and the shrouded blades were faced on the side, at the top and bottom to gauge lengths from a given face.

The end thrust of the steam on the blades in the reaction section of the turbine was taken up by two dummy pistons. They consisted of grooves in the cylinder with brass strip caulked in them, the strip being laid on corresponding grooves in the rotor. The space between the pistons was connected to that between the shrouded and un-shrouded blades in order to equalise the pressures.

The shrouded blades, dummies and glands were all ground to give the same side clearance throughout. This was done by running the machine slowly and pulling the rotor up against the machined faces of the fixed blades. When ground-up, a liner was fitted behind the bottom half of the Mitchell thrust-block to keep the rotor just clear of the faces and the top half in the bearing cap was adjusted to prevent end play in the shaft.

The nozzles were formed by copper vanes cast in gunmetal and were divided into three stages. The first stage was always open; the second stage was opened on full load; and the third stage on overload. The second and third stages were activated by hand operated by-pass valves.

A vertical shaft driven at reduced speed from the rotor by a worm gear, drove the speed governor from its upper end and a rotary oil pump at the bottom. This drew oil from a tank in the baseplate through a filter and a 3-stage cooler and delivered it at 8 to 10 psi to lubricate all bearings, which drained back into the tank by gravity.

Condensing plant

The self-contained surface condensing plant was of novel design. The circulating pump was direct-coupled to the dynamo shaft and the air pump was of the kinetic type. As a departure from usual practice the condensate extraction pump was replaced by a condensate ejector which was supplied with water under pressure from the kinetic pump, the discharge from the ejector going into a vacuum space in the kinetic ejector chamber. The kinetic pump was attached to the pinion shaft. When starting up the turbine a small quantity of circulating water was passed through the tubes of the condenser by means of a steam ejector, which was turned off as soon as the circulating pump started to deliver water at a sufficient rate.

The results obtained from the new turbines were so encouraging that during 1915 Allen negotiated a new licence from C A Parsons covering now unknown aspects of turbo generator design. It seems probable that this licence referred specifically to greatly improved governor designs recently introduced by Parsons.

The War had started with Allens having adequate capacity at Queen's Engineering Works to meet all the demands of the Admiralty and still leave capacity for fulfilling orders for land pumps and other traditional products. This all changed in the early part of 1915 when the Company was urgently called upon by the War Office not only to accelerate and increase production for the Navy, but also to undertake the manufacture of urgently needed aero engines.

The Company's initial response necessitated some major reorganisation at Queen's Engineering Works. A new dynamo shop was built and the pattern shop was removed to temporary accommodation, which meant storing the patterns in the open. This enabled the old dynamo shop and pattern shop to be combined, making a splendid new machine shop to house the greatly increased number of machine tools being made available by the Government. The brassfoundry was removed to the north end of the site, but all this was a temporary expediency.

A new 20-acre site in the Parish of Biddenham at the far end of Ford End Road was purchased for £6,000 and cleared in a very short time. Within three months of the date of purchase a new brassfoundry was built and production established. With present day planning and health and safety at work legislation in force, such speed of action, even in a national emergency, might be impossible. A new, well lit smiths' shop was built and the big hammers and other heavy equipment were transferred and working in record time. This was followed by the completion of a fine up-to-date iron foundry, which enabled the old foundry to be converted to give urgently needed additional space in the very congested Admiralty erecting shop. Finally, a new office building, separate dining halls for men and women and various other auxiliary buildings were built making the Biddenham site fully self-contained by the end of 1916. George Allen, W H Allen's architect son, was responsible for designing all the new buildings and for the supervision of the building contract.

George Pemberton Allen, FRIBA, (1872–1956) W H Allen's second son and for many years the Company's architect.

It was immediately noticeable how much cleaner and dust free Queen's Engineering Works became with the removal of the dirty initial stages of manufacture to Biddenham. This was especially beneficial to the machining and erecting shops where work of great accuracy and precision was demanded. The shop floor environment, where a large number of women were now working, proved very much more pleasant to work in and output was greatly increased.

The Company's involvement in aero engine manufacture started as one of those strange coincidences which have so often developed into success stories throughout our industrial history. Once again it was an example of the network working and of being in the right place at the right time. In the early weeks of 1915, Richard Allen paid a visit to his nephew Major Small who was in charge of the workshops at the Royal Aircraft Establishment at Farnborough. During this visit he was introduced to Colonel Mervyn O'Gorman who was the head of the establishment and, inevitably, the very serious position regarding the supply of aero engines was discussed.

At the outbreak of war no British military aircraft was flying with

The Le Rhone *rotary aero engine. 3221 were produced at Queen's Engineering Works between March 1916 and November 1918 having an aggregate of 386,520 hp.*

British-built engines. Only the Sunbeam company was then sufficiently well-equipped and able to build an acceptable aero engine in this country, but less than 100 had been delivered by the end of 1914. The French were undoubtedly ahead of us in engine design due to the brilliant work of the three Seguin brothers who, in 1908, developed the unique 50 hp Gnome air-cooled rotary engine whose cylinders rotated around a fixed crankshaft. The brothers had a long family tradition in engineering and their grandfather, Marc Seguin, the famous locomotive engineer, patented the horizontal fire-tube boiler in 1827, two years ahead of Stephenson's *Rocket*. Joseph Montgolfier, an earlier descendant, invented the hot air balloon.

Le Rhone *rotary aero engine*

The Gnome engine quickly set new standards for power and lightness in aircraft power units and was adopted by most pioneer aviators, gaining all the records for speed, height and endurance. It was soon followed by more powerful models and produced under licence by other manufacturers, notably Clerget et Blin of Levallois-Peret, near Paris, and the Société des Moteurs Gnome et Rhone. The latter supplied more than 20,000 engines during the Great War. Other licences had been granted to several German manufacturers and variants of the Gnome engine were the principal engine used by both sides during the conflict.

In September 1915, Richard Allen reported to the Board that the War Office had approached the Company with a view to it manufacturing the 80 hp 9-cylinder Le Rhone Gnome engine. Apparently, following an earlier visit to Farnborough the Company had been under consideration for the manufacture of a new in-line aero engine designed by the Royal Aircraft Establishment. This had been rejected by the War Office who now proposed that Allen should take over a contract already placed with Peter Hooker Ltd, of Walthamstow for 100 Le Rhone engines.

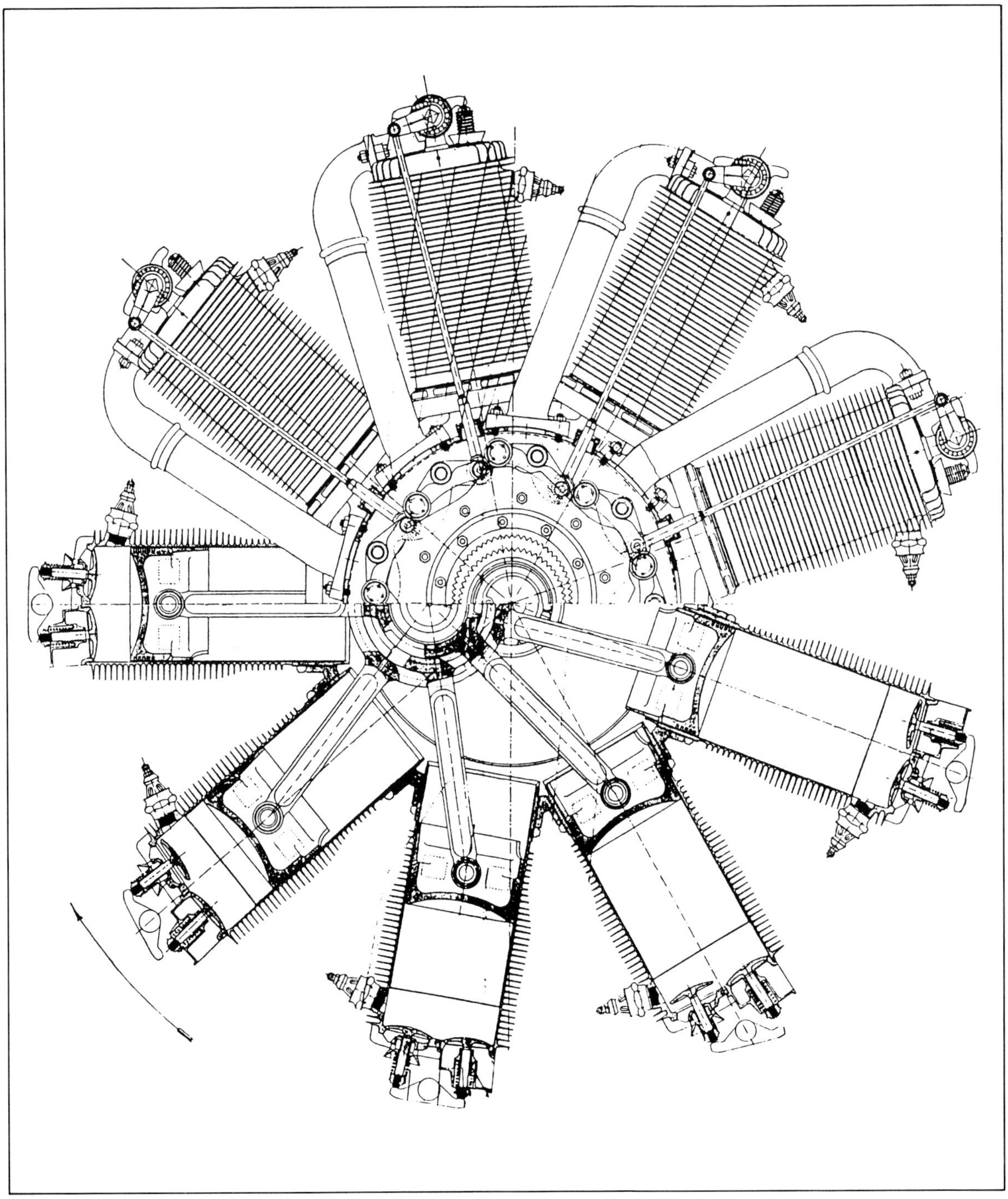

Section through a 9-cylinder Le Rhone *rotary aero engine. The cylinders were manufactured from a solid steel billet.*

The War Office stipulated that the order must be completed by Allens at the rate of three engines per week, starting in February 1916, at a fixed price of £357-10s-0d per engine plus £20,000 worth of spares. Hookers had already paid all the necessary patent royalty fees and purchased £8,000 worth of machine tools and raw materials. Richard identified that additional capital expenditure of £5,500 would be necessary and revised costs, indexed to the price of coal, were agreed. The contract was eventually sealed in November 1915 after obtaining the agreement of the Admiralty to Allens undertaking this work.

The first engine was dispatched from Bedford in March 1916. During the next two and a half years a total of 3,221 engines plus spares were delivered having an aggregate of 386,520 hp, and a value in excess of £3 million. Each engine comprised 1,156 components, the great majority of which were produced in Queen's Engineering Works. Several visits were made to Paris and Lyon by Allen directors and technicians where they were briefed about novel methods of manufacture developed by the French. They were especially impressed by the new methods of heat treatment employed and by the new Brinell test for determining the hardness of metals. At Bedford, E C Ashwell was appointed foreman of the new aero engine shop at a wage of £2-10s-0d per week.

Rotary engines operated on the 4-stroke Otto cycle and were always built with an odd number of cylinders, nine being the maximum, and arranged radially in one plane around the crankcase like the spokes of a wheel. This gave good mechanical balance, and the engine being provided with equally-spaced firing intervals, ran smoothly, spinning round the fixed crank. The propeller was secured directly to the crankcase. The crankcase itself was used to distribute the petrol/air mixture to the whirling cylinders. The carburettor was entirely manual, comprising a petrol jet controlled by the pilot and a flap valve for throttling the air supply. Oddly enough, this crude technique for controlling the engine was easy to learn and was liked by the pilots. A unique feature of the Allen-built Le Rhone engines was that cylinders were manufactured from solid nickel-steel billets.

Sometime in 1917, the engine was modified to give an increased power output to match the performance of captured German aircraft and became known as the 110 hp Le Rhone engine. The swept volume of the pistons was increased from 721 cub.in. to 919 cub.in., the engine revolutions were increased from 1,150 rpm to 1,250 rpm, and the bmep was increased from 62 psi to 87 psi. These modifications increased the power output by 120 per cent from 62 bhp to 137 bhp. Although the engine capacity-to-power ratio was low by the comparative standards of 1915, the power-to-weight ratio was very attractive to aircraft designers and the popularity of the rotary engine was not surpassed until the middle of 1917. The Allen-built Le Rhone engine was installed in the following British aircraft: The DH5, the Sopwith Scout, the Bristol Scout and the Avro.

For running tests in the Works yard the Le Rhone *engines were mounted on an old gun carriage.*

Water-cooled in-line and V-engines began to supersede the rotary engine. By the end of 1918 some 8,200 rotary engines had been supplied to British aircraft manufacturers compared with 6,737 stationary engines of which 85 per cent of the latter were produced in 1918.

By coincidence, W H Allen's former employers, Gwynnes, had secured a contract from the Admiralty in 1914 for the manufacture of the Clerget rotary engine. Reference was made in Chapter I to a disagreement in the Gwynne family which had resulted in the younger brothers John and Henry breaking away from their elder brother James, and establishing their own company at Hammersmith. Due largely to the patient endeavour of Henry Marshall of Gainsborough, who had been appointed by the court, arbitrator in the dispute, the two companies were reunited in 1904. Rotary aero engine production was established in a new factory at Chiswick in 1915.

At this time, a small group of naval officers had expressed concern about the lack of enterprise and spirit among the upper echelons of the armed services. They felt that the monolithic structure and rigid hierarchy of the army failed to encourage original thinking. They soon received the backing of Winston Churchill who was then First

Lord of the Admiralty, and the group became officially known as the Royal Naval Air Service (RNAS). Some officers, in their keen desire to widen their horizons, took to the air concerning themselves initially with defence against Zeppelin raids. Others helped to introduce mechanical traction in warfare and a unit operating in France developed the armoured car. Others examined ideas for armoured troop-carriers and the use of caterpillar tracks as employed on the American Holt tractor. Under the leadership of E. Tennyson D'Eyncourt, Director of Naval Contracts, they played a major role in the formation of Churchill's Landship committee which resulted in the introduction of the military tank in 1916. William Foster & Co. Ltd of Lincoln, the firm entrusted with the manufacture of the prototype tanks, and Gwynnes both became wholly-owned subsidiaries of W H Allen, Sons & Co. Ltd in 1960.

Shortly after joining the RNAS in 1914, W O Bentley of classic car fame, was sent by the Admiralty to Gwynnes as a technical liaison officer with the rank of Lieutenant. Bentley had started life as a steam locomotive engineer at the Great Northern Railway's Doncaster works. He retained a love of steam for the remainder of his life. In 1912, in partnership with his brother, he turned his attention to the internal combustion engine. Prior to joining the RNAS, he had discussions with Ernest Hives, who was then in charge of Rolls Royce's experimental shop, about the design of a prototype 12-cylinder stationary aero engine.

W O Bentley and aero engines

At Gwynnes, Bentley wasted no time in proposing a number of design improvements based on his knowledge of high performance car engines. These included the use of aluminium cylinders with steel liners and aluminium pistons which enabled him to increase the power of the Clerget engine from 82 bhp to 158 bhp. Tests proved entirely satisfactory, but Gwynnes' directors were fearful of the repercussions this might have in France and dared not jeopardise the royalty arrangement negotiated with the French company.

In the midst of this political strife, the Admiralty moved Bentley to the Humber Company in Coventry, allowing him freedom to develop his ideas. This resulted in his famous BR1 rotary engine which went into operational service in July 1917. Almost simultaneously he was authorised to produce an even more powerful 230 bhp rotary engine which became known as the BR2. Orders for this engine were placed with Gwynnes, Daimler, Crossley and Ruston Proctor . By November 1918, 30,000 of these engines had been ordered, but soon after the Armistice many of these orders were cancelled and rotary engines were quickly eclipsed by new designs of stationary engine. The five hundred women engaged at Queen's Engineering Works for aero engine production were made redundant and the department was closed down in the Spring of 1919. Virtually all design and manufacture of the Le Rhone, Clerget and Bentley engines ceased everywhere after the war.

For the Allen family personally, the rotary aero engine spelt tragedy, for in March 1917 W H Allen's eldest grandson Melville, the only son of Richard Allen, was killed in a flying accident. Melville had joined the Royal Flying Corps in January 1915 after having passed through all departments at Queen's Engineering Works. Following a period of active service in France he was seconded for special duties in connection with the manufacture of aero engines. Later, he was appointed to the RFC Testing Squadron and it was whilst so engaged that his plane crashed in Norfolk due to engine failure. He had married in August 1915 and his only child Denis was born six months after his father's death. The Company ceased to manufacture aero engines within a month of the Armistice being signed.

Another war-time tragedy affecting the Allen family was the death at Gallipoli of Lieut. Hugh Crowe serving with the 4th Battalion Royal Fusiliers. He was the only son of W H Allen's eldest daughter Annie and Colonel Percy Crowe. Lieut. Crowe was a military conducting officer at the time of his death and was lost when the warship *Hythe* foundered after a collision in October 1915. Previously, he had seen action in France.

At the time of Melville's death W H Allen was seventy-three years of age, well past the age when many men considered retiring. His health was not good and although he still exerted a very dominant role in the Company's affairs, he left the day-to-day management of the Company to his sons. Undoubtedly he had been emotionally affected by the retirement of James Reid, the Works Manager since 1906. Reid had been with him since 1871 and a close relationship based on mutual trust and respect had developed between the two men. Allen realised that Reid's retirement marked the end of an era and that his like would not be seen again.

James Reid, a former Gwynne employee joined W H Allen in 1880 and remained the Company's distinguished Works Manager and a close confidant from 1906 until his retirement in 1915.

Reid's farewell presentation held in the Pupils' Lecture Hall in June 1915 was an occasion for W H Allen to reminisce. He recalled how forty years earlier he had been called to the factory gate to interview a young man who wanted a job. He realised immediately that here was a man with a high sense of duty and earnestness of purpose, adding that Reid had always fully vindicated his judgement during their long relationship. He reminded Reid how, out of a ruin, they had built up together the York Street Works in the 1880s. He referred to the enormous technical progress that had taken place during their association, and how amazed they were, when in 1871 Mr Bevis of Lairds, the shipbuilders, asked them to produce a steam engine working at 60 psi and how quickly this was followed by the compound engine working at 100 psi and the triple expansion engine working at 150 psi.

He told the amusing little anecdote that when they started business, every man was required to bring his own two-foot rule, adding, 'None of them matched. Now we know that the standard of success is the standard of our gauges.' He praised Reid for the way he had accepted his own sons into the business and how he had helped them to establish themselves and attain the important positions they now held. Although a somewhat severe Presbyterian, Reid appears to have been very good with pupils and apprentices, and always adopted as his theme the three virtues of Truth, Duty and Self-education. For many years to come, many engineers holding high positions referred to James Reid with affection and gratitude.

James Reid

Reid was a modest man of few words and in returning thanks simply said,

> 'I have here a little book which is a link with the old York Street Works, and I do not think the Chairman has seen it for many years. It is the first working number book (Order book) we had there, and while it is only a very small note-book, I think it contains the whole of the orders received for the years 1880 and 1881. Every order is entered up in the Chairman's own handwriting and some of them contain sketches of the work to be done. I have pleasure handing it to the Chairman as a memento of our early days together.'

The first page of the notebook, now in rather a tattered condition, is illustrated in Chapter I.

A few months later, when the Company became a controlled establishment under wartime regulations, Reid, a man without any hobbies and anxious to help the war-effort, rejoined the firm as an aero-engine inspector, a position he held until two months before his death in May 1919, aged seventy-three. His son Watson Reid remained in the Company's employ for many years.

Six weeks before Reid's death another Company stalwart passed away. George Henley, the Company Secretary since 1900 died on 1st April 1919. He had joined Allen at the York Street Works as a clerk in November 1880 and proved himself to be a man of the highest integrity becoming greatly respected by all associated with Queen's Engineering Works. He was succeeded by Robert Anderson, a Scotsman by birth and graduate of Edinburgh University. Prior to his appointment he had been with the Company's auditors, Deloitte, Plender, Griffiths & Company and had been responsible for Allen's audit for several years. He continued as Company Secretary until 1914.

Archibald Carmichael, MIMechE, AMICE, a former Allen pupil, appointed Works Manager in 1915, Works & Engineering Director 1925, retired due to ill health 1937.

Archibald Carmichael, AMICE, MI Mech E, whom both W H Allen and Richard Allen often referred to in glowing terms, succeeded Reid as Works Manager. A native of Ely in Cambridgeshire, he had been a pupil at Queen's Engineering Works from 1898–1902 gaining the coveted Allen Prize in 1902. He spent the next three years at the Central Technical College, South Kensington studying under the guidance of Professor W C Unwin. In 1905 he went to the Royal Arsenal Woolwich for two years to gain further experience, returning to Bedford as personal assistant to Richard Allen. In 1915 upon Reid's retirement he became the Company's third Works Manager. He rendered twenty-one years valuable service in this capacity during an extremely difficult period in its history. His special interest was Fen drainage and he was long remembered for his erudite paper on the drainage of the Bedford Level given before the Institution of Mechanical Engineers.

In spite of the exigencies of war and being at the centre of great events in the engineering world, head of a great company of national importance, suffering poor health and personal tragedy, W H Allen never lost his keen interest in his former pupils. He wrote in the Allen Magazine,

W H Allen's affection for his pupils

> 'I have from time to time received visits from a number of my pupils and apprentices and have been much cheered by what they have done and what they had to say. Many however come to the works without me knowing of their visit. I should like it to be known that I am at all times anxious to see any old students and to do the best I can for them'.

Towards the end of the war, Allen received the honour of being invited to become the President of the Institution of Mechanical Engineers, but sadly due to his poor state of health he felt compelled to decline the invitation. What a sad decision this must have been for the great man.

The catalogue of machinery produced by Allens for the Admiralty during the war is quite extraordinary. The value of sales increased eight fold from £250,000 to over £2 million per annum. We shall see

The Vickers design 800 hp 8-cylinder submarine main propulsion air-blast diesel engine manufactured by both Allens and Belliss & Morcom during the First War.

in a later chapter that this led the Company into grave difficulties without any recompense from the Government. Until the advent of the Le Rhone aero engine, the whole of the Company's manufacturing capacity had been placed at the disposal of the Admiralty which resulted in them becoming involved in the manufacture of machinery not previously made.

Submarine engines

In 1915 due to a critical shortage of engines, the Admiralty requested both Allens and Belliss & Morcom to undertake the manufacture of main propulsion solid injection air blast diesel engines for submarines. These were a Vickers design having 8 cylinders developing 800 bhp at 380 rpm. The cylinders measured 14¼ in. bore x 15 in. stroke and had a piston speed of 950 ft. per minute. Allens completed their first engine in seven months, building a total of three engines. At a subsequent function the Engineer-in-Chief of the Fleet commented, 'Whenever this Company has been called upon to produce machinery out of the ordinary, they have always done it in the time required.'

Other types of main propulsion machinery undertaken by Queen's Engineering Works were sixteen sets of geared steam turbines for 3,500 shp patrol boats; two cruising turbines for destroyers; twenty-four 1,100 hp triple-expansion reciprocating engines for mine-sweepers; fourteen sets of 450 hp trawler engines; and various sizes of compound engines for launches and pinnaces.

Marine main propulsion steam engines manufactured at Queen's Engineering Works for The Admiralty during World War I.

A 450 hp triple expansion main propulsion steam engine for trawlers. One of fourteen sets built at Queen's Engineering Works during the First War.

1,100 hp triple expansion minesweeper engine, one of twenty-four built at Queen's Engineering Works during the First World War.

70 ihp compound launch engine built for the Royal Navy.

160 ihp compound Admiralty pinnace engine.

The following more traditional products were completed for the Admiralty during the war:

645 sets reciprocating steam engines and dynamos ranging in size from 26 kW to 200 kW capacity.

581 sets reciprocating steam engines and turbine circulating pumps having suction and discharge branches from 6 in. to 35 in. diameter.

749 sets of fans and engines, some reciprocating and some turbine driven with fans from 68 in. to 88 in. diameter.

In addition a substantial number of paraffin oil engines were produced by the Company for important subsidiary duties comprising:

> 77 Paraffin oil engines of 45 hp each for driving alternators for supplying current to submersible pumps.
> 82 Paraffin oil engines driving 12 in. diameter salvage pumps.
> 85 Paraffin oil engines driving 6 in. diameter salvage pumps.

In total all this machinery represented an aggregate power equivalent to 162,145 hp.

Salvage pumps

In addition, several new items of plant of a novel character were put in hand. Perhaps foremost in this category was the vertical spindle steam turbine driven pipeless salvage bilge pump. The need for larger capacity pumps, often operating in confined spaces, became urgent. It was decided to produce a self-priming, direct-coupled, vertical spindle multi-stage turbine pump. This would enable the pump to draw direct from the bilge and discharge through the ship's side through a non-return valve. The pump ran satisfactorily when submerged or flooded until the water reached the turbine. It had an output of 1,000 tons of water per hour pumping against a head of 35 ft., and weighed only 43 cwt. complete. The turbine employed was a single stage impulse type running at 950 rpm with a steam pressure of 150 psi and a back pressure of 25 lbs. It was immediately adopted in all new warships under construction.

It became urgently necessary to have equipment able to raise ships sunk by enemy action in comparatively shallow water. Under the superintendence of Commodore Young and Engineer Captain H R Teed RN, who at a later date joined Allen's staff, the firm was commissioned to assist in this work. A small steam turbine driven salvage pump mounted on a trolley was developed for use where ease of transport, small space and weight were important. The turbine was of the radial-flow impulse type connected to a twin parallel pump having an output of 750 tons of water per hour against a head of 35 ft. 167 sets were produced in record time and some were used with great success in operations at Zeebrugge.

Forced-draught fans

During this period, the design section of the pump department devoted a great deal of its time to the development of improved forced-draught fans for ships' boiler rooms. The Admiralty were constantly seeking smaller, lighter boilers with a greater steam output. The advent of fuel oil as a replacement for coal made this a great deal easier, but the ever-present problem of providing sufficient air for combustion remained. Fans were required to supply more air at higher pressures. Richard Allen became acknowledged as an expert in both fan and shuttering design and during the War he presented several important papers on the subject.

All this activity necessitated considerable reorganisation in the works, the burden of which was largely shouldered by Archibald Carmichael. There were acute shortages of skilled labour to contend with and various dilution schemes were successfully introduced. Women were introduced into most departments, including the iron foundry and brass foundry where they were employed making cores and fettling small castings. By the end of the war Queen's Engineering Works employed 2,360 men and boys and 1,034 women. The women were mainly employed in the machine shops and assembling the Le Rhone aero engine.

Internal combustion engines manufactured at Queen's Engineering Works during World War I.

A portable 4-cylinder paraffin oil engine and alternator.

25 bhp paraffin oil engine direct coupled to 16 kW d.c. dynamo.

An Allen portable salvage pump direct coupled to a 4-cylinder paraffin oil engine.

12 in. Conqueror *centrifugal pump fitted with a multiple suction box direct-coupled to a 4-cylinder paraffin oil engine.*

Forced Draught fans built during World War I.

Steam turbine driven forced-draught fan.

An early steam turbine driven vertical spindle forced-draught fan.

In June 1918 Queen's Engineering Works were honoured by a visit of their Majesties King George V and Queen Mary. W H Allen is seen here escorting Her Majesty through the Works yard.

Shortly after the outbreak of war in 1914, it was realised in high places that this war differed from all others in not simply being a war between soldiers, but a war between peoples. A number of key requirements for the successful prosecution of the war were no longer available in the United Kingdom. Britain had for some years been relying upon Germany for some essential scientifically-based products and the supply of these automatically ceased. These included tungsten and special alloy steels and with the sudden call for large numbers of high-performance engines of all types the need for special nickel, chrome and similar high tensile steels became very great.

Science and education

British ingenuity overcame these problems, but this was due largely to firms like W H Allen, Sons & Co. who had placed science and education high on their agenda. Allen's foresight in these matters paid a great dividend to the nation. Wars and economic recession are cyclical as night follows day and this should never be forgotten. We must always think long and hard before cutting back on research, development and education; we must ponder carefully the long-term consequences of selling-off whole industries to foreign investment; the government should not be allowed to abandon enterprises which potentially have a long term strategic importance; for these are as fundamental to our national survival as maintaining a military defence capability.

In June 1918 Queen's Engineering Works was honoured by a visit by Their Majesties King George V and Queen Mary who spent over an hour in the works. They shook hands with a very large number of people and took a keen interest in all that they were shown, leaving behind them feelings of great satisfaction and loyalty. The same year

Richard Allen had the honour of being appointed one of the first to receive the CBE for his services to the Royal Navy.

The day after the Royal Visit, the Company announced the establishment of a new Recreational Club on a 10-acre site it had leased adjacent to the Biddenham Works. They undertook to provide a first class cricket pitch to County Ground standards complete with a splendid new pavilion. An executive management committee was formed and arrangements were made so that employees and their families would be able to enjoy a wide range of sporting and social activities.

A month later, a silver plated Le Rhone aero engine was presented to the Bedfordshire County Council in a ceremony held in the Shire Hall. The engine, which had been closely inspected by the King only a few weeks earlier, was received on behalf of the people of Bedfordshire by His Grace the Duke of Bedford, Lord Lieutenant of the County. Other engines were presented to Imperial College, South Kensington, and Oxford, Cambridge, Liverpool and Glasgow Universities, for educational purposes. Fortunately a specimen still survives in the ownership of the Company.

On 4th January 1919, the Company gave a splendid banquet in the new dining hall which had been specially built for female employees in 1917. Sadly, much to everyone's great regret, the Chairman was unable to attend due to ill-health. In proposing the toast to the Company and its founder, Archibald Carmichael outlined the history of the enterprise. He suggested the success which had attended the Company since its inception was due to one fact, 'that whatever obligations the Company had undertaken it had always legally and morally carried them out to the letter, thereby gaining the complete confidence of the engineering world.' Richard Allen in his reply, after complimenting and thanking the staff for their remarkable performances during the War years, talked of the future. He said, 'IF everybody can be kept fully employed, I have no fear of the future.' It sounded almost as though he had a premonition of what was to come.

The War had claimed the lives of thirty-two Allen employees and pupils and W H Allen made a generous donation to the Bedford Memorial erected in 1921.

CHAPTER V
The Difficult Years 1919–34

THERE is no evidence that the Board, collectively, at any time during the War gave serious consideration to the types of products the Company should be concentrating upon when peace was restored. Many people in authority seemed to think normal trading would be resumed almost as a matter of course. However, events moved quickly following the signing of the Armistice in November 1918 and resulted in the cancellation of most government contracts. Throughout 1919, men were returning from military service expecting the promised 'Land fit for heroes', but this never materialised.

There was not the rush for capital equipment some had forecast and credit was not freely available. Suddenly it was realised that many overseas markets on which British industry had depended for several generations no longer existed. Many companies, especially those previously trading with Germany and its allies and with Russia and Eastern European countries were left with massive debts and in some instances lost their overseas investments. The United States and British Dominions quickly became protectionist and even isolationist in their attitudes to trade.

Serious trade depression 1921

By 1921, the Chairman was reporting the worst year's trading in his living memory. No interim dividend was paid and the Board called for drastic reductions in overhead expenses. It even became necessary to seriously consider a reduction in wages and salaries. The capital of the Company was increased to £400,000 by a Bonus Issue of shares and the capitalization of reserves. The directors also took this restructuring as an opportunity to invest a further £50,000 in the Company in the form of a 4 per cent Funding Loan. At the same time, Harold Allen and Rupert Allen were appointed Managing Directors and in order to comply fully with the requirements of the Companies Act, the name of the Company was altered to W H Allen, Sons & Company Limited.

Widespread labour unrest and damaging trade disputes affected the supply of raw materials to Queen's Engineering Works. Some rationalisation became necessary in the works. The old brassfoundry, the Jig & Tool department, the Automatic Shop, and the Hardening Shop were all closed. All the women engaged during the War and some men were made redundant. But on a more optimistic note, the

Board approved capital expenditure in the Works amounting to £64,000. A new 3-drum Babcock & Wilcox water tube boiler evaporating 20,000 lbs of steam an hour and a new 500 kW turbo generator complete with condenser were installed replacing the reciprocating engines formerly employed in generating electricity; a new cooling tower was built for the Power House; a new Oil Engine Test House, which had been under consideration for some time, was finally authorised; a new Heenan & Froude dynamometer was purchased; and the stores reorganised.

Benefits of volume production perceived

The benefits the Company had derived from volume production during the war quickly became appreciated and understood. Basically, pre-war the Company had been a large scale jobbing shop, manufacturing only what it had already sold. During the War it had been able to sell all it could produce and the benefits of volume production became manifest. It was obvious that the Company could not hope to produce in large quantities the machinery which it had previously manufactured. For example every condenser had to be made to meet the specific conditions for which it was required. The arrangement of marine circulating pumps differed in every ship, affecting their size and branch configuration. The Company was not even its own master in the field of electric lighting and electric power generation. Every shipbuilder had his own special needs. For example, voltages varied necessitating alterations in dynamo design. These special needs prevented the Company using its plant and facilities in the most efficient manner. It was not surprising therefore that during the immediate post-war years there was a strong lobby within the firm to concentrate upon types of machinery which would permit volume production for stock.

The Board sanctioned the production of 500 *Conqueror* pumps for stock in order to keep the iron foundry busy. Immediately the War had ended overseas agencies were re-activated and it was confidently expected that there would be a steady demand for drainage and irrigation pumps in Egypt, India and other overseas markets. The Board further agreed that, henceforth, the Company would concentrate its design and development resources upon the following products:

Post-War product range

Crude Oil Engines
Steam Turbines
Turbine Driven Generators
Turbine Driven Pumps and Fans
Kinetic Pumps for Condensers
Electric motors and starters.

In 1921, in order to strengthen the management team and in recognition of services rendered, Archibald Carmichael, the Works Manager, and Herman Oxlin, then head of the Turbine Department, were appointed Non-executive Directors. These appointments did not automatically carry a seat on the Board. W H Allen paid his last visit to Queen's Engineering Works in October 1922. He was so crippled with acute rheumatism that he was unable to leave his car and a steady stream of his old staff and colleagues lined up to pay their respects to the great old man.

The pupils and apprentices department was also re-activated. During 1919 the first four post-war pupils and seven trade apprentices were engaged. The apprentices weekly wage was increased to

P H S Kempton, appointed Head of the Education Department in 1919, formerly Head of Training at G W R Works, Swindon.

16s 9d for 47 hours work per week and those returning from military service received an additional 21s 6d per week National War Bonus. During the War Oswald Carlton Smith MA had been appointed Demonstrator, replacing his brother Stanley, a former Allen pupil who had succeeded Ernest Lamb. In 1919 Oswald resigned and joined his brother who had established a business in Luton. He was succeeded by P H S Kempton as Head of the Education Department and the normal work of the Lecture Room was resumed. Kempton had graduated from Imperial College, London, then held a research scholarship at the Royal College of Science and gained his initial experience in the education and training of engineering students at the Great Western Railway's Swindon Works.

Since 1913 he had been on the staff of the Department of Naval Education at Portsmouth Dockyard, which handled nearly 1,000 students a year. The Dockyard school system was probably the oldest works school system in the country dating from the year of W H Allen's birth in 1844. Numbered among its students were the great engineers and naval architects Sir William White, Sir George Carter and Vice-Admiral Sir George Goodwin. In February 1920 HRH The Duke of York, later to become King George VI, visited Queen's Engineering Works as President of the Industrial Welfare Society. So renowned had Allens become for their enlightened attitudes to education, training and good industrial relations, that the Duke wished to see for himself the Company's Welfare and Education facilities.

Internal combustion engines

During the war the Company had acquired considerable experience in the design and production of internal combustion engines. The engines produced between 1906 and 1919 had an aggregate output of 15,000 hp. Immediately after the war a large potential market for hot-bulb semi-diesel engines had been identified to supersede the original petrol/paraffin engines. It was believed that concentration upon this type of engine would go a long way to satisfying the Work's need for a product suitable for quantity production.

An agreement was concluded with S Z Hall, the well-known Consulting Engineer, to undertake the design of a new generation of heavy oil engines. He was to be paid £100 per annum for 5 years, plus the cost of drawings.

The intention was to produce a 2-stroke low compression single cylinder engine in four sizes developing 25, 35, 50 and 80 bhp and to offer these in multiples of up to four cylinders. This gave a range of power units from 25 bhp to 320 bhp, but it was soon found that there was a large demand for smaller engines and a 15 bhp model was introduced. The engines proved economical and reliable and the fewer number of working parts was welcomed by users.

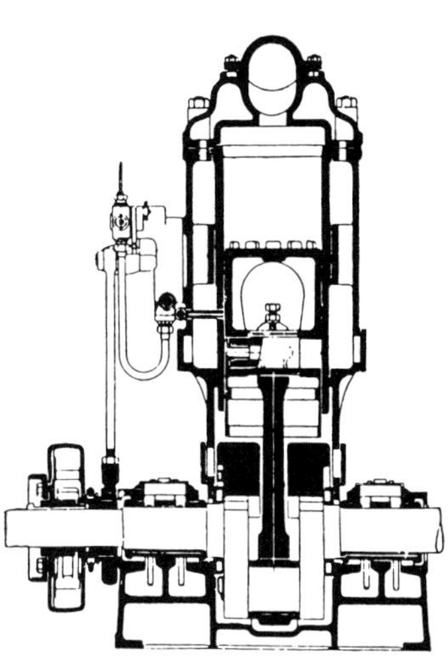

A section through the 2-stroke, low compression heavy oil engine to S. Z. Hall's design introduced in 1921.

Working on the now well-known 2-stroke cycle using solid ignition, the fuel was injected into the combustion chamber immediately before ignition occurred by means of a pump activated by an eccentric on the crankshaft.

The stroke of the fuel pump was controlled by a governor so that the quantity of fuel injected during each revolution was proportional to the load on the engine. The sequence of operations during each working cycle was as follows: The piston was driven down from the top of the cylinder by the force of the explosion, at the same time compressing the air in the crankcase. When the piston had travelled downwards to within a short distance of the bottom of its stroke a

A 4-cylinder version of Allen's 320 bhp, 2-stroke heavy oil engine.

series of exhaust ports were uncovered in the cylinder wall allowing the burnt gases to escape. When the piston reached the bottom of its stroke a further series of scavenging ports in the opposite wall of the cylinder were uncovered. These were in direct communication with the crankcase allowing the compressed air it contained to rush through the ports into the cylinder. Any remaining burnt gases in the cylinder were displaced through the exhaust ports by the special shape of the piston head as the piston began to move upwards. The rising piston closed the scavenging and exhaust ports compressing the charge of air. At the same time it drew a new charge of air into the crankcase through the automatic air inlet flap valves situated at the back and front of the crankcase. When the piston reached approximately the top of its stroke, the fuel oil was injected into the combustion chamber in the cylinder head and immediately ignited driving the piston down to commence another cycle.

Crude oil engines

The engine worked satisfactorily on any type of crude oil having a specific gravity not exceeding 0.92. Provided the fuel was free from acids and impurities, a calorific value of 18,500 BThU was obtained. The engines worked equally well on kerosene and other refined petroleum products.

To start the engine from cold it was necessary to heat up the ante-chamber to a dull red heat as the compression itself was too low to ignite the fuel spontaneously. For this purpose a special blow-lamp was provided on each cylinder. The first impulses at starting were given by the admission of compressed air and if the temperature of the combustion chamber was sufficiently high to effect the combustion of the fuel injected by the fuel pump, the engine started readily. Thereafter the heat generated in the cylinder by successive compression and combustion was high enough to keep the engine running continuously without further application of external heat.

Special attention was paid to the design of the pressure lubricators feeding oil to the cylinders, pistons and connecting rods. The pumps were driven by a rocking shaft and ratchet coupled to the fuel pump levers. The crankshaft main bearings were ring lubricated. The cooling water to the cylinder jacket was either pump driven by a belt off the crankshaft or by means of the thermo-syphon system.

The new oil engine was first exhibited at the Motor Boat, Marine & Stationary Engine Exhibition held at Olympia in 1920. Others were

Engineer Captain H R Teed RN (Rtd) became the Company's representative for all diesel engine marine applications.

exhibited at the Royal Show held in Darlington and at various other agricultural shows held throughout the country where their application as drainage pumps and small electric generators aroused considerable interest. Within two years, orders for over 200 engines had been received including orders from Egypt, India, Japan, China, Australia and South Africa. Over a period of forty years Allens had built up an enviable reputation for their steam-engine driven machinery. Now, they were becoming internationally acknowledged as manufacturers of economical and totally reliable robust oil engine driven machinery.

It was then decided to apply the engine to marine propulsion, constructed on essentially the same principle as the land engine, adding only reversing gear, a thrust block and shafting. Engineer Commander B W Knoff RN was appointed on a five year contract to head the Oil Engine Department, which was now located in the old brassfoundry. Engineer Captain H R Teed RN became the Company's representative responsible for all oil engine marine applications and Richard Allen personally made contact with all the leading shipbuilders. As if to set the seal on the Board's faith in the new engine, it authorised the building of fifty for stock and the installation of a 200 bhp engine and generator at Biddenham. This engine supplied all the Work's electrical power requirements.

The Board decided, however, to decline the opportunity to manufacture under licence the Tyler and the Straker Squire petrol engines. Board minutes at this time also refer to an agreement to manufacture Carbon Dioxide compressors driven by Allen engines, for E G White & Company of London. No further details of this agreement appear to have survived.

Harlé diesel engine licence

Shortly after the successful introduction of the semi-diesel engine, the question of what sort of diesel engine the Company should manufacture in the future was carefully examined. The French Harlé design, about which we know very little, appears to have had only a limited success. It was Company policy that only proven products should be offered for sale and nothing in the nature of an experimental product was passed on to the customer. At this time the output of the Danish Burmeister & Wain type engine greatly exceeded that of other makes and seemed best suited to meet the market needs and satisfy the Company's policy.

Burmeister & Wain licence

Burmeister & Wain had acquired Dr Diesel's patent rights and commenced manufacture of both 2-stroke and 4-stroke engines on a large scale in 1904. By 1918 they had built engines for twenty-four ocean-going motor vessels and were able to supply air blast diesel engines up to 8,000 hp. They licensed various other manufacturers worldwide and Harland & Wolff secured the U.K. licence. In 1921 Allens obtained, at a cost of £5,000 a sub-licence for 4-stroke engines from Harland & Wolff through the good offices of W H Allen's old friend Lord Pirrie. Richard Allen, Commander Knoff and Herman Oxlin visited Copenhagen and received enormous help and encouragement from both Burmeister & Wain and Harland & Wolff engineers. The first 4-stroke air-blast injection diesel engine produced at Queen's Engineering Works was completed in April 1922. This was a 2-cylinder engine developing 100 bhp at 300 rpm having a 325 mm bore x 350 mm stroke. A 3-cylinder 150 bhp version having the same bore and stroke followed, and within four years the range was extended to include sizes up to 675 bhp. The remarkable contrast between a 1906 petrol/paraffin oil engines and the 1925 675 bhp

A 1,200 hp 6-cylinder Burmeister & Wain built air-blast diesel engine for Copenhagen Power Station.

engine will be noted in the accompanying illustrations.

Initially, the licence imposed limitations on the size of engine which Allens could build. The largest engines manufactured by Harland & Wolff at this time were of 1,200 bhp and exceeded 250 tons in weight, but the largest which could be physically handled at Queen's Engineering Works was about 600 bhp. The Board agreed that Allens would concentrate on engines of 100, 150 and 200 hp and that larger engines would be purchased from Harland & Wolff. But by 1924 we learn that the Bedford Works had produced a 600 bhp engine and that production facilities were being reorganised to permit the construction of three 1,000 bhp engines for a big pumping contract in the Sudan. Each engine was required to drive a 40 in. centrifugal pump delivering 1.9 million gallons of water per hour. The Board agreed also that they would not quote for main-propulsion diesel engines or marine auxiliaries actually installed in the engine room. Nevertheless, the Bedford built engines were an immediate success and several important contracts were received from water-

200 bhp, 4-cylinder air blast diesel engine direct coupled to a 130 kW electric generator.

works and drainage schemes in the U.K. and for various projects in South Africa, Egypt, the Sudan and China. The limitations on the size of marine engines appear to have been removed by 1927 which was a record year for diesel engine production. We learn that eight 460 bhp engines driving 275 kW generators were built for the Shaw Savill Line's new ships and that 675 bhp engines driving 450 kW generators were supplied for two new Canadian Pacific liners being built in Japan. By this date there were clear indications that many ship owners preferred the diesel engine to other power sources for marine auxiliaries and records show that 100 vessels employed 280 Allen diesels for a variety of duties. This was a considerable achievement in a period of general trade depression.

Marine diesel engine applications

The operation of all diesel engines depends upon compression pressures being sufficiently high to produce the temperatures required for spontaneous combustion of the fuel oil injected into the

950 bhp air-blast diesel engine and 40 in. twin series centrifugal pump for the Gezira Irrigation Scheme, Sudan.

cylinders. The Burmeister & Wain engines operated on the air-blast injection system. The fuel was forced into the engine cylinder against the compression pressure by a supply of high pressure air. It was necessary to have a continuous supply of compressed air available for this purpose. This was obtained, once the engine was running, from an air compressor, usually of the 3-stage type, integral with the engine. For starting purposes the compressed air was obtained from previously-charged storage cylinders. Initially, the baseplate, trunk and individual cylinders were separate castings. During 1926, the separate cylinder construction was dispensed with and the trunk and cylinders were incorporated in a single casting. The vertical drive shaft from the end of the crankshaft to the camshaft was replaced by a chain drive. These modifications made the engines more compact by reducing the centres between the cylinders; they also reduced the number of component parts and cheapened the cost of manufacture.

Air-blast diesel engines

Both the hot-bulb semi-diesels and the air-blast injection engines remained in production until 1930 and were replaced by entirely new designs of solid injection airless diesel engines, but they belong later in our story. Large numbers of the air-blast engines were built but space precludes the mention of the many fascinating and highly successful applications upon which they were employed both upon land and sea.

Before considering the firm's progress in the field of steam turbines in the years following the Great War, it is necessary to catch up with certain miscellaneous events not previously mentioned which occurred at Queen's Engineering Works.

During the early 1920s, a great deal of the Directors time was spent pursuing claims against the Admiralty Contracts Department amounting to £87,500. The main burden of this work fell on Harold Allen and he was only able to recover some £20,000, which at first sight appears a poor reward for the Company's remarkable achievements. Few would argue that at sea it had been very much an engineers' war and Allens had been at the forefront of the conflict.

On an entirely different subject, we learn that at some time during 1923 W H Allen received a statement from his bank indicating that his current account was in credit. So pleased was he with this news, that he resolved there and then to establish a scholarship enabling a promising young student to read Mechanical Sciences at Trinity College, Cambridge, the immortal Isaac Newton's old college. The prize was first awarded to Christopher Hinton, later to become Sir Christopher Hinton, the 'Father of our nuclear power station industry'. It was he who led the team of engineers and scientists who produced the celebrated Calder Hall atomic reactor. The *Daily Mail* described Calder Hall in 1957 as, 'Probably the greatest technological triumph Britain has achieved in the present generation. What a wonderful investment for the country Mr Allen made in the 1920s when he saw the need for top-class scientific engineers 30 years on'.

The Christopher Hinton saga

During the War, Herman Oxlin had been appointed head of the Steam Turbine Department as a result of the excellent work he had done on pre-war turbine pump designs. In 1919 the Board approved the construction of a new drawing office for the department and turbines were placed high on the list of post-war products. Undoubtedly, the firm had gained much valuable experience in this field during the war especially in connection with the work they had done for the Admiralty on fast patrol boat main propulsion engines. These were of the disc and drum Parsons type and were supplied complete

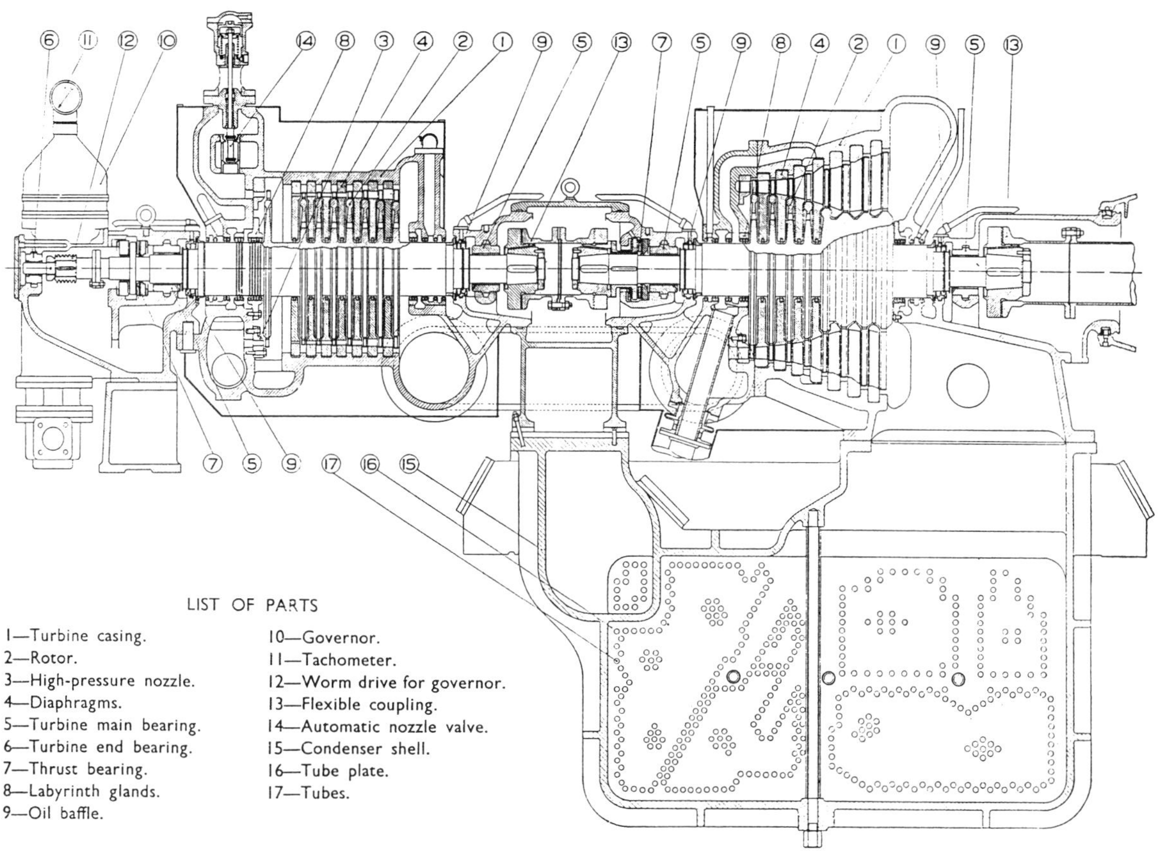

Sectional arrangement of a 2-cylinder condensing turbine with the Awlinwun *condenser.*

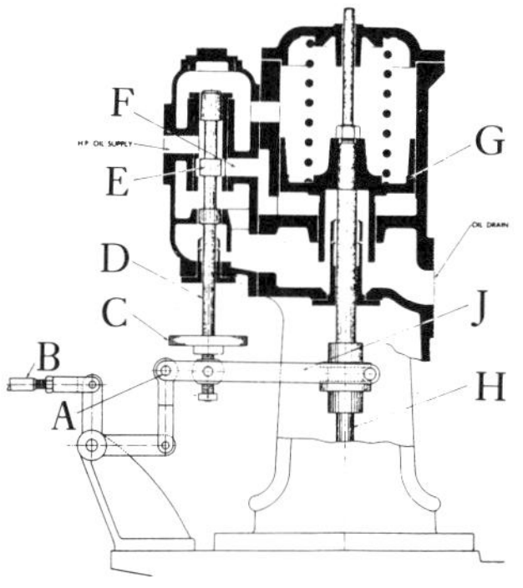

ALLEN DESIGN OF FLOATING LEVEL OIL RELAY.
OPERATION – suppose the governor to have moved the pivot 'A' downwards as the result of a slight decrease of speed. The pilot valve is lowered and the valve beat 'E' admits high-pressure oil to the relay cylinder. This raises the relay piston against its spring and increases the throttle valve opening. While this is going on, the floating lever swings about the pivot 'A' and raises the pilot valve again until the beat 'E' has shut off the high-pressure oil supply. The movement then stops with the pivot valve back in its original position but with the throttle valve lifted higher to correspond with the lowered position of the pivot 'A'.

with gearing manufactured at Queen's Engineering Works. The high-pressure and low-pressure turbines were combined on a single shaft developing 1,750 bhp and proved very successful.

During the War, turbines had become more or less universally adopted on large ships for driving electric light generators. It became urgently necessary that Allens should give their closest attention to the post-war development of turbines for driving all types of marine auxiliary machinery. Their use at sea provided the most arduous conditions under which a turbine could be called upon to operate. The need was for a new generation of turbines giving improved economies in steam consumption combined with savings in space and weight.

It is, perhaps, not surprising that Swiss-born and educated Oxlin consulted the work of Heinrich Zoelly, who had produced his first turbine in Switzerland in 1903. The resultant Allen design was based on the Zoelly machine manufactured by Escher Wyss who had already produced several hundred of these turbines on the Continent. At this time Parsons type turbines were considered unsuitable for the smaller variable load machines and German, Swiss and American designs were considered to be technically in the lead. However, Allens continued to maintain close liaison with Parsons and derived much help from them especially in connection with impulse turbine design and reduction gearing. They purchased a Parsons gear-hobbing machine which eliminated the pitch errors which had been responsible for an undesirable scream in large spur wheels. Zoelly-type turbines were also produced in the United Kingdom by English Electric Co. who, uniquely, used nickel steel strip metal blades for the simple impulse stages of their turbines.

275 kW geared turbo-generating set.

Steam turbine driven direct-coupled boiler feed pump.

400 hp steam turbine direct-coupled to a Reavell Blower.

Steam turbine driven circulating pump as supplied to post-World War I Cunard ships.

The Zoelly turbine generally employed fewer stages than the popular French Rateau design also introduced in 1903. Consequently, the Zoelly design was extremely compact, clearances were large and a relatively smaller number of blades were employed, which resulted in a lower initial cost. When used for driving d.c. generators the problem of alternator periodicity was eliminated which permitted the use of smaller scaled-down dimensions with a resultant saving in weight without affecting the machines' robustness. Competition was severe at this time. Fraser & Chalmers of Erith and Metropolitan-Vickers of Manchester had taken up Auguste Rateau's designs as had Westinghouse in America. Charles Curtis patented his designs in the United Kingdom and these were produced by the General Electric Company of America. The Swedish Ljungström turbine having two contra-rotating rotors and no conventional stator, was taken up by the Brush Electrical Engineering Company and several other British firms were seeking a corner of the market.

Turbine competition

The design features of the new Allen turbines which continued in production until the late 1930s and worthy of special mention are as follows:

The wheels and shafts were produced from nickel steel, instead of mild steel used by most manufacturers, and were forged in one piece in machines running at 6,000 rpm or more. In the case of larger diameter wheels running a lower speeds, the wheel forgings were separate from the shaft. A bronze ring was interposed between the wheel and the shaft making the wheel more readily removable and ensuring its tightness when submitted to running stresses. While the end thrust in an impulse turbine is negligible a Mitchell thrust

2,500 kW high pressure direct-coupled turbo-alternator. Supplied to Eastbourne Corporation Power Station.

bearing was always provided for positively locating the wheels and nozzles.

The governor gear consisted of a centrifugal governor of the type used on the high-speed reciprocating engines. It operated the throttle valve through the medium of an oil relay and piston which gave the necessary power to the throttle valve while keeping the centrifugal governor within reasonable dimensions. The oil pot containing the piston was supplied with oil by a forced-lubrication pump working at 25/30 psi, the oil being admitted under the piston by means of the piston type relay. Oil pressure held the piston against a spring and the position of the relay valve was regulated by the action of the centrifugal governor. An emergency governor of the ordinary unbalanced ring type was mounted on the countershaft driving the speed governor and forced-lubrication pump. When the speed exceeded a pre-determined limit the unbalanced ring overcame the spring and in so doing struck a trigger thereby releasing the emergency valve.

Turbine construction

The steam belt of most turbines was divided into two or more sections, the additional sections being controlled by hand operated valves allowing some nozzles to be shut-off according to the condition of the load. This ensured better economy than if the steam were reduced in front of the total number of nozzles.

In the case of turbines operating with superheated steam, all parts in direct contact with the high temperature steam were produced in cast steel.

The turbine blades were held in grooves in the periphery of the wheels by means of positive serrations in the grooves and on the root of the blades. All blades were inserted at one point in the periphery and moved round into their ultimate position. In later machines the blade and its adjacent spacer were made in one piece which allowed higher peripheral speeds due to the greater strength of the blade root.

The turbine casing was extended beyond the bearing in machines driving through reduction gearing ensuring the accurate alignment of the turbine bearings and pinion shaft. The shaft was provided with bronze or stainless steel sleeves under the carbon packings eliminating the problem of rust found in earlier models.

In smaller sizes of geared turbine a single helical gear drive was employed. This was adopted mainly on turbines driving forced-draught fans where the alignment was simpler. When double helical gearing was employed the pinion was made of nickel steel integral with the shaft. Usually the spur wheel was of cast iron with mild steel rings shrunk on, but in the smaller sizes the spur wheel was produced as a solid steel forging. In all but the smallest machines an intermediate bearing was provided on the pinion shaft. Reduction gearing was especially applicable to turbo generators eliminating commutation and other troubles encountered in high speed direct current machinery.

Within eighteen months of the introduction of the new turbines Allen secured orders for geared turbo generators from many of the leading steamship companies operating on the Atlantic service as well as those operating to South America, South Africa, India and the Far East. In addition orders were received for turbine-driven main circulating pumps for new vessels being built for the Atlantic service. 400 hp geared turbines were supplied for driving gas boosting blowers in a large gas works. A 500 hp geared turbine was ordered for driving the circulating pumps at a large power station in London; and a 500 kW geared turbine complete with condensing plant was supplied to one of HM Dockyards. Small turbines of the new design were beginning to be extensively used for driving kinetic rotary pumps in large condenser plants.

2,500 kW turbo-generator

An especially prestigious contract received in 1923 was for a 2,500 kW direct-coupled turbo generator set driving a single phase alternator for Eastbourne Corporation. This operated under exceptional steam conditions with superheated steam at 250 psi and 250 °F giving a total temperature of 650 °F, necessitating all the parts of the turbine in contact with the superheated steam being produced in cast steel. The machinery was supplied complete with condensing plant. Concurrently, two 950 bhp turbines were supplied to South Africa for driving centrifugal pumps through double helical reduction gearing. Together they pumped 5½ million gallons of water per day against a head of 510 ft.; and a 1,000 kW generator was supplied to Perth Municipality in Australia.

The largest geared turbo generator sets produced in 1923 were a 1,500 kW set for the Indian Government Arsenal and a 2,000 kW geared single phase turbo-alternator capable of transmitting 3,600 hp through the gears. Within the four year period to the end of 1923, the Company built geared steam turbines having an aggregate output of 85,000 bhp which combined with the sets produced for marine propulsion was a record with few equals, made all the more remarkable when one remembers that trade worldwide was still generally in recession.

Herman Oxlin

Under the stewardship of Herman Oxlin, the Company made a special study of the needs of industry, where steam might be required for various processes, including heating, as well as for power generation and driving various types of machinery. They developed the back-pressure reciprocating engine and for turbines the pass-out-concept. By the mid-1920s Allens were able to claim with every justification that its experience in this field was second to none. For small and medium outputs Allen's high speed totally-enclosed forced-lubrication back-pressure reciprocating engine continued to be available in sizes from 5 to 500 bhp. The back-pressure and

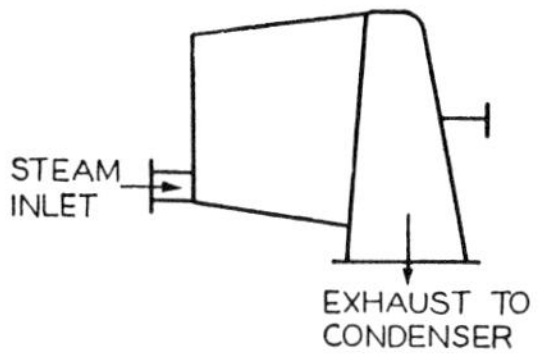

'Straight' condensing turbine.

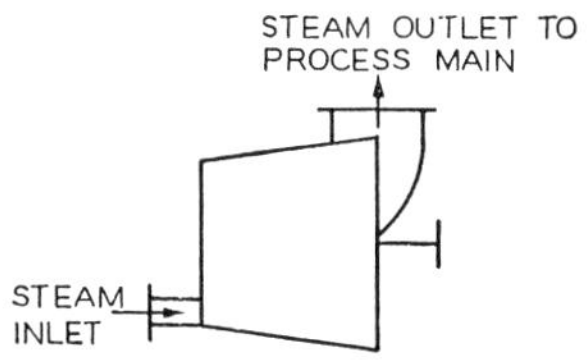

Back pressure turbine.

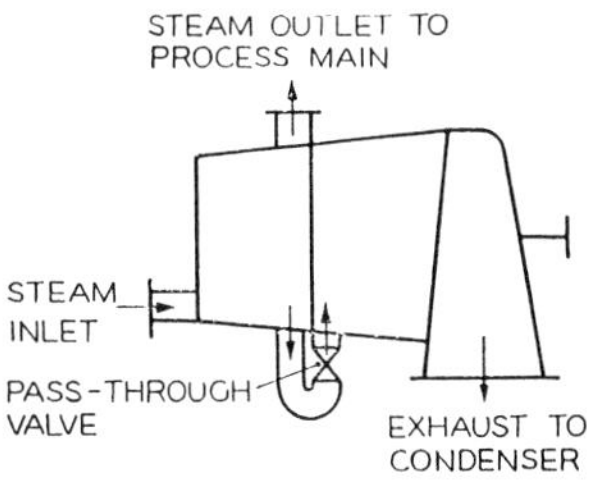

Single pass-out condensing turbine.

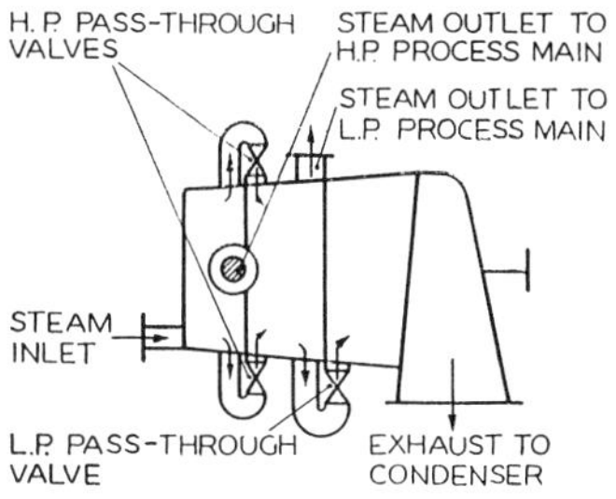

Double pass-out condensing turbine.

pass-out turbine in sizes from 50 to 10,000 bhp was developed for use with process and heating steam.

Cheap power was of vital importance to all industries and any manufacturer having boilers already installed for process purposes could, with the new technology being developed, produce power at negligible cost as a by-product from heating and process steam. By combining power generation and heating systems together it was possible to use practically all the heat present in the steam. When power only is generated in a condensing turbine, as in the case of electricity power stations, over sixty per cent of the heat originally present in the steam is wasted in heating the condenser circulating water. Whereas by using a back-pressure engine or turbine as a reducing valve power can be generated at a fraction of the fuel cost.

The turbine could readily be designed to overcome problems where the demand for power was in excess of the process demands or where the two requirements did not synchronise. The pass-out turbine allowed the steam to do a portion of its work and when reduced to the requisite pressure pass it out in sufficient quantity to meet the process needs. The remaining steam was then passed through the low pressure stages of the turbine producing the required amount of power before being exhausted to the condenser. In many processes, absolutely clean steam is necessary and the absence of rubbing surfaces in the turbine within the steam spaces makes lubrication unnecessary, ensuring perfectly clean process steam even with initial superheat.

In certain cases it was found more convenient to use a combination of back-pressure and condensing turbines, so arranged that the back pressure turbine took the load which could be generated from the steam required for process purposes. If the demand for electrical power exceeded the amount obtainable, the excess steam was automatically passed to the condensing unit.

Another alternative successfully used at this time was the running of back-pressure turbines in conjunction with the public electricity supply with excess power automatically being taken from the mains in the event of the demand exceeding that which could be generated by the process steam. In this case the public supply acted virtually as a condensing turbine. Later, in the 1930s, with the development of the airless injection diesel engine, pass-out turbines were in special circumstances used in conjunction with diesel engines. The concept of utilising the total heat of the steam available for dual purposes soon became very popular. Many industries traditionally using separate reciprocating engines for power generation installed new Allen pass-out turbines to great economic advantage. These included:

Dye Works	Chemical Works	Rubber Factories
Breweries	Oil Refineries	Linoleum Works
Pulp Mills	Spinning & Weaving Mills	Laundries
Sugar Factories	Paper Mills	Brick Works

A typical single pass-out condensing turbine is shown diagrammatically. It will be seen that the steam after passing through the main steam chest and the high pressure stage of the turbine is led by a branch to the pressure main and also to a pass-through valve chest. From the pass-through valve chest the steam that is required by the low pressure turbine is admitted by the pass through valve whose opening is controlled by the pressure in the process main. This serves to maintain a constant pass-out pressure, more or less steam being

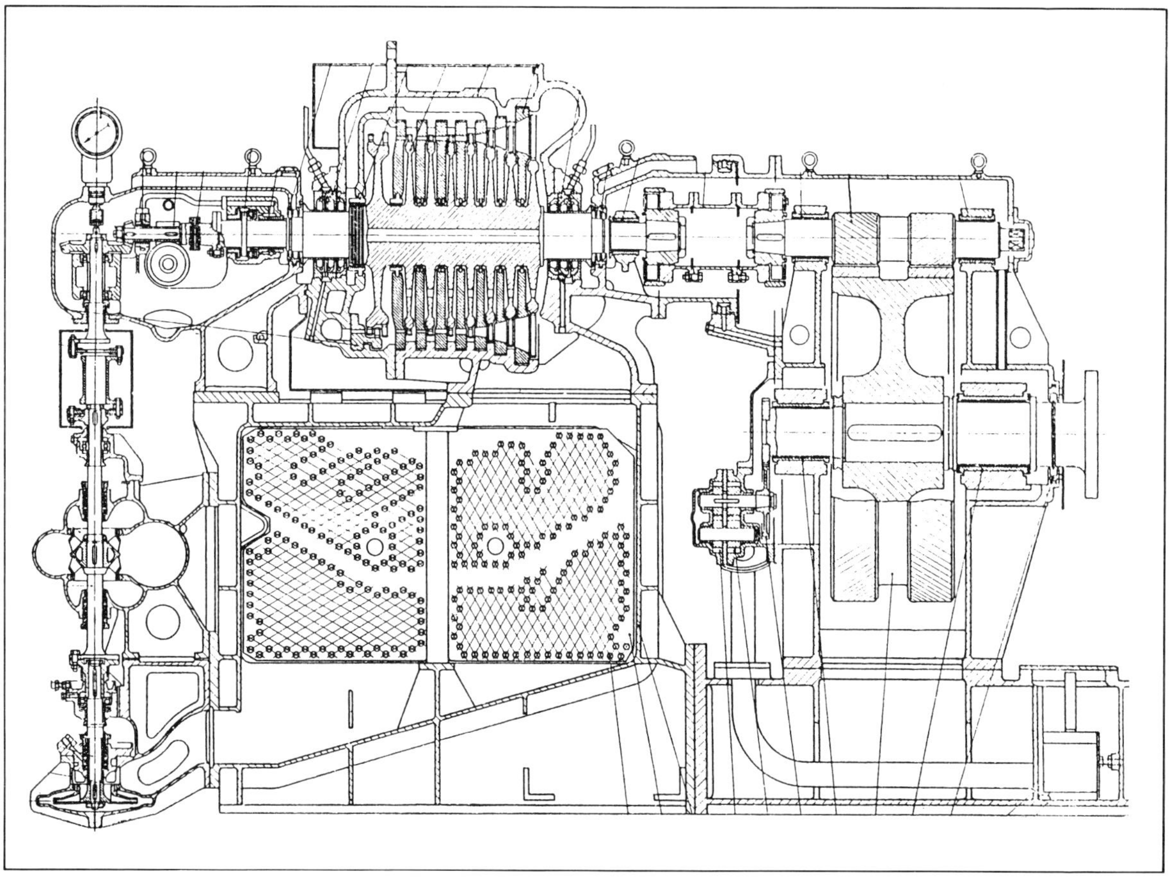

Sectional arrangement of a condensing turbine with speed reduction gears, Awlinwun *condenser and mechanically driven auxiliaries.*

passed through to the lower stages of the turbine as the pressure rises or falls. The effect of an increase in load is to cause a slight fall in the turbine speed whereupon the speed governor immediately opens the main throttle valve to admit more steam to the high-pressure turbine. This increases the power output and increases the flow to the pass-out main. If concurrently there is no increase in the pass-out main demand, the pass-out pressure rises as a result of which the pass-through valve admits more steam to the low-pressure turbine which then takes up its own share of the increased load. If there is a decrease in the pass-out main demand a reverse sequence of events occurs.

Two safety devices were mounted externally to the turbine. Firstly, a relief or surplus valve was connected to the pass-out main in order to protect the turbine casing from the effects of sudden surges in pressure; and secondly a non-return valve was fitted in the pass-out branch. If two different supplies of process steam are required, the turbine could be adapted as a double pass-out type by duplicating the pressure control mechanism.

Awlinwun *condenser*

Later in the 1920s, Allens developed a combined turbine and surface condenser which became known as the *Awlinwun* system. Previously, installations had required two floor levels with the turbine mounted above a barrel-type surface condenser situated in the basement. This layout involved heavy and costly foundations. The *Awlinwun* arrangement soon became standard for both land and marine installations up to 2,500 kW. The above diagrammatic illustration shows a typical *Awlinwun* condenser installation with its mechanically driven auxiliaries.

Allens resumed the manufacture of surface and closed-feed condensing plant immediately after the war and at an early date important orders were received from Australia and Japan. Another important Allen installation was at the new Portobello electricity generating station in Edinburgh which was opened by HM King George V in 1923. This comprised three large condensing plants of 15,500 sq.ft. each. Within a year a 35,000 sq.ft. plant was completed for a power station in Japan, and an even larger plant of 45,000 sq.ft. was under construction. This was supplied for use with a 35,000 kW turbo generating plant at Nagoya in Japan. The four boilers employed were the largest ever built in the world and operated at 350 psi and 750 superheat total temperature. Richard Allen visited the site in 1926 during his 24,000 mile world tour and his comment upon returning home was 'I have never seen anything like it before!'.

Undoubtedly Richard Allen was a very great expert in this field as well as marine work, and projects such as the Tokyo Power Station were his first love.

A huge 45,000 sq.ft. surface condenser supplied to Japan in 1924 for use with a 35,000 kW turbo-alternator.

Large increases in turbine power output, steam pressures and temperatures in the search for improved overall efficiency in power stations involved a great deal of investigation into questions associated with heat balance all of which had a major effect on condensing plant design. The design of feed pumps, circulating pumps, air pumps, water heaters, evaporators and de-aerators all involved a great deal of know-how and mathematical calculation. The technical competence of Allens was indeed very remarkable and only few firms could match them. One suspects that it was questions of financial realignments and commercial groupings which subsequently diluted and weakened their position in the market place, rather any decline in their technical excellence. But the technical considerations and complexity of this type of work goes far beyond the scope of this book.

During the 1920s, over 400 condensing plants were built at Queen's Engineering Works, the largest being two 46,000 sq.ft. plants for Leeds Corporation Electricity Generating Station for dealing with 480,000 lbs of steam per hour. This work continued, although on a reduced scale until the outbreak of war in September 1939.

Rotodynamic pumps

The manufacture of all types of rotodynamic pumps continued as an important branch of the Company's activities in the 1920s and 1930s. Small pumps for irrigation and land drainage work continued to provide a steady flow of 'bread and butter' orders and it was not uncommon to receive single orders for 200 pumps at a time. The name *Nile-Conqueror* pump had become a household word in Egypt. Throughout the forty years since W H Allen supplied his first pump to this market designs had been steadily improved. Five sizes of high efficiency pump were available in the 1920s with branches ranging from 4in. to 10 in. delivering from 200 gallons to 3,500 gallons per minute at heads varying from 10 ft. to 50 ft.

A similar pump, the *Tigris Conqueror*, which had been first introduced in 1906, met the preferred needs of Iran and Iraq. This differed only in the positioning of the branches and the use of independent pedestal bearings for the pulley drive. Substantial orders were received for this pump in the post-war years.

In 1923 an entirely new range of high-lift multi-stage pumps was introduced utilising new high-quality steels and bronzes developed during the war. The result was a more compact, robust design permitting the greater use of standardised components which could

Two 52 in. Conqueror *circulating pumps supplied to the London Electric Supply Company for their Barking Power Station.*

be manufactured for stock whilst ensuring complete interchangeability. This attracted valuable orders from mines in many parts of the world. As an example two 7-stage pumps were supplied to a gold mine in South Africa driven by 350 bhp squirrel cage a.c. motors. Each delivered 337 gallons of water per minute against a head of 1,980 ft. The total lift from the lowest mine level to the surface was made in two stages involving two complete units against a total head of 3,960 ft. The casings of these pumps were made from cast steel and all the high velocity water passages were lined with special acid-resisting bronze.

Multi-stage pumps were being increasingly employed by waterworks as replacements for old beam engines. These could be direct-coupled to a steam turbine, diesel engine or an electric motor, some of which were arranged with vertical spindles. An interesting contract was received from Worcester Corporation who installed two electrically-driven pumps. When working in parallel they delivered 2,200 gallons per minute against a head of 165 ft., or when coupled in series they delivered 1,000 gallons per minute against a head of 350 ft.

Vertical shaft pumps for bore holes and deep wells became a speciality of the Company. They were usually driven by a.c. motors and the shafting was fitted with special bearings mechanically

21 in. axial-flow sewage pump.

An Allen-Thompson gravel pump with electric motor drive.

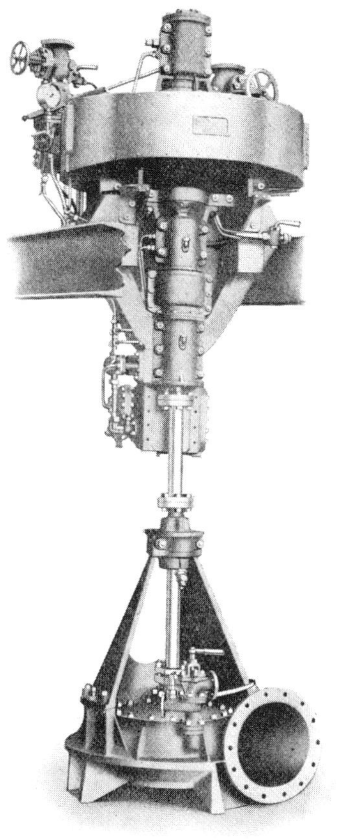

Steam turbine driven salvage bilge pump.

lubricated by a plunger-type pump driven through bevel gearing from the vertical shaft. An early example was a complete installation supplied to the London Electricity Company's super power station at Barking. The plant comprised three 36 in. vertical shaft pumps able to deliver 24,000 gallons per minute against a total head of 37 ft.

An interesting borehole pumping plant was supplied to Le Grand Sutcliffe & Gill for installation in Central London. The 17-stage pump was situated 250 ft. below pavement level and the overall diameter of the pump did not exceed 10¼ in. Running at 1,200 rpm each impeller generated a head of 21.5 ft. Portable installations were also developed for de-watering deep mine shafts. The whole weight of the pumping machinery including the motor was suspended from the colliery winding gear at the pit head.

Apart from continuing the development of many and varied types of rotodynamic pump for waterworks, sewage plants, docks and power stations; and a multitude of special pumps for steam plants and marine applications, the firm introduced several special-purpose pumps during the period under review. These included pumps for handling abrasive substances where the wear resisting properties of the casing and impeller were of paramount importance. Sand pumps were in considerable demand for dredging and salvage work and a major contract for gravel pumps was signed in 1930. The casing liners were made of 'white' iron, a material so hard as to be unmachinable.

A special vertical-type engine piston cooling pump was developed for cooling the pistons of large marine diesel engines. This involved designing a special rolling-drum type of exhauster to overcome problems arising through the loss of cooling water when the ship was rolling violently.

Vertical lubricating oil pumps were also developed for diesel powered vessels. Each pump consisted of a number of stages each with its own impeller and guide vanes. Four pumps supplied for a new motor vessel built in 1925 were each capable of pumping 250 tons of lubricating oil per hour against a pressure of 60 psi.

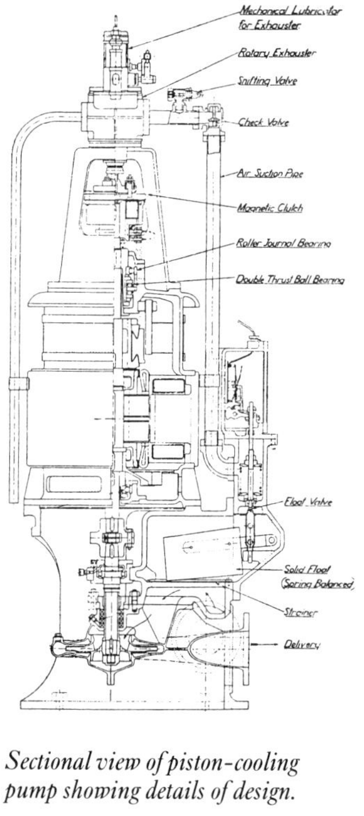

Sectional view of piston-cooling pump showing details of design.

Any reference to the Company's pumping activities in the period following the First Great War would be incomplete without reference to the great Vaal River Scheme at Vereeniging in South Africa. This was undertaken to ensure adequate supplies of water to the rapidly growing city of Johannesburg and was probably one of the most interesting engineering projects undertaken in the world in the 1920s. The Bill granting rights to impound the River Vaal was passed in 1914 thereby ensuring a supply of up to 20 million gallons a day to the City.

Allens were awarded the contract for two complete pumping sets each comprising high pressure impulse-type turbines developing 920 bhp, driving high lift pumps through double helical gearing, complete with condensing plant. When working on full load each plant was designed to deliver 6 million gallons of water a day at a head of 565 ft. The turbines ran at 5,000 rpm reduced to 955 rpm through the gearing. Under these conditions the guaranteed steam consumption was 12.78 lbs per pump hp, per hour. The firm also supplied two 350 kW geared turbo alternators and condensers for the 2,200 volt 3-phase electrical supply. The official opening was performed by HRH Prince Arthur of Connaught, the Governor General of the Union of South Africa.

Finally, mention must be made of a large sewage plant built at

Almeria in Egypt and completed in 1928. This was notable because diesel engines were used to provide the motive power. Three 5-cylinder 550 bhp air blast diesel engines drove the 4-stage 18 in. pumps. The actual pump impellers were 51 in. diameter which gives some idea of the massive proportions of the pump casings. Additionally, a 330 bhp air blast diesel drove a 14 in. mains pump through double helical speed increasing gears. These increased the speed of the engine from 240 rpm to give 1,175 rpm at the pump shaft. Allen's ability to supply completely integrated plants of this nature was almost unique.

Death of W H Allen

Within three months of Richard's return from his world tour William Henry died peacefully at his home, Bromham House, in the early hours of 3rd September, 1926 in his eighty-third year. He had belonged to a generation in which character was developed at an early age and from the moment he left the Wern Foundry as a young man he did many things which older men would have feared to attempt. His remarkable business achievements permeate throughout the story of Queen's Engineering Works. From the very onset he had visualised the great possibilities in developing inter-related mechanical and electrical engineering equipment.

Back in his days in South Wales he resolved that when he became his own master, training and education would be high on his agenda. He never forgot that resolve and was amongst the first in British industry to systematise the training of pupils and apprentices. He appointed a manager responsible for all aspects of training and the welfare of young men in his charge. He set up excellent classroom facilities in his works and encouraged further education at all levels. He always strove to maintain contact with his old pupils and continued to do what he could for them. The success of his plan is demonstrated by the large number of pupils from all walks of life who went on to important posts in the community throughout the world.

He was a truly public spirited man and served for long as a Justice of the Peace and became High Sheriff of Bedfordshire in 1904. He contributed generously to All Saints Church, Bedford. He threw himself with his customary energy and generosity into the development of Bedford town following his removal from London. He continued to support many scientific bodies and technical institutions and rendered great service as a Council Member of the Institution of Mechanical Engineers. He was responsible for the establishment of their Benevolent Society.

He loved his family dearly but nevertheless maintained a rather Victorian aloofness. He regularly saw his grandchildren, but always by appointment and he never ate with them. His first question to them was always 'What have you learnt today?' He never really recovered from the loss of his eldest grandson, Melville, and was always quite determined that his son Richard should be a worthy successor well-prepared to face the tasks ahead.

He enjoyed travelling abroad and became frustrated when illness restricted his activities. His network of many friends and acquaintances was very important to him and he was enormously respected by his peers.

It was impossible to come into contact with W H Allen without being impressed by his strong personality. His character was firm and his integrity beyond reproach. Quick to make decisions, his resolve was enormous, but he did not readily brook opposition. Yet he had a warm and kindly heart especially for the many long-serving men that

Richard W Allen, CBE, eldest son of W H Allen. Chairman W H Allen, Sons, & Co. Ltd 1926–55. President Institution of Mechanical Engineers 1928. Knighted for services to Royal Navy 1942.

grew up around him. They loved him as much as they respected him.

At the Board Meeting held on 18th October, 1926 Richard Allen was appointed Chairman of the Company, an acting role he had fulfilled admirably for several years during his father's last long illness. A year later, in October 1927, a bronze tablet was unveiled on the outside wall of the main machine shop facing the main offices, to perpetuate the memory of the founder of the Company. Today the same memorial tablet may be inspected on the wall of the new multi-storey office building adjacent to the imposing front entrance.

In December that year, tradition was broken and for the first time a lady was invited to distribute the prizes at the annual distribution to pupils and apprentices. In former years this pleasant task had been fulfilled by a long list of distinguished male guests. In 1927 Mrs Richard Allen performed the task giving the occasion a greatly appreciated family feeling. A new premier award presented by the Past Pupils Association was created and named the William Henry Allen Memorial Prize. It was to be presented annually to the best all-round graduate or student during the previous year. The first recipient was Herbert Faulkner, a twenty year old apprentice.

Record sales per employee

1927 was a very busy year for the new Chairman. A protracted miner's strike culminating in the General Strike had seriously dislocated industry during 1926. The iron, steel, and engineering industries were particularly badly affected and left the Company with large arrears of work outstanding. In each of their six areas of specialisation, namely steam engines, turbines, condensing plant, centrifugal pumps, oil engines and electrical machinery, a greater output by weight was achieved in 1927 than ever before. The oil engine department was especially busy and at one period during the year, eighteen large new air-blast diesel engines were being completed simultaneously in the recently enlarged engine test bay. The average value of sales exceeded £500 per man employed per annum for the first time. This was considered to be a good result when due allowance was made for the depressed prices ruling at the time.

In the following year Richard Allen was elected President of the Institution of Mechanical Engineers. Founded in 1847 with George Stephenson as its first President, election to this office remains one of the greatest honours that can be bestowed upon an engineer. In his Presidential Address Richard struck a note which typified the very ethos of Queen's Engineering Works. He commented, 'The inventive genius of Parsons and Diesel and the improvements in materials effected by metallurgists, would have been of little value had not workshop conditions kept pace with the exacting demands made by the new designs and new materials. Efficient management must take account in equal measure of the training and welfare of the men and the proper use of machine tools and machinery generally.' Three years later he was made an Honorary Life Member of the Institution.

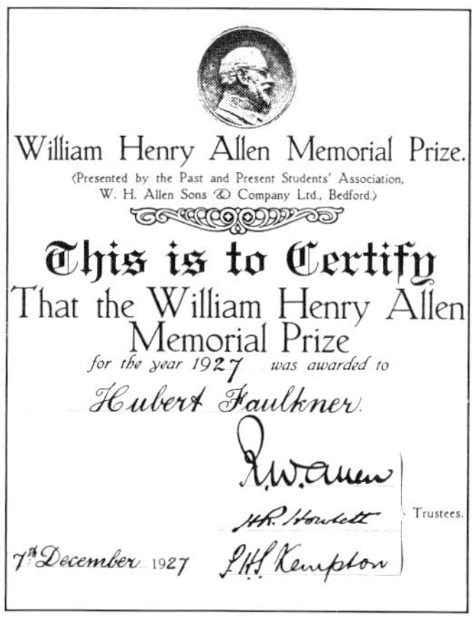

William Henry Allen Memorial Prize.
(Presented by the Past and Present Students' Association, W. H. Allen Sons & Company Ltd., Bedford.)

This is to Certify
That the William Henry Allen Memorial Prize
for the year 1927 was awarded to
Hubert Faulkner.

Trustees.

7th December 1927

The William Henry Allen Memorial Prize Certificate awarded annually to the best all-round graduate or student during the previous year, introduced in 1927.

In June 1928 the Company was honoured by a visit from members of the Institution of Civil Engineers. This visit formed part of its Centenary celebrations to mark the granting of its Royal Charter in 1828. The very fact that Queen's Engineering Works was selected for such a visit was the clearest possible indication of the high esteem in which Allens were held by the members of the most senior branch of the profession.

Richard was further honoured in 1929 by being invited to represent Oxford and Cambridge Universities and the Institution of Mechanical Engineers at the World Engineering Congress held in

Richard Allen inspecting the 45,000 sq.ft. condensing plant at Toho Power Station, Japan during his 1926 world tour.

Tokyo. He had undoubtedly made a good impression and acquired many friends during earlier visits to Japan, and during this visit he was made an Honorary Life Member of the Japan Mechanical Engineering Society.

At home, Harold Allen was appointed Deputy Chairman thereby relieving the sixty-year-old Chairman of as much work as possible enabling him to concentrate on his many public duties. Harold had been responsible for the administrative side of the business for many years and his great tact and acumen had won the respect and goodwill of all with whom he came into contact. The third brother, Rupert Allen concentrated on the Company's commercial affairs. On the mechanical engineering side of the business, the processing of enquiries, tendering, design and drawing office work was entrusted to Project Managers, but they had no direct involvement with manufacturing. It is interesting to note that at no time was a Director specifically responsible for the Company's sales and marketing. This was the joint responsibility of the three managing directors, who travelled widely and at all times maintained close personal contacts with all important customers. It operated as the personification of a well-run family business at its best.

Shipyard production

This period saw a short-lived resurgence in the shipbuilding industry, but this was soon overtaken by worldwide depression. Before the First World War the Clydeside yards alone had an annual capacity of 750,000 tons per annum; during the War production exceeded 1 million tons; and by 1927 it slumped to 450,000 tons. The 1928 up-turn in trade was of great benefit to Queen's Engineering Works who supplied a considerable amount of marine auxiliary machinery both at home and abroad. The increase in the numbers of air-blast diesel engines supplied was particulary marked, the largest of which developed 700 bhp. By 1931 most industries were in the depths of recession and the number of new ships ordered was the smallest in living memory. So serious was the situation that the Allen Board reluctantly decided to take no action to mark publicly the Company's Jubilee year.

Major ship work executed by the Company in 1928/29:

1) The ships *Countess of Bedford, The Countess of Atholl, The Countess of Richmond* and the *Countess of York* for the Canadian Pacific line.
2) Other major liners completed were the Royal Mail *Asturias* and the Union Castle *Carnarvon Castle.*
3) Important orders for Shaw Savill and the Holt Line.
4) Important orders for the Chilean, Argentine, Japanese and Spanish Navies, for forced-draught fans and pumps.
5) Motor tankers *British Valour, British Glory* and *British Courage.*
6) MV *Staffordshire* and *Shropshire* for the Bibby Line.
7) MV *Port Fairy* and *Port Alna* for the Commonwealth & Dominion Line.
8) MV *Manunda* for the Adelaide Shipping Company.
9) MV *West Lynn* for Sir William Reardon Smith of Cardiff.
10) MV *Clan Macdonald* and *Clan Macdougal* for the Clan Line.
11) MV *Asama Mara* and *Tatsuma Mara* for the Nippon Yusin Kaisha Pacific Service.

Large ships were by this time complete electrical power stations in themselves. Although Allens did not manufacture a.c. machinery, nor any longer carry out electrical wiring installations in ships, the Electrical Department continued as an important integral function of the works. The rebuilding of the British mercantile fleet after the war produced many problems. Steam turbines required higher-speed generators and the oil engine lower speeds. There were problems to be dealt with of rapidly-varying electrical loads and the sharing of the load between sets. Other problems concerned torsional oscillation and cyclic irregularity, and greater attention had to be paid to the mechanical strength and rigidity of generators. The effects of centrifugal force and current collection from the commutator became increasingly important as the capacity of sets increased.

The magnet system of early dynamos was steel bar, this gave way to cast iron and later to cast steel. Eventually, these were succeeded by fabricated steel made possible by the enormous advances made in electric welding techniques which permitted great savings in weight and size. Considerable progress was made in the ventilation and cooling of motors. Fan-cooled motors offered further material savings in size and weight.

Since the early days of the Electrical Department, the firm had manufactured a wide range of mechanical and fully-automatic contactor starters, control panels and switchboards. In the post-war period many automatic control panels were produced to meet the special needs of large electrically-controlled pumping installations on land and sea. Year by year the degree of sophistication in control gear requirements increased and it was not unknown for this auxiliary equipment to cost more than the motors. The Company's Tidal Basin Depot in London's Dockland continued to provide a service to shipowners. It held substantial stocks of electrical components and carried out some electrical maintenance and repair work.

Roman Strub, a Swiss born engineer, Chief diesel engine designer Queens Engineering Works 1926 to 1939.

In 1924, Herman Oxlin developed tuberculosis and upon his doctor's advice retired to Switzerland, but he continued to act in a consultative capacity for the firm. In 1926 he interviewed a remarkable young Swiss engineer, Roman Strub, who had graduated in mechanical engineering at Zürich and Berlin. Strub's father, Emil Vicktor Strub, was a well known and greatly respected engineer in Switzerland. He was a close friend and collaborator of Roman Abt, the 'Father of Rack Mountain Railways' and named his son after Abt.

A large early type 6-cylinder 750 bhp airless injection engine installed in a brickworks.

Emil designed and built the Jungfrau mountain railway and while employed by the Rolleschen Ironworks built other unique rack railways in Switzerland, Germany, Italy and France.

Roman Strub

Roman Strub was employed by the great locomotive builders the SLM company at Winterthur at this time and eventually he accepted the appointment as Chief Diesel Engine Designer at Queen's Engineering Works, a position he held until 1939. He died in 1944. His son, Ulrich Strub, graduated in mechanical engineering at Lausanne University and became a highly-respected pupil at Queen's Engineering Works. He left Bedford in 1938 and joined the Anglo Iranian Oil Company.

Work on a new solid-injection airless diesel engine was started in 1926 and production was commenced in 1929. It was realised that the air-blast diesel would eventually become a thing of the past. Airless solid injection engines were cheaper to manufacture since no integral air compressor was required. They had fewer working parts, fuel consumption was improved, engine speeds were increased substantially and the new designs were lighter and much more compact than the air-blast engines. The marketing and distribution of diesel fuel oil worldwide was in the process of being greatly improved and clearly there were many excellent new opportunities for the diesel engine manufacturer.

By 1930 Queen's Engineering Works was producing 4-stroke diesel engines having 2, 3, 4, 5 and 6-cylinders with 320 mm stroke

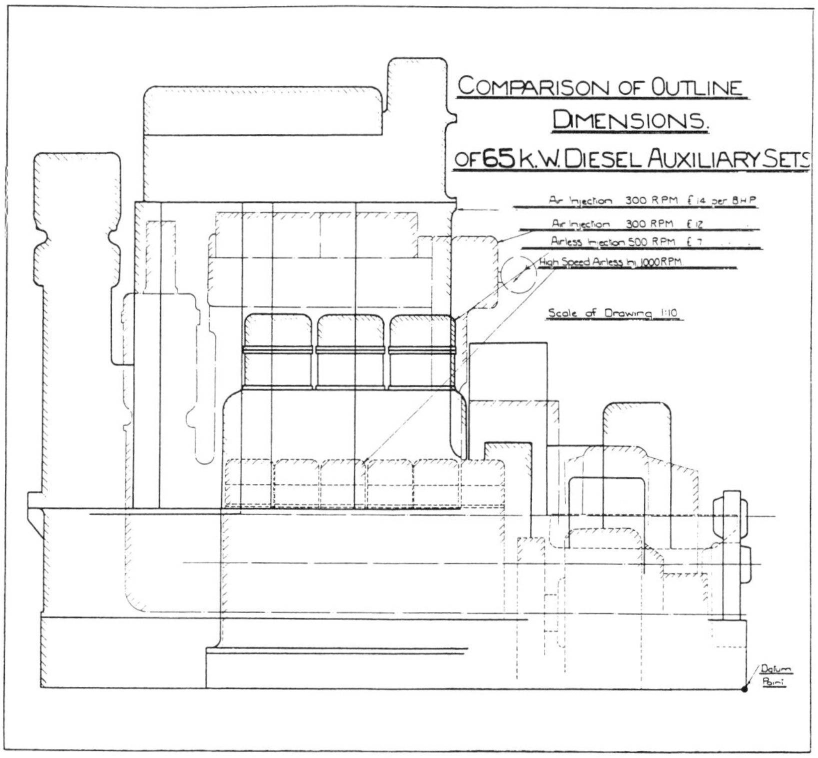

A diagrammatic representation of the space saving and reduction in cost per bhp of diesel engines developed in the decade 1920 to 1930.

running at significantly higher speeds and giving a greatly improved power-to-weight ratio than comparable air-blast engines. Burmeister & Wain came to much the same conclusions as Allens and began to phase out their range of large air-blast engines in favour of the airless injection engine. In 1931 Allens concluded a new licence agreement with Harland & Wolff giving them access to the Danish company's extensive research and development facilities. The subsequent developments which took place at Bedford laid the foundations of Allen's work in this field for the remainder of their independent existence.

Airless injection diesel engines

It is perhaps necessary to refer to the nomenclature employed by the firm in describing their diesel engines. All air-blast engines had the prefix A. The number following referred to the engine stroke in centimetres. The first air-blast diesel built just after the War was a 4A85, a 4-cylinder engine with a 850 mm stroke. The airless engines all had the prefix S. With one exception, the number following the prefix gave the stroke in centimetres, the exception being the S12 engine which had a 12 in. stroke. When pressure charging was introduced in 1956 a prefix B was added to the S and similarly when intercooling appeared in 1962 the prefix became BC. In due course other prefixes were used, G indicating dual fuel engines, H heavy residual or crude oil engines, and P main propulsion engines. When 2-stroke engines were introduced shortly after World War II, the prefix S was altered to T and the letter V was added to the prefix when V-form engines appeared in 1956. The final alphabetical suffix used after the stroke indicated the stage of development the engine had reached. Mark B engines were introduced in 1938, C in 1942, D in 1956, E in 1964 and F in 1968. Thus, it will be seen that a 6BS37D was a 6-cylinder airless injection engine having a 370 mm stroke pressure charging and incorporating all modifications introduced up to 1956.

6-cylinder 500 rpm airless injection diesel engine direct coupled to d.c. dynamo.

The first Strub engine which became classified as the S30 developed up to 45 bhp per cylinder at 600 rpm. It employed a C-frame cylinder block giving excellent accessibility to the crankshaft but was less rigid than the conventional A-frame and not perpetuated. Inspection doors were fitted on both sides of the engine giving it an extremely clean-looking external appearance. There were two valves per cylinder and the valve springs were provided with a safety clip preventing the valve from fouling the piston in the event of spring failure. Each cylinder head was provided with a relief valve.

Wet-sump lubrication was standard and the cam and followers were provided with separate flood lubrication. For starting, an air distributor driven by the camshaft delivered compressed air to the appropriate cylinders. A water-circulating pump was usually mounted on the engine frame without disturbing the standard components thereby enabling customer special requirements to be met at low cost.

Several orders were received at an early date for a variety of land applications, but as was to be expected with Strub's background, consideration was soon given to the application of the diesel engine to transport duties. The War Office commissioned the conversion of a battery-driven shunting locomotive to a diesel-electric drive with

Type S30B 8-cylinder 302 bhp diesel engine driving a gasoline pump through speed increasing gears. The pump duty is 1,280 gallons per minute against a head of 240 psi.

traction motors mounted on the axles. The conversion was carried out entirely at Queen's Engineering Works and a 5-cylinder 110 bhp airless injection engine running at 1,200 rpm was installed direct coupled to a d.c. generator. This conversion is known to have given many years satisfactory service at the department's Shoeburyness range.

Shortly afterwards an important order was received from BTH Ltd, Rugby for S27 airless injection diesel engines for three Bo-Bo diesel electric shunting locomotives for the Ford Motor Company. These were the first 'All British' standard-gauge diesel electric locomotives ordered by an industrial organisation in the United Kingdom. They weighed 44 tons in working order; had an axle loading of 11 tons; a tractive effort of 24,000 lbs; and were capable of speeds up to 35 mph. The Allen 6-cylinder airless injection diesel engines developed 550 bhp at 550 rpm and were direct-coupled to a generator driving the four traction motors. The main generator was uniquely wound so as to provide a novel starting motor, a battery carried on the locomotive providing the means of motoring the generator for cold starting.

The fabricated welded construction C-frame cylinder block used in early Allen airless injection diesel engines. Later superseded by A-frame castings.

The diesel engines were novel at the time in that they were entirely of fabricated welded steel construction. The question of weight was of paramount importance since the electrical transmission equipment was itself heavy and reduced considerably the permissible weight of the engine. Extensive preliminary tests were carried out with different welds which included a series of Izod tests. The designs finally adopted comprised seven steel plates arranged vertically to the axis of the crankshaft supporting the main bearings. The plates were left open at one side for the erection of the crankshaft. The distinctly Swiss-looking appearance of the finished locomotive will be noted. Fortunately one of these interesting locomotives is preserved on a private railway in Kent.

Diesel locomotives

At this time the four main line railway companies were considering the introduction of diesel-powered locomotives. The Hunslet Engine Company exhibited an engine with mechanical transmission and a pre-selector gearbox at the British Industries Fair in 1932. The claimed savings in fuel costs, increased availability and suitability for one-man operation were very attractive to the railway companies. A fierce debate ensued regarding the relative advantages of mechanical versus the alternative hydraulic and electric transmission systems being developed. The Board of the London, Midland & Scottish Railway authorised the expenditure of £30,000 in order to determine the most suitable system for standardisation and orders were placed with Hunslet, Armstrong Whitworth, Harland & Wolff, Hudswell Clarke and Drewry. An 0-4-0 diesel mechanical shunting locomotive was ordered from Drewry, who were then associated with English Electric Co., and the L.M.S. No. 7400, later changed to No. 7050, was built at the latter's works at Preston. The locomotive was fitted with Allen's new and very promising S18 high speed diesel engine introduced in 1933. This had 8 cylinders and developed 160 bhp at 1,200 rpm. The diesel electric system using a Sulzer engine advocated by Armstrong Whitworth won the day and after a period on loan to the Air Ministry, No. 7050 was sold to the War Office in 1943.

Concurrently with the railway projects the works turned their attention to small main-propulsion marine diesel engines for small vessels. During 1932 the 60 ft. 28 ton Lowestoft trawler *Dusky Queen* was converted to a motor vessel and fitted with an Allen 3S30 engine

The War Office battery-driven locomotive converted by Allens to diesel-electric drive and fitted with a 5-cylinder 110 bhp at 1,200 rpm airless injection diesel engine and d.c. generator.

One of three diesel-electric shunting locomotives built for the Ford Motor Company fitted with Allen 6-cylinder 550 bhp airless injection diesel engines and 95 kW d.c. generators.

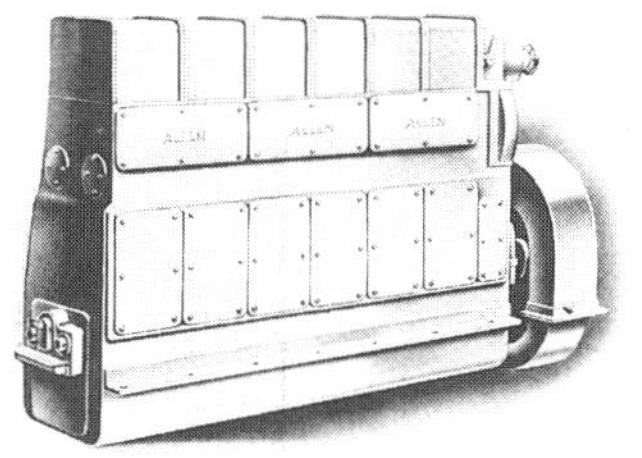

The S27 6-cylinder 150 bhp airless injection engine installed in the Ford Motor Company's three diesel-electric shunting locomotives.

An experimental 25 ton mechanical transmission shunting locomotive built for the L.M.S.R. fitted with Allen's new S18 160 bhp at 1,200 rpm airless injection diesel engine.

developing 100 bhp at 500 rpm. The propeller shaft was driven through a heavy-duty reversing gear which was operated by a hand wheel, rack and pinion, and manufactured at Queen's Engineering Works.

The only departures from a standard engine were alterations to the lubricating system in order to make due allowance for the pitch and roll of the vessel, a wider and smaller diameter flywheel, and the provision of circulating and bilge pumps and an air compressor driven from the engine crankshaft. A quick speed governor was fitted to control the engine when changing direction from full ahead to full astern. Roman Strub attended the successful sea trials held in June 1932 and further orders soon followed. Up until this time Strub had designed his diesel engines to suit the individual needs of the customer. This policy was changed by Kenneth Allen, who was responsible for the introduction of a range of standard engines with the minimum number of variations, whilst retaining facilities for the easy addition of auxiliaries specified by the customer. The Diesel Engine Machine Shop continued to be separate from the General Machine Shop but all diesel engine spares were carried in the General Stores.

Marine propulsion diesel engines

Two other 82 ft. Lowestoft vessels, *Boy Clifford* and *Helping Hand* were converted to diesel propulsion and fitted with Allen 4S30 engines developing 134 bhp at 500 rpm. The sea trials of *Helping Hand* took place in August 1933 and on that occasion the Company was represented by Kenneth Allen, a young man whom we shall learn a great deal about in subsequent chapters, as a leading player in the Company's affairs for the remainder of its independent existence.

These were followed by the conversion of a twin-screw trawler. The existing 2-stroke Deutz engines were replaced by more economical Allen S30 engines, making it the most powerful trawler operating in British east coast waters. Within a few years more than 50 small vessels, including trawlers, tugs and coasters were fitted with Allen airless main propulsion diesel engines. This class of work continued as a major activity at Queen's Engineering Works until the 1940s.

A welcome order received from John J Thorneycroft & Co. in 1933, called for two 5S27 engines and generators for the outstandingly beautiful private yacht *Trenora*. The engines were of fabricated steel for lightness and mounted on specially designed spring-mounted baseplates. The special base consisted of a cast iron housing in two parts, the upper floating part to which the engine was attached and the lower fixed part secured to the seating. A number of adjustable helical springs were contained in the housing, and special anti-vibration pads were arranged in pockets in the housing to guard against the inertia effects of the vessel pitching and rolling.

In 1936, a very similar arrangement was supplied for two 6-cylinder S27 diesel engines driving 90 kW d.c. generators for Mr Tommy Sopwith's 1614 ton luxury motor yacht *Philante* built by Camper & Nicholson. The essential feature of this contract was an absolute minimum of noise and vibration as the engines were located directly beneath the owner's stateroom. The project was closely supervised by Kenneth Allen personally. *Philante* featured prominently in the popular press during 1937 when Tommy Sopwith competed in the great America Cup yacht race held in the United States. Later the yacht was acquired by the King of Norway. A third privately-owned luxury yacht built by Thorneycrofts in the 1930s and

The special baseplate developed by Allens for the S27 diesel engine installed in Mr Tommy Sopwith's luxury yacht Philante *in order to reduce noise and vibration to an absolute minimum.*

fitted with Allen diesel generators was Sir Bernard Docker's much publicised *Shemara.*

Years of depression

1932 was an appalling year for British industry, and Queen's Engineering Works was no exception. Output slumped to an average of £30,000 per month, establishment charges were limited by the Board to £160,000 per annum, and orders in hand rarely exceeded £200,000 in value. Exports were particularly badly affected. Allen's neighbours, J & F Howard, very old-established agricultural engineers, were forced into liquidation. Britain had a National Government under Ramsey MacDonald and any tangible results from the International Conference on Trade held in Ottowa were slow in materialising.

It is perhaps of interest to note that in 1930 the Government published a census of industrial prime movers. The recorded capacity of prime movers in use in factories was: reciprocating steam engines 7 million hp; steam turbines 3 million hp and oil engines 290,000 hp. The capacity of prime movers in electricity generating stations was said to be 10 million hp, the majority of which was developed by steam turbines, but these figures illustrate the continued importance of the reciprocating steam engine in the national life.

During the depression, Queen's Engineering Works lost a number of good friends. Percy Crowe, W H Allen's son-in-law died only twelve months after his retirement. Sir Charles Parsons died during a cruise to the West Indies. Andrew Laing, the head of Fairfields, Sir Alfred Yarrow, Sir Archibald Ross and P H S Kempton, the Pupils' Demonstrator all died. Described as 'A scientist and engineer with a deep knowledge of human nature', Kempton was sorely missed by the Company, but such was the state of trade that the Board reluctantly decided to suspend the new entry of pupils and apprentices for the time being.

Here and there, there were glimmers of hope for better times to come. A 3,000 kW steam turbine-driven generating set complete with a regenerative type condenser was completed for the Bloemfontein Corporation in South Africa. The 250 psi turbine drove a G.E.C. alternator capable of producing 3,750 kVa, 3,000 kW, 2,200 volt, 3-phase 50 cycles electricity at 3,000 rpm. Another interesting order completed in 1932 was for a 2,000 kW pass-out geared turbo-alternator for a large paper mill. The turbine speed was 6,000 rpm and was complete with a 2,000 sq.ft. *Awlinwun* condenser. The alternator, generator and exciter motor were arranged in tandem and ran at 1,000 rpm. The pass-out provided up to 35,000 lbs of steam an hour with a bleed for feed heating up to 4,000 lbs per hour at 7 psi.

By 1934 the Company was poised for a period of growth and prosperity due principally to the Naval re-armament programme.

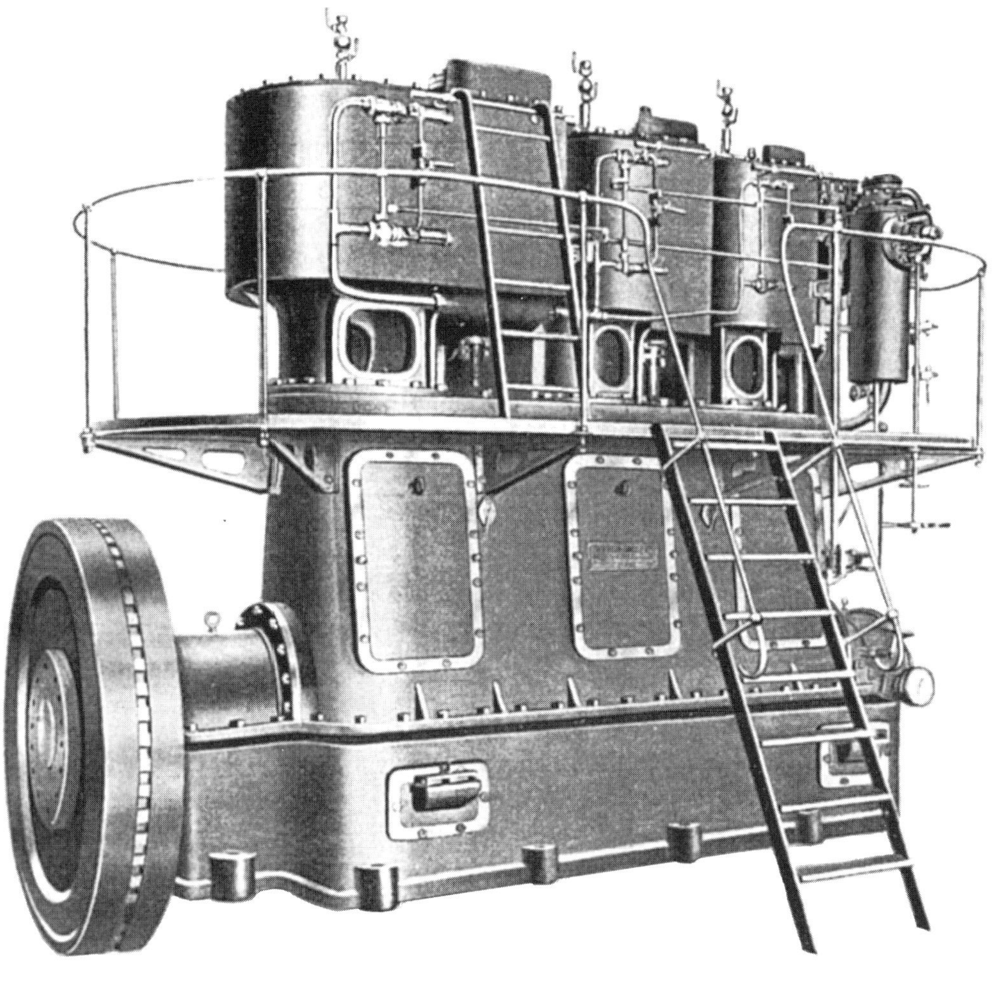

An Allen triple expansion totally-enclosed reciprocating steam engine for direct coupling to a 500 kW d.c. generator produced in the 1930s.

CHAPTER VI

Recovery and Growth – 1934–50

At the beginning of 1933 the recovery was still fragile and after much heart searching the Board took the bold decision to transfer all production from the Biddenham Works back to Queen's Engineering Works. This necessitated the re-erection of the iron and brass foundry, the smiths and plateworkers shop, and the pattern stores at the north end of the site. There was now little demand for the slow-speed, 2-stroke heavy oil engine and the diesel engine test bay was re-erected as an extension to the fitting shop, where the new airless injection engines were assembled. This work was all completed by the end of October and immediately showed worthwhile cost savings.

Recession ends

A feature of the Bedfordshire landscape was the plethora of brickworks' chimneys. A visitor to Bedford at the end of 1933 would have noticed that once again they were belching black smoke, a sure sign that the recovery was becoming a reality as the new house-building programme got under way.

The total value of orders received by Queen's Engineering Works for the airless diesel engine by the end of 1933 was double that received in 1932; by the end of 1934 the increase was five-fold. In many areas of Allens specialisation, especially in mercantile marine applications, the high-speed diesel engine was undoubtedly replacing the steam engine. In road transport in particular it was replacing the petrol engine and the steam wagon, and engineers in both Britain and Germany were seriously considering a diesel aero engine. It showed great savings in both size and weight. Within less than a decade engine speeds were progressively increased from 250 rpm to over 1,000 rpm.

The ending of the recession brought a breath of fresh air throughout the organisation and morale at all levels greatly improved. Each day brought forward new ideas, and thanks to the foresight and careful planning by the Board, the Company was able to take full advantage of new opportunities which presented themselves. In all spheres of activity, whether steam or diesel, renewed emphasis was placed on achieving better fuel consumption, savings in weight and space and an absence of vibration and noise. The need for continued research and investigation was never in doubt, and Allens were determined to lead rather than to follow. But all this proved to be very expensive in new pattern, jig and tooling costs.

300 bhp vertical spindle drip-proof electric motor.

The reduction of noise was a subject of much concern at this time. Although the country had not yet embarked upon the rearmament programme, the Admiralty in particular, were very much alive to the need for continued research and development. They commissioned Allens to build a new high-speed diesel engine where the elimination of noise was of first importance in order to make detection by an enemy more difficult.

The Company launched a big sales drive aimed at industries using steam for process and space-heating purposes. They were able to demonstrate conclusively that an Allen turbo-generator incorporating back-pressure and pass-out systems could supply the electricity needs of the user at a fraction of the cost of relying solely upon National Grid electricity. Smaller plants continued to use successfully the high speed totally-enclosed reciprocating steam engine with a back-pressure facility, and a large range of these engines were available throughout the 1930s. Orders for this type of machinery came mainly from laundries, dye works and textile mills in this country and from sugar plantations overseas.

70 hp windless motor fitted with disc brake and slipping clutch. The deck mounted master controller is shown on the right.

Several important new water and sewage contracts were undertaken, and pumps, which were becoming ever bigger and more efficient, formed a very important part of the Company's activities at this time. The Electrical Department was busy also and new improved ventilated, totally-enclosed drip-proof motors were introduced. New control gear was developed and valuable orders were received for motors and controllers for application to such duties as ships' steering gear, circulating pumps, refrigeration machinery, air compressors, fans and winches. Stothert & Pitt of Bath had recently acquired the patent rights of the well known J H Wilson of Birkenhead winch. They concluded an agreement with Allen for the supply of the electric motors and control gear, leaving themselves to manufacture the mechanical parts. The main feature of this winch was that the motor and transmission gear were integral and concentric with the winch barrel shaft.

A three ton winch fitted with 28 hp Allen motor and control gear.

It has already been noted that during the dark days of the recession it was felt necessary to suspend the training scheme and no new pupils or apprentices were engaged for a couple of years. Fortunately this painful decision was short-lived and the scheme was reinstated as soon as the recession ended. One pupil to be affected by these events was Christopher Cockerell, who later became famous as the inventor of the hovercraft. In Kempton's report dated 1931, Cockerell was described as, 'A sound, healthy and intelligent fellow, a good type of pupil. He has brought some very good ideas in the Test Bay.' Cockerell left Queen's Engineering Works in 1934 to undertake a further course of study at Cambridge University where he had already graduated and where his father was the Director of the Fitzwilliam Museum.

That year, the very popular Annual Childrens' Fête was reinstated in the Allen Park on St Swithin's Day. As a measure of the progress made during the past sixty years it is worth recalling that this was the first occasion on which a public address system had been used in Bedford and it was the very first occasion in which Richard Allen had spoken into a microphone. Such happenings are taken for granted today and we tend to lose sight of many interesting local and national events. That year the mighty *Queen Mary* Atlantic liner was launched on the Clyde; Scott and Black flew their D H Comet from Mildenhall to Melbourne in 71 hours; and the Belisha beacon began to appear in the streets.

The Chairman once again felt free to broaden his activities. He paid an extended visit to Canada and had the honour of being appointed Chairman of the Engineering Section of the British Association for the Advancement of Science. He presented a masterly paper before their Annual Meeting held in Leicester entitled 'Experiences in mechanical engineering'. He reminded his audience that fifty years ago there had been no steam turbines, no diesel engines, no petrol engines, and that electricity generation and transmission were virtually unknown. The mind boggles at the progress he might have identified today as having taken place in mechanical engineering during the past 50 years; but one thing is certain, Queen's Engineering Works would feature prominently in the list.

Product developments

During the 1930s, the Company took every opportunity of improving and extending its product range by the acquisition of manufacturing licences and the extension of its technical 'know-how'. W F W Millington's patents Nos. 253302/03 covering improvements to centrifugal pumps were purchased. Richard Allen acted as Chairman of the British Standards Institution committee BS599, which produced a new British Standard for testing centrifugal pumps. The splendid service given to the Institution by thousands of scientists, engineers and businessmen entirely voluntarily should never be forgotten in this age of highly-subsidised quangos. The Company purchased the Mierbe Steam Circulation System patents and obtained a licence from Modern Wheel Drive Ltd in connection with main propulsion gearing for marine application. They financed a research project at King's College, London who were developing new instrumentation for monitoring quieter running of diesel engines. They acquired a licence from the consulting engineers Ricardo & Company for the use of certain of H R Ricardo's diesel engine patents. This remarkable engineer probably did as much as anybody in the United Kingdom to develop the internal combustion engine. During World War I he designed aero engines and military tank engines and after the War he devoted much time to the development of combustion chambers for compression ignition engines. At this time Allen engineers were developing the diesel engine for use with a wide range of alternative fuels. In 1936 Allens renewed their licence from Parsons and donated generously to the Hon Sir Charles Parsons' Memorial Fund.

French licensees

Allen licensed two French companies to manufacture their products on the Continent. Société de Condensation et d'Applications Mecaniques of Paris were licensed to manufacture forced-draught fans on a royalty basis. The second French licence was granted to the old-established concern Jean Crepelle et Cie of Lille. They manufactured all types of reciprocating machinery and were responsible for the development of the American Corliss stationary engine in France, as well as an extensive range of multi-stage air compressors. They had had some experience with hot-bulb heavy oil engines. The need for this arrangement arose because another French company, Petroles Jupiter, a part of the Royal Dutch Shell Group, had adopted the Allen airless diesel engine as standard equipment for its fleet of petrol barges. Being a company classified as of national importance, it was compelled by a decree passed in October 1934, to use only machinery manufactured in France. Within days of this becoming

Type PS30B 8-cylinder 340 bhp marine propulsion diesel engine with 230 kW Allen d.c. generator installed in a salvage vessel.

law, Harold Allen met Monsieur Pierre Crepelle in Lille and an agreement to manufacture the 'S' type airless injection diesel in France was concluded. By December 1935, a total of 12 engines had been satisfactorily completed by the licensees and the arrangement worked well until the outbreak of war in 1939.

Fifty members of the Institution of Marine Engineers visited Queen's Engineering Works in June 1935, a happy occasion coinciding with a large influx of new orders from the Admiralty. Many of the items ordered were classified as secret and few details have survived, but at a stroke the value of orders in hand increased by nearly a third. The Navy were by now committed to a full-scale rearmament programme and new capital ships of all kinds were on the stocks. Allens also supplied auxiliary machinery for a new Dutch cruiser, *De Ruyter* and a new Argentine cruiser and destroyers being built in Britain.

Marine diesel auxiliaries

Orders received during the previous twelve months from the Mercantile Marine for diesel generating sets were also extremely encouraging. No less than 125 vessels using 330 diesel auxiliary sets had by now been completed and four types of airless injection engines – the S18, S27, S30 and S47 were in regular production. These provided a range of power output from 17 bhp to 100 bhp per cylinder. Four sets of large 6-cylinder S47 engines each developing 550 bhp and driving 375 kW generators had been recently installed in new Commonwealth and Dominion Line motor vessels. Others were installed in the Adelaide Steamship Company's new motor vessel *Manoora*.

1936 started on a sad note with the death of HM King George V, but events at Queen's Engineering Works remained buoyant. All departments were extremely busy and output in both monetary terms and by weight continued to grow. The largest single order ever received by the Company was placed for Britain's largest waterworks pumping station at Hampton by the Metropolitan Water Board. This order alone provided the factory with two years work and the contract was valued at £211,800. The combined output of the pumps specified for this project was 268 million gallons of water a day and the aggregate continuous output of the turbine pumps and generators exceeded 20,000 bhp – but more of this as our story unfolds. Suffice it to say that the total capacity of all the pumping installations ordered from Queen's Engineering Works in 1936 equalled 1.9 million gallons per day which was equivalent to 35 gallons per day for each member of the population.

But not all pumping installations were associated only with water. The world's growing oil industry provided a big market for pump manufacturers. For example, Allens supplied the Anglo-Iranian Oil Company with three steam turbines direct-coupled to pumps capable of delivering 34,000 gallons per minute against a total head of 160 ft. Each set comprised two 42 in. double suction pumps arranged in tandem and driven through gearing. The pump efficiency on normal load was 84 per cent and the total power absorbed was 3,930 bhp. The turbines had 1 Curtis wheel and 13 Rateau stages and all had special stainless steel blades.

1936 was an exceptionally good year for the Electrical Department. 1,200 motors and dynamos were produced for marine applications alone. They were mainly used for driving fans, for refrigeration and for the Stothert & Pitt Wilson type winch which was proving very successful and was produced in batches of fifty. Seventy motors and their associated controllers were supplied for the P & O liner *Orcades* for driving a variety of auxiliaries.

Sadly, in the midst of all this activity, Archibald Carmichael, at the age of 55, was found to be suffering from a progressively debilitating disease. After several months absence from work, the Directors reluctantly decided that he should be relieved of his duties as Works Manager. In December 1936, W G Poole, a long serving employee and one time superintendent of the Biddenham Works, was appointed as the Company's third Works Manager since its formation in 1880. Carmichael's complete retirement was confirmed three months later and armed with a generous pension he settled in Bexhill-on-Sea.

The Board, at its meeting held on 2nd July 1937, discussed various proposals for the conversion of a part of the Company's Ordinary shares into Preference Shares in order to facilitate the winding up of the late Chairman's Estate. It was ultimately agreed that conversion of the Company's status from that of a Private Limited Liability Company to that of a Publicly Quoted Company would best achieve their purpose. It was felt that a Stock Exchange quotation would be in the best long term interests of all shareholders and would enable the capital of the Company to be increased to £450,000. The Company's solicitors were instructed to proceed but, for reasons now unknown, the matter appears to have been deferred until 1952.

W G Poole, Works Manager Queen's Engineering Works 1936–54.

Seen in retrospect, an equally important long term decision was taken at the next meeting held on 19th July. The Chairman, Richard Allen proposed that William Kenneth Allen, the founder's eldest surviving grandson should be appointed to the Board as an Executive Director. Kenneth, as he was always known, was born in 1907, the eldest son of Harold Allen. He was educated at Westminster School and at the University of Neuchatel in Switzerland. He became a pupil at Harland & Wolff's engine works at Finnieston Street, Glasgow, followed by a period in their Belfast engineering works and shipyard, and subsequently at Queen's Engineering Works. He spent some time in London working in the offices of the firm's auditors, Deloitte, Plender, Griffiths & Company and this was followed by a period in the various commercial departments at Queen's Engineering Works.

His first appointment within the Company was as a representative at the firm's Manchester office. He was charged with, as he put it, 'calling upon industrial premises wheresoever a smoking chimney was to be seen.' His object was to secure business for modern high-speed totally-enclosed reciprocating steam engines and turbines and to develop the concept of low-cost electricity generation by the use of Allen back-pressure and pass-out machinery. Involved as he was with relatively high-cost capital equipment, he realised the importance of establishing contact with the principals of firms. He was dismayed to find how often he was told that Mr So-and-so was out golfing, shooting or fishing instead of attending to the affairs of his business. He realised that these people were in most cases the second or third generation of the founding families and his experiences undoubtedly affected his personal attitudes to his responsibilities in a family business. As a result of the reorganisation that took place at Queen's Engineering Works during the depression he became head of the Diesel Engine Department, a role he fulfilled with great energy and distinction.

Kenneth Allen

In July 1931 he married Eleanor Mary Eeles, the daughter of Henry Eeles, a director of Smith Docks Ltd of South Shields. In due course Kenneth and Eleanor had two children, Charles born in 1936 and Caroline born in 1938. Some years ago Kenneth wrote a scholarly and fascinating biography of all the members of the Allen family in which we learn that Henry Eeles died when his children were very young and his widow, Florence, married again. As an amusing diversion to our story we learn that her stepson, James Bond, became a world famous ornithologist. Without leave the writer Ian Fleming, himself a keen bird watcher, coined the name James Bond for the hero of his extraordinarily successful series of books and films. In 1966 Mary Bond, James' wife wrote an amusing book *How 007 got his name*, which was published by Collins, in which she described the effect upon their lives caused by this.

H E Boyd rendered the Company over fifty years continuous service and rose from junior clerk to Company Secretary, a position he held for twenty-five years.

Following its reorganisation in 1937, the Board comprised Richard Allen (Chairman); Harold G Allen and Rupert S Allen (Managing Directors) and Kenneth Allen (Executive Director). H E Boyd, who had succeeded R Anderson, was Company Secretary. One of their first actions was to arrange the sale of fifteen acres of land at Biddenham for a new housing estate but the tempo of things changed dramatically in 1938. Throughout the months prior to the Declaration of War in September 1939 there was enormous activity at Queen's Engineering Works in order to ensure that production was maximised and that everything possible was done to prepare for what most people now regarded as the inevitable. Few had much faith in the Prime Minister's declaration of 'Peace in our time' following his meeting with Herr Hitler. The re-armament programme and air raid precautions became central to most people's lives. Gas masks were issued to everybody, sand bags appeared on most public buildings, and air raid shelters were constructed. Spitfire and Hurricane fighter aircraft were just beginning to come off the production lines, and the expansion of air defences was given top priority.

Admiralty work received the highest priority at Queen's Engineering Works and by the summer of 1939 60 per cent of output was devoted to the navy's requirements. £50,000 had been expended on new machine tools and considerable improvements were made in the manufacture of items such as turbine blades by the introduction of

Block Plan of Works – Circa 1934.

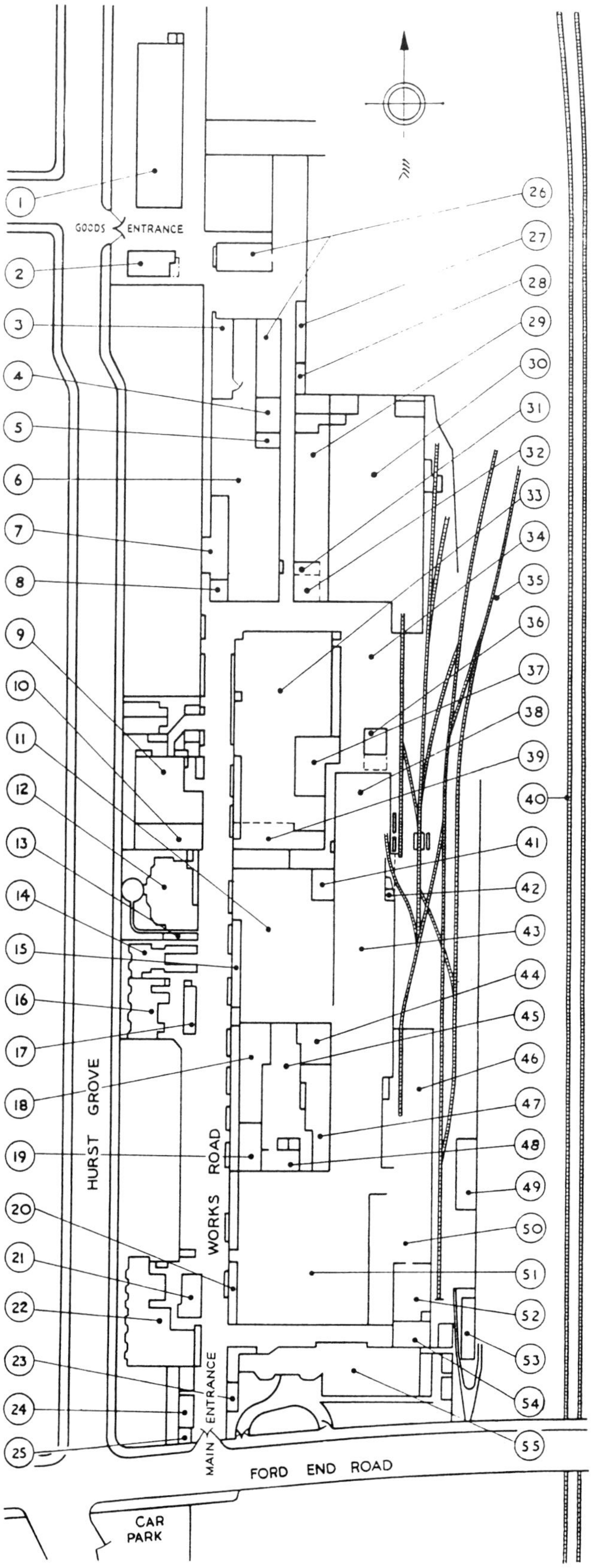

LIST OF DEPARTMENTS AND OTHER SECTIONS AT THE QUEEN'S ENGINEERING WORKS, BEDFORD

1. General Stores
2. General Stores Offices
3. Pump Erecting Shop
4. Millwrights' Shop
5. Garage (workshop vehicles)
6. Sheet Metal and Welding Shop
7. Hardening Shop
8. Metal Spraying Shop
9. Canteen
10. Laboratory
11. Light Machine Shop
12. Men's Institute
13. Library
14. Allen Junior Club
15. Whitemetal Shop
16. Education and Welfare Dept.
17. Surgery
18. Steel Stores
19. Gear Cutting Shop
20. Jig Stores
21. Works Management Offices
22. Design Offices
23. Reception and Conference Rooms
24. Fire Station
25. Gatehouse
26. Pattern Stores
27. Chain Stores
28. Oil Stores
29. Pattern Shop (first floor)
30. Iron and Brass Foundries
31. Sand Blast Shop
32. Compressor House
33. Electrical Shop
34. Moulding Boxes
35. Railway Sidings
36. Cooling Tower
37. Wiremen's Shop
38. Diesel Engine Test Shop
39. Electrical Test Bay
40. Main Line – LMSR
41. Coppersmiths' Shop
42. Paint Shop
43. Fitting and Erecting Shop
44. Stores
45. Tool Room
46. Packing and Despatch Bay
47. Detail Assembly Shop
48. Tool Stores
49. Cooling Tower
50. Steam and Pump Test Bay
51. Heavy Machine Shop
52. Boiler House
53. Research Dept.
54. Power House
55. Commercial and Technical Offices

The ubiquitous Pickfords Scammell low-loader, a familiar sight around Bedford transporting the finished products of Queen's Engineering Works.

new high production profile milling machines. A new Yarrow water tube boiler was installed in the Power House capable of producing 20,000 lbs steam per hour at 600 psi. A completely new test house was built for testing pumps and fans and the Electrical Test Bay was doubled in size.

During this period the staff was increased to 376, the increase being mainly in the technical and production departments. To a large extent this was made possible by the steady flow of highly competent pupils and apprentices trained by the Company. A staff pension and life assurance scheme was introduced offering benefits which at that time were largely unheard of in the engineering industry and an employees holiday accumulation fund, providing holidays with pay was introduced in the works.

Airless injection diesel engines

During this period the range of diesel engines was reconsidered in the light of market needs and it was decided to concentrate on three basic types. The smallest of these was the S30B engine designed to develop 44.5 bhp per cylinder at 600 rpm. The design embodied several improvements resulting from previous operating experience and particular attention was paid to the accessibility of parts, such as the valve operating gear, governor drive and assembly, and the camshaft drive and control mechanism. The crankshaft was provided with double bearings at the flywheel end. Dry sump lubrication was adopted so that the engine could be installed well down on restricted depth of seatings for marine propulsion and other applications, resulting in an engine of low overall height. The larger S37B and S47B engines also embodied improvements in the chain-drive layout, unit governor construction and totally-enclosed camshaft drive. Some difficulties had arisen in shipping the larger S37 and S47 engines to overseas destinations resulting in serious damage to the engines. It was decided to abandon the C frame construction in favour of the more rigid A frame which permitted a lighter maximum lift.

Another decision was to add a 2-stroke engine to the range of airless solid injection engines in order to meet the requirements for the largest engine capable of being built by the Company. Designated type T47, it developed 135 bhp per cylinder at 375 rpm. The largest unit built had 8 cylinders and developed 1,080 bhp.

T47 6-cylinder 2-stroke diesel engine direct-coupled to 500 kW Allen alternator.

Once again the company turned to Harland & Wolff for a licence to base their new design on the Burmeister & Wain Uniflow scavenge system. This was arranged on a royalty basis of 5 shillings (25p) per hp for engines under 1,000 hp and 6 shillings (30p) per hp for engines over 1,000 hp. It was at this time that the famous firm of international patent agents and patent lawyers, Marks & Clerk, were appointed to act for the Company.

The scavenge air was supplied by a Rootes type three-lobe blower located at the back of the engine. It was driven from the crankshaft through a flexible coupling and speed-increasing gears. An effective silencer could be fitted on the suction side of the blower if required.

T47 2-stroke diesel

The cylinder heads were fitted with two exhaust valves operated by a single push rod, permitting the use of a single central fuel injector, greatly simplifying the fuel distribution in the combustion space. A separate fuel pump was employed for each cylinder. The pistons had concave crowns giving efficient turbulence and the gudgeon pins were inserted underneath. This gave a larger bearing area than would have been possible if they had passed through the pistons. The gudgeon pins were force-lubricated and the pistons were oil-cooled.

The cylinder liners were made from a special close-grained cast iron with the scavenge air inlet ports machined to give the correct amount of swirl to the air. The forced-lubrication oil pump was gear driven from the crankshaft and supplied the engine pressure lubrication system and piston cooling through an oil cooler.

The exigences of war retarded the development of the T47 engine until 1946 but we must not lose sight of two very important mercantile marine contracts completed in 1938 for Swan Hunter. The Shaw Saville motor ship *Dominion Monarch* was the largest powered motor vessel in the world at the time of her maiden voyage to the Antipodes in February 1939. Powered by four Duxford opposed piston diesel engines each rated at 8,000 shp she was capable of 22 knots. Five sets of Allen 6S60 engines were installed side by side in an auxiliary engine room ahead of the main engines and it is said that the combined output of their generators, amounting to 3,000 kW, was the largest of any ship afloat. The cylinders measured 430 mm x 600 mm and each engine developed 900 bhp when direct-coupled to Allen's marine-type multipolar compound wound 220 volt d.c. generators having a normal full load output of 600 kW. These were the largest diesel generators made by Queen's Engineering Works prior to World War II.

The *Sobieski* built by Swan Hunter for the Polish Gydnia America Line had three 450 kW generators powered by 6S60 engines running at 275 rpm. Over forty Allen electric motors ranging from 3 to 85 hp were installed in this vessel for dredging pumps, fans, compressors and other auxiliary machinery.

Norman Gwynne Allen

During 1939, Norman Gwynne Allen, Kenneth's younger brother was invited to attend Board Meetings. Whilst recognising his wise counsel as an expert in engineering matters, they wished to acknowledge the splendid work he had done supervising the great Hampton Pumping Station contract placed by the Metropolitan Water Board. He was born in Bedford in 1912 and educated at Westminster School and Trinity College, Cambridge. He did his practical training at Whites of Cowes and at John Brown's great shipyard on the Clyde. Later, joining Queen's Engineering Works he gained further experience in most departments. From an early age he demonstrated his remarkable technical knowledge, practical ability and humanity. Throughout his career he was always greatly respected and liked by his colleagues. In 1938 he married Marjorie Brown of Cowes, Isle of Wight; they have four children.

In many respects, the Hampton Pumping Station contract was unique. Apart from being the largest order ever received by Queen's Engineering Works, when completed, it was the largest of its kind in the world. Its total output was 138 million gallons of water a day. In the 1930s the distribution of water in England and Wales was

The machinery hall at the Metropolitan Water Board's Hampton Station showing the Allen turbine-driven pumping and generating units.

7,000 bhp Allen steam turbine-driven pumping unit installed in the Rand Water Board's Vereeniging Pumping Station in South Africa. Normal output 1,875,000 gallons per hour against a total head of 530 ft.

controlled by some 1,250 public and private bodies. Consequently, since the areas supplied were comparatively small, only moderate capacity pumps were required. Following the successful introduction of the National Grid in the 1920s for the distribution of electricity, some advanced thinking engineers began to turn their attention to a similar network of water service pipes. A committee was formed to investigate the problem but little progress was made. In this country only the Metropolitan Water Board felt justified in establishing a large central pumping station.

Fortunately, Allens had previously had experience supplying similar machinery for a major scheme in South Africa. The impounding of the River Vaal by the Rand Water Board in 1921 was a 'show piece' project handling over 50 million gallons of water a day. Competition for the Hampton contract was very severe and twenty-two competing tenders were submitted. Shortly before their tender was completed, Allens were able to carry out extensive tests at Bedford on two large steam turbine driven pumps, one of 5,000 hp for the Anglo-Iranian Oil Co., the other a 4,000 hp set for the Rand Water Board. These tests made possible substantial increases to the turbine efficiency by altering the nozzle and diaphragm designs and resulted in improvements to the pump designs which enabled the company to offer the Metropolitan Water Board guarantees with absolute confidence. The difference between Allen's successful tender and their nearest rival was only 0.04 lbs of steam per hp per hour, illustrating the closeness of tendering.

River Vaal project, S Africa

It is difficult to describe in a few words the equipment and functioning of this enormous pumping station. The machinery was required for pumping filtered water through a number of mains varying in size from 30 in. to 42 in. diameter distances up to 17 miles at heads up to 170 ft.; and two 36 in. diameter mains a distance of 10 miles at a head of 80 ft. The maximum power required exceeded 20,000 hp. This was supplied by eight steam-driven turbines; one water-driven turbine; and one electric motor driven unit for both filtered and unfiltered water pumps. The four largest units had 2-cylinder steam turbines and the four smaller units had single-cylinder turbines. Two of the latter drove 300 kW generators and four of the larger units drove in addition to the pumps, a 450 kW generator when the pumps were not in operation and a 300 kW generator when pumping and generating. All the turbines operated at 300 psi, at a total temperature of 650°F and exhausted into a vacuum of 29 in.

The condensers were the normal surface type housed in a basement below the turbines. Steam jet air pumps were used and the circulating and extraction pumps were motor driven. Arrangements were made for them to be driven also by water turbines. Allens supplied the closed feed water system and complete heating and evaporating plant including the three turbine driven and two motor driven boiler feed pumps.

The works had to make special arrangements for testing the machinery on full load. They acquired a dynamometer brake capable of absorbing 3,600 hp. The large filtered water pumps which absorbed 1,900 bhp were tested with a turbine, the reading being taken by a torsion dynamometer. Other pumps were tested by one of the 450 kW generators used as a motor. Models were made of all the pumps and no effort was spared to ensure Hampton was the most efficient pumping station in the world.

Hampton low-lift Pumping Station

In 1939 the company was awarded the contract for the separate low-lift Hampton Pumping Station. This comprised 13 Allen vertical-spindle conical flow pumps, 11 of which were driven by Allen 220 volt d.c. motors and 2 by Gilbert, Gilkes & Gordon water turbines. The normal duty of each of the four larger pumps was to deliver 18.75 million gallons a day against a head of 15.75 ft. driven by a 160 hp motor running at 350 rpm. The contract was finally completed in 1941.

Another important pumping contract undertaken by the firm before the outbreak of war was the new 4,000 ton floating dock constructed by the Furness Shipbuilding Co. for the port of Durban in South Africa. As the war progressed, involving the transportation of vast quantities of men and materials round the Cape en route to Egypt and elsewhere in the Middle East, this became of great strategic importance. The dock had an overall length of 350 ft. and an overall width of 64 ft. The whole of the machinery was electrically operated, the supply being taken from the shore.

The main pumping machinery consisted of four 16 in. Allen vertical, conical-flow centrifugal pumps each being designed to deliver 28 tons of sea water per minute against a head of 16.4 ft. The centre line of the pumps was 23 ft. below the motors and the 2½ in. diameter shafts were supported in lignum vitae lined bearings. The impellers were cast in gunmetal. Each pump was driven by a 45 bhp motor running at 580 rpm. The completed dock was towed out to Durban, the 7,000 mile journey taking nearly three months.

The 36th edition of the splendid Queen's Engineering Works Magazine appeared in January 1939. This was supplemented by the Allen Engineering Review which was originally intended to be published quarterly, but wartime restrictions meant its suspension from 1942 to July 1946.

Preparations for War

A committee was formed in the early part of 1939 to plan the Company's air raid precautions in order to protect both people and property. 20,000 sand bags were prepared to protect buildings and men were trained in fire fighting and first aid. A scheme for totally blacking out the factory was formulated, enabling the night shift to continue working, and steps were taken to make a duplicate record of all important documents essential to the continuance of the business. 60,000 drawings and 21,700 documents were copied and stored at Biddenham. A third machine shop was established at the north end of the Bedford site. Jigs and fixtures for such items as forced-draught fans, which were of particular concern to the Admiralty, were duplicated and arrangements were made to transfer production to Biddenham if necessary. Norman Allen, having completed the Hampton contract was transferred to the works as Assistant Works Manager in order to provide additional back-up for Mr Poole. In true British style an especially successful Annual Summer Fête was held in Allen Park. Most employees and their families attended including 55 Company pensioners, who between them had a total of 1,840 years service. Each was presented with a long service certificate by the Chairman.

On 18th September 1939, the Board considered at length its future policy in the light of current events. Harold Allen had submitted a very erudite report shortly before the declaration of War in which he emphasised that the Company's policy during World War I had led them into enormous difficulties from which it had taken them twenty years to recover. They had accepted a great deal of new work from the Admiralty and other Government departments outside their normal activities and output had increased from £250,000 to £2 million per annum involving enormous capital expenditure. Subsequent Acts of Parliament, which they could not have anticipated, resulted in years of losses and anxiety.

He pointed out that many of their friends and competitors had been able to carry on with their normal activities with only a limited involvement in new work of a defence character, whereas Allens had forsaken all their commercial friends and concentrated 100 per cent on Government work. He regarded this as the Company's great mistake.

Government contracts reviewed

Between 1910 and 1914 27 per cent of the Company's output went to the Admiralty. Before the present emergency the figure had dropped to 25 per cent. Now, following the launching of the rearmament programme, 60 per cent of their output went to Admiralty contracts. He advocated that this proportion should not be exceeded thereby protecting their other commercial interests.

He concluded by reminding the Board that no matter what they had embarked upon during World War I, legislation was forced upon the company by the raising of taxes, duties and other impositions, the consequences of which had had repercussions for many years to come.

The outcome was a resolution that 'The policy of the Company be to continue producing machinery to the normal designs of its various specialities. Not to embark on any new work requiring capital expenditure, new buildings, etc. with its corresponding responsibilities. To regulate the output so as not to exceed to any great extent the present rate, the Admiralty output being approximately 60 per cent of the total.'

1940 was the Company's Diamond Jubilee year and a dividend of 15 per cent was declared. An impressive list of new machinery exported to the four corners of the world during the year was published in the January 1941 issue of the Allen Engineering Review. But this could not continue. May 1940 saw Holland and Belgium overrun and the defeat of France. Winston Churchill became Prime Minister and Britain braced itself for total war. The Ministry of Supply declared the company 'A controlled undertaking'.

Richard Allen, now in his 74th year, was living in Hampstead. He decided that London was too dangerous and that in any event he should be more readily available in Bedford. He leased Turvey Abbey, a pleasant residence a few miles outside Bedford with the understanding that it should provide emergency office accommodation in case of need.

In January 1942, Richard was knighted for his services to the Royal Navy. This honour was undoubtedly well-deserved for he had devoted a great part of his fifty years in business to working with and for the Senior Service. He knew, personally, every Engineer-in-Chief of the Fleet this century, and it is extremely doubtful if there was a single capital ship afloat without some Allen machinery.

During the difficult years 1940 and 1941 it was estimated that over 100,000 productive man-hours were lost at Queen's Engineering Works due to enemy action. Then a system of 'Spotters' was introduced whereby work continued during an air-raid alert until enemy aircraft were known to be within 10 miles radius of Bedford. By this method the loss of production was greatly reduced and a tremendous momentum was built up in the works. The workforce grew to a total of 3,034 in spite of the loss of 279 Allen employees to the armed services. Of this total, 512 were women who were employed mainly in the machine shops and Electrical Department. Turn-over was increased from £1.4 million in 1940 to £1.97 million in 1943. During this period the Admiralty made available to the company machine tools to the value of £1.25 million at a rental of 12½ per cent per annum. Subsequently, following lengthy negotiations with E C Jubb, the Director of Navy Contracts it was agreed that these should be acquired for a sum of £163,400.

Norman Allen's elevation to the Board was confirmed in 1943 and for the first time a female was granted indentures in the works being offered four years training in the laboratory. Rather as the British advocated eating carrots as a means of improving night vision, the German propaganda machine stressed the importance of the Industrial Psychologist in improving morale in the German Navy. The Admiralty took up this theme and no doubt under their influence W H Allens appointed an Industrial Psychologist, but this seems to have been a short lived expediency. Of much more benefit to the workforce was a gracious visit of HRH The Duchess of Gloucester to Queen's Engineering Works in February 1944.

The list of conventional auxiliary machinery manufactured for the Navy was impressive and may be summarised as follows:

Wartime production

Steam turbine driven electrical generating machinery
Reciprocating steam engine driven electrical generating machinery
Steam turbine driven main circulating pumps
Steam turbine driven forced-draught fans
Electric motor driven pumps of various designs
Electric motor driven forced-draught fans
Steam turbines for steering gear
Closed circuit feed water machinery, comprising steam turbine driven extraction pumps, steam jet air ejectors and automatic feed control valves.
Electrical machinery including generators and motors, steering gear, capstan and winch motors and associated control gear.

In addition, a large volume of orders were received for more specialised equipment not in regular production. For example, ten sets of specially designed steam turbines and condensers driving 'VSG' hydraulic pumps for operating the big guns on the '*King George V*' class battleships were produced. In order to combat the menace of

An Allen 500 kW turbo-generator with self-contained condensing plant as installed in British battleships, aircraft carriers and cruisers.

An Allen 200 kW turbo-generator with self-contained condensing plant as installed in Battle *class and* Weapons *class destroyers.*

An Allen 60 kW back-pressure turbo-generator as installed in Hunt *class destroyers.*

Steam turbine-driven general service unit for steam gunboats. The turbine drives a 10 kW generator, the hydraulic pumps for gun turret operation and the steering gear.

the German E-Boats Allens were commissioned to produce machinery for a new class of steam gunboats. It was extremely important that the machinery should be as light as possible and entirely new designs were produced in record time. Increased operating speeds were employed, the turbine casings were of welded construction and hardened steel helical gears of a special design were incorporated in the General Service Units, circulating pumps and forced-draught fans. These subsequently provided the basis of design for an entirely new steam turbine driven ventilating fan installed in ships' engine rooms and auxiliary compartments of vessels earmarked for service in the Far East. Over a three year period nearly 200 sets of these turbines and fans were produced.

Other specialised Naval work included items for a new submarine detection system produced in conjunction with Fraser & Chalmers Engineering, and 200 mm Oerkkon gun mountings. A total of 1,200 of these gun mountings were produced at the Biddenham Works. 700 sets of oil-operated marine reversing and reducing gears for use in Tank Landing Craft were produced for Modern Wheel Drive Ltd; and 500 sets of crankshafts were machined and balanced for small diesel engines produced by Victor Oil Engines Ltd of Coventry.

The first contract for diesel engine driven generating sets for the Navy was received in 1942. Twelve 200 kW sets were installed in new

A typical jet condensing plant with steam turbine driven rotary air pumps.

Light Fleet Carriers and others were supplied to Naval Shore Establishments and Dockyards Power Stations. In addition several mercantile vessels taken over by the Admiralty and converted to aircraft carriers for escort duties were fitted with Allen diesel generating sets. These orders represented a development of considerable significance to the company in the post war years. The production of diesel engine driven generating sets for the Mercantile Marine under the aegis of the Ministry of War Transport continued at a pace and numerous sets were supplied to most of the leading British shipping companies.

In the early days of the war the Company received an order from the Metropolitan Cammell Carriage & Wagon Company for machining and assembling *Valentine* Mark V tank turret assemblies and the main suspension assemblies. This Company, together with William Foster of Lincoln, had been main contractors for the supply of first-generation military tanks during World War I. During 1942 the Government decided that Naval construction must be given top priority and Allens had to decline further contracts for work associated with the tank programme.

Special wartime production

Mention must also be made of other important contracts for essential services completed during the war years. Five sets of 500 kW transportable turbo-alternators and condensing plant were supplied for service in the Soviet Union. Others having various outputs ranging from 15 kW to 550 kW were built for relief work in recently-liberated and needy countries. Two sets went to Rangoon in Burma; three sets went to Hyderabad; two sets went to the Punjab; and others were placed at the disposal of UNRRA. Two 1,000 kW turbo-alternators and condensing plant complete with associated equipment went to China. Three sets of 315 kVa diesel engine driven alternators were installed in a new bomb-proof General Post Office at Faraday House in London. Other 200 kW diesel sets were supplied for the Military Short-wave Radio Station at Droitwich and three sets were installed in the bomb-proof Admiralty Citadel in Whitehall. From 1942 – 45 Norman Allen assumed responsibility for a satellite

A portable emergency diesel generating set supplied to the Metropolitan Water Board during World War II.

shell factory located at Letchworth in Hertfordshire.

The supply of pumping machinery for maintaining essential services also received a high priority. Plant driven by diesel engines, steam turbines and electric motors was built for a score of leading water undertakings. The Metropolitan Water Board took delivery of several portable units mounted on four-wheel pneumatic-tyred trailers. Some of these were driven by steam turbines and others by electric motors and were intended for the restoration of water supplies damaged by enemy action. Other important contracts contributing to the nation's essential needs were the construction and installation of several major land-drainage schemes in East Anglia. Large orders were received from the Anglo-Iranian Oil Company for steam turbine driven pumps, condensing plant and de-aerating plant. These were required to assist with the maintenance of vital oil supplies from the Iranian Oilfields.

No review of events at Queen's Engineering Works could be complete without reference to the achievements of the Electrical Department. Literally thousands of electrical machines comprising dynamos, motors, starters and control gear of many different types were produced and a sustained rate of 150 machines per month, excluding starters and control gear was achieved. In order to meet this demand, most of the work associated with starters and control gear was transferred to the Biddenham Works.

Electric generators

Some 2,400 main generators having a combined output of over 200,000 kW were constructed at Queen's Engineering Works during the war years. Although mainly used with prime movers of Allen design, many were supplied to other leading manufacturers such as Peter Brotherhood, F Perkins, Ruston & Hornsby, National Gas & Oil Engine Company and Harland & Wolff. The largest single order destined ultimately for the Mercantile Marine was placed by the Carron Iron Works, Falkirk in 1942 for 152 deck winches.

Several specialised Navy contracts are worthy of special mention. In November 1939 the cruiser *Belfast* sustained severe damage as the result of an under-water explosion, and the Admiralty immediately demanded a revision of all existing designs of electrical equipment used in capital ships. This resulted in the substitution of cast iron by cast or fabricated steel and a new system of resilient mounting

A batch of 10 kW single cylinder enclosed steam engines and generators use for de-gaussing purposes in merchant vessels.

embodying corrugated steel plates and rubber pads. Particular attention was paid to overspeed governors and the risk of them shutting down the machinery at a moment it was of vital importance that they should remain in operation. Allens undertook detailed research into the problem and, in conjunction with the Admiralty Research Laboratory at West Drayton, proposed a new double-ring shock proof emergency governor. Eventually, the Admiralty accepted the design for all its turbine driven auxiliary machinery.

De-gaussing equipment

In 1940 the magnetic mine menace necessitated fitting vessels with de-gaussing equipment in order to neutralise the ship's magnetic field. During the next two years Allens built 950 sets of single-cylinder reciprocating steam engine driven 10/15 kW generating sets complete with switchboards and circuit breakers. In spite of the Naval authorities strenuous endeavours to neutralise the effects of the magnetic mine, a significant number of vessels were damaged which increased the demand for portable salvage pumps. Later similar types of equipment was used for bilge pump duties in Tank Landing Craft and a total of 1,950 units were manufactured at Queen's Engineering Works.

Other electrical equipment was produced for ammunition hoists, boat and paravane winches, ships' capstans and combined seaplane and mine hoists. These accounted for 6,058 separate units having an aggregate of 85,626 hp. At least 95 per cent of steering gear motors and the control gear required for Destroyers and Escort Vessels were produced at Bedford. These comprised some 1,200 units each of between 10 and 20 hp for the smaller vessels and as high as 130 hp for the largest ships, having an aggregate power of 26,000 hp.

Once supplies for the European War were assured, the Admiralty concentrated its attention upon the needs of the Far Eastern theatre. They developed an ocean going tank carrier and landing craft fitted with watertight bow doors and a draw-bridge type vehicle ramp. Working in conjunction with the Sentinel Wagon Company of Shrewsbury, Allens designed a fool-proof system of control for the bow doors and lowering ramp. Orders were received for 250 sets which included 500 electric motors and associated equipment totalling some 3,740 assemblies. The majority were completed before the unexpected abrupt termination of the Far Eastern campaign. The

An Allen 275 kW back-pressure turbo-generator. One of nine units for vessels of the British India Steam Navigation Co. Ltd.

requirements of the entire ship. The use of pass-out turbines for land installations had been established practice for many years and *Caronia's* turbo-generators embodied the results of many years development work. Each set comprised a multi-stage impulse turbine mounted directly on its surface condenser driving a compound-wound, specially-ventilated, d.c. generator through double helical reduction gearing. Improved materials developed during the War were extensively used for the steam cylinders, rotor and blades, carbon-molybdenum steels replacing the high tensile steels formerly used. Steam from the pass-out stage of the turbine was re-admitted to the low-pressure blading by a pass-through valve under the joint control of the pass-out regulator and a new improved design of speed governor, the action of which maintained the pass-out pressure constant.

Turbine Design Department

Arthur Fitt, the Chief Turbine Designer, who came to Allens from Parsons in 1925, died in 1948, although he had ceased to function in this capacity in 1939 due to ill health. He was succeeded by Roderick McLeod, who successfully dealt with several difficult design problems during the War years. Eventually, he left the Company and became a right-hand man to Frank Whittle, the pioneer of the gas turbine at his newly established company, Power Jets in Leicester. The post-war turbine and gearing scene was brilliantly handled by Alick Hutchinson, the Chief Steam Turbine and Gearing Engineer. He had been with the Company since 1922 and eventually, in 1956, was appointed Engineering Consultant to the Company.

By mid-1947 exports to the four corners of the world began to flow once again from Queen's Engineering Works. New ships of fourteen nations were fitted with Allen auxiliary machinery and diesel engines, steam turbines and pumps of all kinds were supplied for land installations in over twenty countries ranging from the Argentine to Australia, from South Africa to Russia and most European countries. The list was impressive and just as the Company had responded to the Nation's call during the War, so did it respond to the urgent call for exports.

At home, times were difficult. There was an acute fuel crisis and very severe weather to contend with during February and March 1947. Food rationing and shortages of most consumer goods affected the daily lives of the people, and industry had difficulty obtaining the raw materials it required. As if to cap it all, serious flooding occurred in the Fens during the year. Although planned before the great flood, the River Great Ouse Catchment Board authorised the construction of a new pumping station at Welches Dam on the drain between Earith and Downham Market as part of an important flood prevention scheme in the Cambridgeshire Fens. Allens supplied two very large 45 in. pumps capable of pumping 5 million gallons of water per hour against a head of 13.5 ft. The pumps were driven by 6-cylinder 500 bhp airless injection diesel engines running at 475 rpm through double-helical reducing gears. The scheme, designed to allow flood water to flow into the sea through the Denver Sluice and the River Great Ouse at Kings Lynn, represented the largest drainage pumping plant order received at Queen's Engineering Works for Fen drainage for over fifty years.

Major pump contracts

Another important pumping contract fulfilled in the post-war years was the Bournemouth Gas and Water Undertakings' new pumping station on the banks of the River Avon in Hampshire. The two Allen vertical double-suction pumps were designed to handle 14 million gallons of water per day against a total head of 308 ft. The 6-cylinder diesel engines were the new type T47 2-stroke engines developing 125 bhp per cylinder at a speed of 345 rpm. Each engine was connected to the speed increasing gears through *Ambiflex* couplings which the firm had recently introduced. The exhaust gases from the engines were utilised in waste-heat boilers which served the central heating system in the pump house and four adjoining cottages, in addition to providing domestic hot water. The Allen machinery was painted eau-de-nil picked out in black. The green terrazzo flooring combined with the fine architectural design of the building made the installation somewhat of a show piece.

The T47 2-stroke engine was based on the Burmeister & Wain patent and was licensed to Allen by Harland & Wolff. It was of the uniflow scavenge type and available with 3, 4, 5, 6 or 8 cylinders. The bore and stroke of the cylinders was 290 mm x 470 mm and each cylinder developed 135 bhp at 375 rpm. These engines were of robust, compact construction, special attention having been paid to accessibility. During the next two decades many were built for a variety of applications.

In May 1947, the North Bedfordshire College of Further Education was opened and Queen's Engineering Works revised its training programme. Soon over 100 students and apprentices attended the College on Day Release schemes, but the Company's great tradition, as regards engineering training was maintained. In 1948 they employed six post-graduate pupils, nine senior engineering students, seven junior engineering students, and 160 trade apprentices. Several of the students were from overseas, coming from as far afield as Iran and China. During 1949, the Allen Memorial Prize for the best all-round graduate or student during the year was re-introduced.

Revised training programme

Although it was clear that there would be many social, economic and technological changes in the second half of the 20th Century, the Board faced the future with quiet confidence.

CHAPTER VII

The Final Years of Independent Existence 1950–68

SHORTLY after the ending of hostilities in Europe, the Admiralty contacted W H Allen, Sons & Co. Ltd in connection with the work of an eminent German engineer, W G Stoeckicht of Munich, who was an acknowledged expert in the field of epicyclic gearing. Norman Allen was requested to go out to Munich and, following memorable, and at times difficult negotiations, Stoeckicht was persuaded to come to Bedford for further consultations. Allens had already acquired a high reputation for the design and quality of their turbine reduction gearing, and their parallel shaft gears manufactured at Queen's Engineering Works were regarded as being among the best and most accurate manufactured in the United Kingdom. However, during the War, Stoeckicht had been responsible for some striking developments in the use of epicyclic gearing for the transmission of high power which were of great interest to the Admiralty. Working in conjunction with the Royal Naval Scientific Service, Allens lost no time instituting an investigation into Stoeckicht's work and in due course a five year design consultancy agreement was signed in which Stoeckicht received royalties on a horse power transmitted basis.

Epicyclic gearing

It was soon found that internal gears could be cut and ground with the same degree of accuracy as external-toothed gears. Engineers realised also that by allowing the annulus to float, the planet gears shared the load equally. By 1950, when up to 20,000 hp was being successfully transmitted, it was confidently expected that many users of power machinery would in future specify epicyclic gears where previously parallel shaft gearing had been used. Of course, this was not possible where a change of centres between the input and output shafts was necessary, but the growth of this new business was rapid and profitable. Soon Allen-Stoeckicht gears were being manufactured under licence in the United States, France, Italy and Germany.

A view of a typical high-speed planetary gear with planet carrier cover, the coupling ring and coupling flange all removed.

In 1955, Allens decided to concentrate the manufacture of all types of gearing at the 70,000 sq. ft. Atlas Works at Pershore in Worcestershire which they had purchased from the old-established agricultural engineers, Fisher Humphries & Co. Ltd. When production started in 1956 some 25 people were employed in the works but by 1961 the number had risen to 271. Considerable investment was

HMS Brave Borderer, *a fast patrol boat built by Vosper Ltd of Portsmouth. Powered by three 3,500 Bristol Siddeley marine* Proteus *gas turbines with integral Allen-Stoeckicht primary reduction epicyclic gearing.*

made in new plant and machinery and in 1961 further machinery was installed for the manufacture of small turbines. Norman Allen had overall responsibility for this branch works, the local management being headed by E R Yoxen, Works Manager, and T P Jones, OBE, a brilliant gearing engineer who was appointed Chief Engineer.

The completion of the Australian-built *Bass Trader* in 1961 represented a landmark in the development of epicyclic gearing for she was the first ocean-going commercial vessel to be fitted with main propulsion gearboxes of this type. Powered by two Napier *Deltic* 18-cylinder high-speed diesel engines coupled to Allen-Stoeckicht double-reduction double-helical type gearboxes through a *Fluidrive* hydraulic coupling, which gave a speed reduction from 1,580 to 175 rpm. This was the forerunner of the '*Brave*' class fast naval patrol boats, the first of which *Brave Borderer* was built by Vosper Ltd of Portsmouth. She was of a very advanced design powered by 3,500 hp Bristol *Proteus* marine gas turbines with integral Allen-Stoeckicht primary reduction gearing, driving forward through Allen-Stoeckicht epicyclic reverse/reduction V-drive gears.

However, the path of such exciting developments does not always run smoothly and when the large tanker building programme got underway in the 1960s difficulties arose. It was found that the Stoeckicht design rules proved inadequate for the transmission of power in excess of 30,000 hp and some failures were encountered. Needless to say, the competence and integrity of Allen engineers overcame these problems in due course. Stoeckicht died in the 1960s.

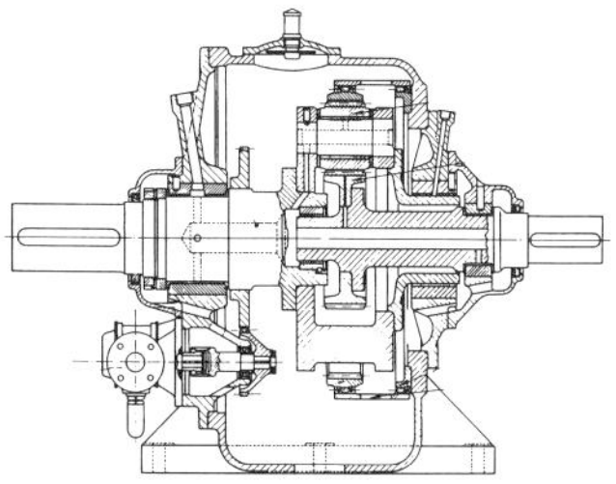

Sectional arrangement of typical epicyclic gearbox having a gear ratio 3:1.

During World War II, the gas turbine was developed as a jet engine for the propulsion of high speed aircraft. The power produced by the turbine was sufficient only to drive the air compressor and the hot gases from the combustion chamber were then passed out direct to atmosphere in the form of a high-velocity jet the reaction forces of which provided the motive power. It was therefore in its original form unsuitable for low-speed land and marine applications. However, it was found that by introducing one or more turbines into the gas

Prototype 1,000 kW gas-turbine alternator built to Admiralty specifications in 1951 working in conjunction with the Bristol Aeroplane Company. Shown with the outer lagging covers removed.

stream, the heat energy of the gases could equally well be employed for driving a propeller, electric generator or other forms of auxiliary machinery. Several alternative arrangements were proposed, the most common of which were either to mount the compressor and turbine on a single shaft to which the load was coupled; or the mount the compressor and H P turbine on one shaft with a separate L P turbine coupled to the load on another shaft.

Gas turbines

Naturally the Admiralty soon became interested in these developments, although several private sector market surveys carried out at the time were somewhat sceptical about its value for commercial applications. A warship steams predominantly at its economical cruising speed and only occasionally is full power required. In the high ranges of speed the power required varies roughly as the cube of the speed. The Admiralty found that a gas turbine could be used as a booster unit to supply the extra power occasionally needed, using a conventional steam or diesel engine to supply the normal cruising speed power requirements. This resulted in a very large saving in weight and space.

In 1947, W H Allen, Sons & Co. Ltd under the aegis of the Admiralty, became involved with the Bristol Aeroplane company, and supplied an Allen-Stoeckicht epicyclic gearbox for a Bristol *Theseus* gas turbine being developed for marine auxiliary and industrial purposes. The *Theseus* was the first gas turbine to pass the 500 hour endurance test. The distinguished Technical Director of the Bristol Aeroplane company, Roy Fedden, knighted in 1943 for his work on aero engine designs, was a cousin by marriage of four members of the Allen family. W H Allen, his elder sister Anne, his son Richard, and his daughter Anne, all had married Feddens. In 1945, after a period with Frank Whittle of Power Jets of Leicester, Fedden established his own business, Cotswold Turbine Company, with Arthur Pope, a former Power Jets technician and brilliant mathematician, as his right-hand man. Following the intervention of a Commander Baker of the Admiralty, Pope joined Allens in 1947 and a Design Con-

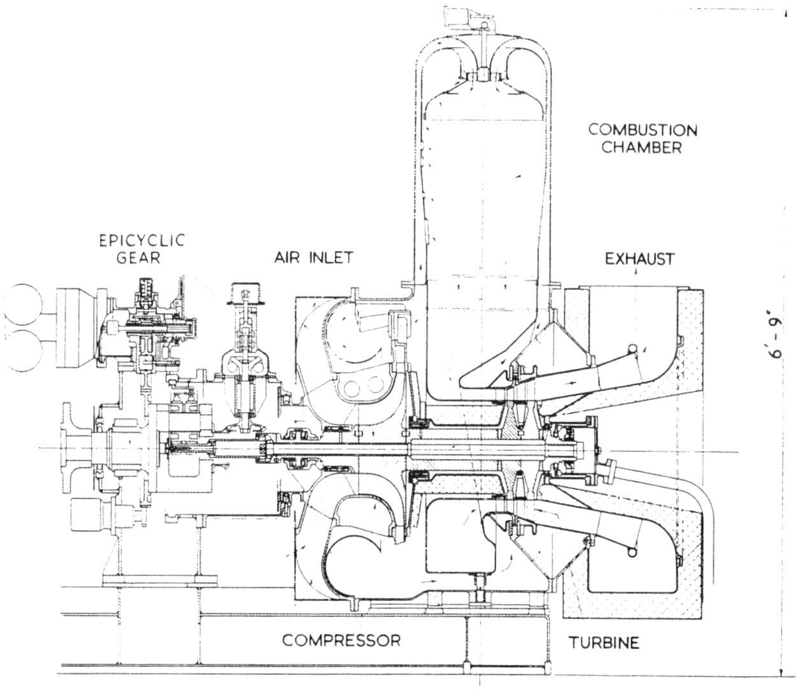

Allen 200 hp gas turbine with a single stage centrifugal impeller driven by a two-stage axial flow turbine. Six sets were supplied to Alfred Holt's Blue Funnel vessels for driving 350 kW d.c. generators.

sultancy Agreement was concluded with the Bristol Aeroplane Company.

1,000 kW gas turbine

This was followed almost immediately by a contract from the Admiralty to develop a 1,000 kW gas turbine and generator for base load operation. Allens commenced their design work at the beginning of 1948 and the unit was successfully run at full speed and full power early in 1951. A section of the Biddenham works was set aside for the assembly of gas turbines and special machine tools were installed for blade manufacture. A fully-equipped and instrumented test house was built on behalf of the Admiralty. Later, Pope was awarded the Thomas Lowe prize for his paper on naval gas turbines.

Having carefully balanced the conflicting requirements of low weight and space with an acceptable efficiency, Allens decided upon a comparatively simple open-cycle set having an axial flow compressor with a compression ratio of 4.25:1 driven by a two-stage turbine; an annular two-pass cross-flow heat exchanger; multi-chamber combustion chambers arranged symmetrically round the engine; and a separate single-stage power turbine driving an Allen alternator through Allen-Stoeckicht epicyclic gearing. This was a scratch design built within the height restriction of 7 ft. specified by the Admiralty. The overall length was 16 ft. and the width 8 ft. 6 in. The total weight, including the heat exchanger but excluding the alternator, was 8½ tons, the set being carried on resilient mountings in order to minimise the effect of shock loading due to under-water explosions. Because of alteration in the design specification of HM ships at this time only one set was built.

This was followed three years later by another Admiralty contract to develop a 200 hp emergency gas turbine. A comprehensive series of performance, governing and endurance tests were carried out at the end of 1952. Due to the short periods of running expected from

SS Rotterdam, *the 37,500 ton flag ship of the Dutch mercantile marine launched by HM Queen Juliana of the Netherlands in 1958.*

the engine, fuel consumption and long life were relatively unimportant considerations and it was therefore possible to construct a simple cycle single-shaft type engine. It embodied a single-stage compressor, a single combustion chamber and plain bearings. The compression ratio was limited to 2.5:1 so as to enable the use of a single-stage turbine.

350 kW gas turbine

In 1954, a similar but larger gas turbine was ordered by Alfred Holt & Company for auxiliary duties on board their Blue Funnel liners. Rated 350 kW and deck mounted, a total of twelve sets were ordered. The simple single-shaft two-stage axial flow gas turbines were coupled to a d.c. generator through 10:1 reduction epicyclic gearing and ran at 15,000 rpm. The total weight of this unit was only 5 tons 7 cwt.

These were much lighter and less bulky than the equivalent diesel powered equipment and could consequently be deck mounted without fear of upsetting the trim of the vessel. This allowed the engine room to be made smaller and the cargo capacity to be correspondingly increased enabling the capital cost of the gas turbine to be quite quickly recovered by the additional revenue earned. The *Dolius*, owned by the Blue Funnel Line, made her maiden voyage in January 1956 and was the first ship in the mercantile marine to use gas turbine emergency equipment.

The 350 kW Allen gas turbine generating set installed in SS Rotterdam *(37,500 tons), the pride of the Dutch mercantile marine.*

About the same time the Admiralty decided to build a new generation of anti-submarine and general purpose frigates which required compact, light-weight 500 kW base load generators. After an intensive design study, a two-shaft, open-cycle, straight compound machine of Allen's design was chosen. This had an axial compressor and turbine on each shaft and a tubular intercooler between the two compressors. The power output from the H P shaft was taken through an Allen-Stoeckicht epicyclic reduction gear to an Allen water-cooled alternator. A single reverse-flow combustion chamber was fitted after the H P compressor. The intercooler not only produced a useful gain in efficiency, but prevented surge in the L P compressor when load was applied. A heat exchanger was considered unnecessary and would have added considerably to the overall weight of the unit. The prototype engine was installed in *Llandaff*, a new diesel-engined air direction frigate. The subsequent successful development of the engine involved continued close collaboration with the Bristol Aeroplane Company and with Joseph Lucas Ltd, who were responsible for the fuel system.

A prestigious order was received from Holland in 1957 for Allen auxiliary machinery for the new 37,500 ton liner *Rotterdam*, flag ship of the Holland-America Line. Launched by HM Queen Juliana of the Netherlands in 1958, she made her maiden voyage to New York in September 1959. Electricity for the auxiliary power, lighting and other services was supplied by turbo-alternators. In addition an Allen 350 kW gas-turbine-alternator was installed for emergency power requirements and located within the boiler casing adjacent to the sun lounge. The gas turbine was a single-shaft open-cycle type consisting of a single stage compressor, reverse flow combustion chamber, and two-stage axial flow turbine. The standard, ventilated, drip-proof, revolving field marine-type alternator was driven through Allen-Stoeckicht double-helical, single reduction epicyclic gearing running at 1,800 rpm. But this was the last great ship to employ the Allen gas turbine. In spite of its technical success, the introduction of turbo-charging on diesel engines followed a few years later by intercooling, resulted in ship owners focusing their attention on the new range of greatly-improved diesel engines for ships' auxiliary power. The situation was further complicate by the decision of the Bristol Aeroplane Company not to renew the design consultancy agreement with W H Allen.

A total of about thirty-five gas turbines were produced at Queen's Engineering Works, but the department was finally run down in 1964 following the completion of a contract for gas turbine generators installed in *County* class destroyers. One final machine of special interest was a gas turbine installation for student instruction commissioned by the Imperial College of Science and Technology, South Kensington, for the newly completed Gas Dynamics Laboratory. It comprised an Allen type B1 gas turbine designed to develop 170 bhp at 23,000 rpm coupled through epicyclic gearing to a Heenan & Froude dynamometer and suitably modified to include a wide range of instrumentation in order to measure and analyse performance.

A number of important changes occurred at Queen's Engineering works during the 1950s affecting the management and financial structure of the Company. In 1952 the Company sought a Stock Exchange quotation and became a Public Company under the terms of the Companies Acts. The capital was increased from £500,000 to £1.25 million by the creation of 750,000 new £1 shares. At this time the net current assets were valued at £3.126 million, of which £1.179 million was accounted for by stock and work-in-progress.

Denis W M Allen, Richard Allen's Grandson. Joined the Company after service as Engineer Officer in the Royal Navy. Director 1953.

In 1953, Denis W M Allen, Melville Allen's son, was appointed to the Board. Born in 1917, only a few months after his father's tragic death in a flying accident, he was educated at Canford and Trinity College, Cambridge. He received his practical training at Queen's Engineering Works and during World War II served as an Engineer Officer in the Royal Navy. Later he became the Company's Personnel Manager and was very much liked by all with whom he came into

The Board of Directors. (left to right) *H Norman G Allen; Harold G Allen; Sir Richard W Allen, CBE, DL; Rupert S Allen; W Kenneth G Allen in the Board Room beneath the portrait painting of the late Mr W H Allen, the Founder and first Chairman of the Company.*

contact. Sadly, ill health forced his early retirement in 1970.

In the 1950s, Queen's Engineering Works employed, on average, 2,500 people and to mark the Queen's Coronation the Company gave a celebration dinner in a huge marquee erected in Allen Park, at which over 2,000 people sat down. William G Poole, the popular and greatly-respected Works Manager, retired in March 1954 after forty years continuous service. Formerly an apprentice at the London & South Western Railway's Nine Elms Works when the great William Adams was Chief Mechanical Engineer, he spent the greater part of his working life at Allens in Bedford. In recognition of his strenuous efforts during World War II he was appointed an Officer of the Order of the British Empire (OBE). It was a source of great satisfaction to him that in the year he retired he attended the presentation of the Allen Prize to his nephew, Eric Poole, awarded to the best all-round Pupil of the year.

W A Train Works Manager

W A Train was appointed to succeed Poole as Works Manager. His long practical training in the Works, his proven engineering ability and extensive knowledge of the Company's products made him the ideal choice for this important appointment. At the same time a number of other important appointments were announced. Ken Rowell became the Commercial Manager with responsibility for the Engineering and Sales Development Department; A C Hutchinson was appointed Chief Steam Turbine and Gearing Engineer; C W Hayes became the Principal Steam Turbine Designer; T P Jones became the Principal Gearing Designer; A W Guppy, Chief Pump and Fan Engineer; and L Leigh became responsible for the Diesel Engine Design Department. Norman Allen had overall responsibility for this team as the Director in charge of all technical departments. Together these people represented a remarkable galaxy of talent.

Death of Sir Richard Allen

The Chairman, Sir Richard Allen died in July 1955 in his 89th year. As an act of great magnanimity and wisdom Harold Allen, in his 81st year, and Rupert Allen, in his 76th year, resolved to stand down in favour of the next generation and Kenneth Allen was unanimously elected by the Board as the Company's new Chairman. Although there was universally enormous affection and respect for both brothers, this decision was applauded by staff and shareholders alike.

Richard's death, like the passing of the founder of the Company twenty-six years earlier, marked the end of an era. In every way Richard had proved himself a worthy successor to his father, a good businessman and a first-class engineer. It is difficult to recall any great honour that by-passed him. Anything to do with ships and the Navy were his great love. He proudly boasted that he had known and worked with every Engineer-in-Chief of the Fleet to hold office since the position was created, as well as all the leading personalities in the shipping and shipbuilding world. He was a prominent member of most of the leading technical institutions including the Civil and Mechanical Engineers, the Marine Engineers, the Institute of Metals, the Aeronautical Society and the Engineering & Allied Employers National Federation. Like his father, education and training were high on his agenda and he took a keen interest in the work of the Industrial Welfare Society. He played an important role in the affairs of the town and country, he was a Deputy Lieutenant of the County and High Sheriff of Bedfordshire; a J.P. and Member of the Quarter Sessions. He loved flowers and was a Fellow of the Royal Horticultural Society, the Zoological Society and a Governor of the Royal Agricultural Society of England. In his younger days he enjoyed travel and circumnavigated the world four times, decades before the advent of jet aircraft. His great personality, foresight in business, directness in method and kindness was long remembered by all who came into contact with him. An outside interest close to his heart was the part he played in the founding of the Bedford Eisteddfod, an annual event which brought much pleasure to the people of Bedford.

Kenneth Allen appointed Chairman

The new Chairman and his colleagues lost no time tackling the many problems facing the Company. It was realised that considerable capital expenditure would be necessary in the coming years if the Company was to retain its market share. Over a period of years a high proportion of the profits earned had been ploughed back into the business, but it was clear that it would no longer be possible to finance future capital expenditure, on the scale required, from taxable profits. The importance of maintaining the correct relationship between loan capital and issued capital was also fully understood. With these factors in mind it was decided to raise £800,000 by the issue of 5¾ per cent First Mortgage Debenture Stock repayable 1979/81 and this was wholly subscribed to by the Prudential Assurance Company. It was decided also to make a Script Issue of shares by offering shareholders one £1 Ordinary Share for every £1 share held.

For the first time in the Company's history, non-family appointments were made to the Board. T Golding, OBE, Manager of the

took part in many important outside activities linked with the Company, which included the formation of the Confederation of British Industry. Norman concentrated upon technical and engineering matters.

155 bhp Allen motor-driven vertical spindle circulating pump. Duty - 12,000/16,000 gallons per minute.

During 1960, the organisation of Queen's Engineering Works was re-structured and strengthened. Five quite separate product departments were established and made self-contained. A Manager was appointed for each of the departments dealing with turbines, pumps, diesel engines, electrical machinery and gearing. The Manager was responsible for sales, tendering, contracts, design and drawing office work. The actual manufacturing operation remained independent and centralised. Preceding this reorganisation, the Board approved considerable capital expenditure upon buildings, plant and machinery, thus ensuring the Company remained at the very forefront in its fields of specialisation. In the years 1958 to 1961 over £1.63 million was expended, including the building of a handsome multi-storey office building on the site of part of the original offices fronting on Ford End Road. This was formally opened by HRH The Duke of Edinburgh in May 1959.

New pump test house

Since the ending of World War II both Allens and their old competitors Gwynnes had been heavily involved with the Central Electricity Board (CEGB) in the design of large circulating pumps for the cooling systems in the new generation of large power stations being planned. These soon became too large for either company to test satisfactorily and the CEGB Chief Pump Engineer, L O Wild, a former Gwynne employee, insisted this be rectified. The cost of a suitable Test House was clearly going to be enormous and it was decided to investigate the possibility of building a jointly-owned facility, rather as the pre-nationalisation railway companies had done for testing locomotives. G A Wauchope, Gwynne's Managing Director, and Norman Allen, who were old friends and co-founders of the British Hydromechanics Research Association, initiated talks. These were held in great secrecy in a Peterborough hotel, but suddenly the talks were stopped. A few months later, Allens made a formal bid for William Foster & Co. Ltd of Lincoln, then owners of Gwynnes.

Shortly after World War I Gwynnes had begun manufacture of the Albert and the Gwynne 8 hp motor cars in their Chiswick factory which had been established during the War to manufacture French-designed Rotary aero engines. This venture proved disastrous and in 1927 a receiver was called in. The Company was eventually purchased by William Foster, whose Managing Director, Sir William Tritton, was another former Gwynne apprentice. Traditionally, Fosters, a private limited company had manufactured, at their Wellington Foundry, Lincoln, steam traction engines and threshing machinery. During the War, as a result of Winston Churchill's Landship Committee's initiative, Fosters were awarded the contract to build the first military tanks which made their debut on the Somme in 1916. This work resulted in the Company building up a healthy bank balance and during the depressed post-war years they were looking for diversification. Located near the Fens, where major land drainage schemes were planned, pumps provided the ideal answer.

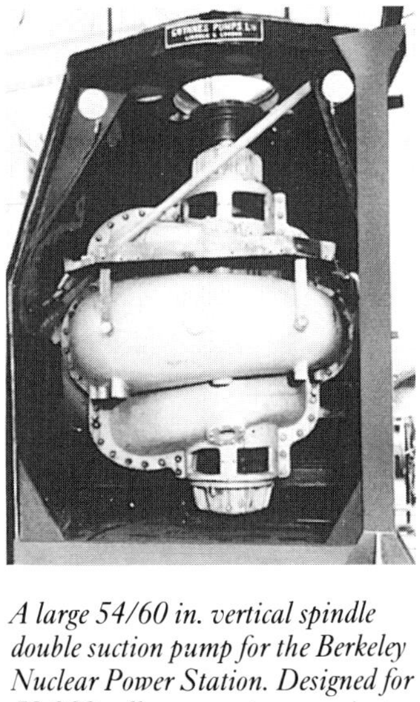

A large 54/60 in. vertical spindle double suction pump for the Berkeley Nuclear Power Station. Designed for 58,300 gallons per minute against a head of 41 ft. Built at Lincoln and tested at Biddenham.

Thus Gwynnes became a wholly-owned subsidiary of William Foster. Gwynne's Hammersmith factory was transferred to Lincoln and the Chiswick factory was sold off by the receiver. A new company, Gwynnes Pumps Ltd was formed and continued trading as manufacturers of centrifugal pumps, although all materials and

The Allen-Gwynne Pump Test House, Biddenham, completed in 1962. Designed for testing large pumps conforming with the revised BS599 specification with flows up to 150,000 gallons per minute.

services were purchased in Foster's name while their traditional products were phased-out. By 1943 over 120 pumping stations in Lincolnshire and the Fens were using Gwynnes pumps.

William Foster of Lincoln acquired

In May 1960, William Foster applied for a quotation on the Stock Exchange and proposed that its existing shares be sub-divided into four 5 shilling (25p) shares and that 458,460 5 shilling shares be issued as fully paid to shareholders in the proportion of two 5 shilling shares for every £1 share held. This was achieved by the capitalisation of reserves. In September 1960, S W Warburg & Company, acting on behalf of W H Allen, Sons & Co. Ltd offered £1.46 million for the share capital of Fosters. This was accepted by the Foster Board. In due course, Kenneth Allen was appointed Chairman of Fosters.

Immediate benefits were felt by increased production of pumps for waterworks, sewage plants and power stations. Whereas Gwynnes had sub-contracted prime movers for the majority of their pumping installations, the take-over resulted in a welcome increase in the sale of Allen diesel engines and electric motors for these applications. Queen's Engineering Works continued independently to manufacture pumps, mainly for marine applications, and forced-draught and ventilating fans for British and Commonwealth ships. The iron foundry at Queen's Engineering Works had been closed down in 1957, ending a seventy year tradition in iron founding. The Lincoln iron foundry proved to be a useful addition, for it was well-known as a pioneer in loam moulding which was particularly well suited for the production of pump casings.

George Andrew Wauchope, one of the foremost personalities in the pump industry for many years, formerly with Gwynnes and latterly with Allen-Gwynne Pumps Ltd

The building of a new Research Laboratory at Biddenham was approved by the Allen Board in 1961 and a contract was placed with Balfour Beatty for the construction of a large new Pump Test House. A smaller version was also built at Lincoln. The Biddenham Test House was designed to test large, medium and low head pumps with both horizontal and vertical suction branches. Three measuring legs were provided, each containing a venturi meter designed to cope with a combined flow of 150,000 gallons per minute. Suction conditions could be varied for −20 ft. to +20 ft., whilst the pipework permitted working up to a 200 ft. head. Arrangements were made to test all pumps with their own driving motors for which electric power was supplied by an Allen diesel-alternator set, having a voltage range from

Sir Kenneth Allen at the CBI Headquarters shortly after his appointment as Chairman of the influential Labour and Social Affairs Committee.

380–11,000 volt. An extensive instrument panel and the latest types of control gear were installed on a platform overlooking the test area. The site also included two gas turbine test cells and two wind tunnels for turbine blade development, as well as numerous test rigs for the development of bearings and governors. The official opening in May 1962 was performed by Sir Richard Powell, the Permanent Secretary to the Board of Trade, before a large gathering representing many branches of the engineering industry.

Kenneth Allen knighted

The Birthday Honours List published in June 1961 announced the conferring of a knighthood upon the chairman, Kenneth Allen. This news was received with great pleasure by all associated with him in the Company and, indeed, by the engineering industry in general. The honour was felt to be well-deserved recognition of the drive and initiative he had shown, not only in his own Company, but greatly benefitting the engineering world as a whole. The list of his appointments, covering a wide spectrum of British industry, makes impressive reading:

A member of the Engineering Advisory Council appointed by the Board of Trade.

Chairman of the Council of British Internal Combustion Engine Manufacturers Association.

President of the Council of the British Engineers Association.

Chairman of the British Electrical & Allied Manufacturers Association.

Chairman of the Nuclear Energy Trade Association Conference.

Vice-President of the Engineering Employers' Federation.

First Chairman of the influential Labour and Social Affairs committee of the Confederation of British Industry.

In October 1961 the Board was further strengthened by the appointment of W A Train, the Works Manager, and F J Goodall, the Chief Accountant, as Directors. This was the first time in which the number of non-family members of the Board exceeded the number of family members. Train's appointment was especially interesting in that for the first time it established the principle that the door to the Board Room was open to former trade apprentices. Good industrial relations remained high on the Board's agenda and the Chairman encouraged the publication of the Company's financial results in a form that could be readily understood by the workforce. It was a source of great pleasure to the Board when Lord Carron, the outspoken and often controversial President of the Amalgamated Engineering Union (AEU), accepted their invitation to present the prizes and the Annual Prize Giving.

During its first ten years as a Public Company, W H Allen, Sons & Co. Ltd pre-tax profits rose steadily year by year to peak at £1.039 million in 1958; thereafter they declined to £444,000 in 1961. Taxation and interest rates were high, inflation was reaching unacceptably high levels and there was great pressure on wages, all of which placed an enormous burden on companies like Allen. Generally, borrowing increased substantially from 1961 onwards and it became evermore difficult to forecast future trends. Competition became more severe particularly in export markets. Government policy generally did not help industry, and in some cases nationalisation had upset the balance of trade and the trend was more and more towards the re-structuring of heavy industry which resulted in a growing number of take-overs and mergers. The prospect of a Common Market in Europe only complicated the issue. Allens were caught in the middle of all this, being neither very big, nor very small. By 1961 the Directors must have seen the beginning of the ending of their independent existence. But the Company had many strengths and every effort was made to capitalise upon these.

Nelson Engineering acquired

In this period several acquisitions were made. Nelson Engineering, a small electrical manufacturer in Nelson, Lancashire was purchased and arrangements were made with them for the manufacture of small electric motors. J P Hall & Sons (Holdings) Ltd of Peterborough, manufacturers of small pumps was acquired together with its subsidiary Thames Marine Propulsion. Within a short time both Allen's Tidal Basin premises in London's Dockland and the Thames Marine Propulsion Company were closed.

J P White & Company's Pyghtle Works adjoining Queen's Engineering Works was acquired in 1961. Whites, old-established ecclesiastical and architectural joinery manufacturers had merged with a company in Reading, and their 3½ acre site became surplus to their requirements. It is interesting to note that W H Allen originally sold the land to them for £10,000 and Kenneth Allen paid £110,000 to repossess it. During the War, Whites manufactured axial flow blower blades for the *Ark Royal* and *Daring* class warships for Allens, as well as producing large quantities of components for *Spitfire* and *Mosquito* aircraft.

In the space available, it is difficult to do justice to the many interesting contracts fulfilled by Queen's Engineering Works in the years 1955 to 1968. All products became technically more sophisticated and efficient in performance. It is possible only to make superficial references to the many remarkable improvements incorporated in the Company's wide range of specialised products, but the origins of most of these can be traced to the excellent foundations laid by generations of mechanical and electrical engineers brought up in the Allen tradition.

The range of products produced by Queen's Engineering Works at this time may be summarised as follows:

Product range

POWER PLANT
Airless injection diesel engines from 100 bhp to 1,080 bhp. Steam turbines, high pressure, low pressure, mixed pressure, back pressure and pass-out types up to 10,000 bhp. Reciprocating steam engines of the totally-enclosed forced-lubrication type, 10 bhp to 500 bhp.

Condensing plant, including closed-feed systems, de-aerators, feed water heaters and associated equipment.
Gas turbines up to 3,500 hp.

PUMPING PLANT
Centrifugal, mixed and axial-flow pumps for marine applications, for waterworks, land drainage, irrigation, docks, power stations, sewage works and other industrial applications.

AIR SUPPLY TO BOILER ROOMS
Turbine driven forced-draught fans; steam engine and electric motor driven fans and power operated louvre-type shutters.

ELECTRICAL EQUIPMENT
D.c. generators up to 3,000 kW.
A.c. generators up to 1,500 kW.
Electric motors up to 4,500 hp.
Control gear, automatic and drum types.
Switchboards and complete electric equipment for winches, capstans, windlasses, etc.

GEARING
Epicyclic gears, straight reduction and special reverse/reduction gears for ship propulsion, up to 10,000 shp and for auxiliary machinery applications.
Helical gears, single reduction up to 10,000 bhp.

By the end of the 1950s there were signs that the post-war shipbuilding boom was coming to an end. The volume of industrial work received at Queen's Engineering Works was beginning to exceed marine work which had been the mainstay of the Company's business for so long. The prospect of large new orders for both the Mercantile Marine and the Navy did not look encouraging. The world demand for big tankers had originally looked promising, but it was only a matter of time before most of this business went to new shipyards in the Far East.

Fine ships

However, mention must be made of some of the fine ships built in British yards and equipped with Allen machinery. In 1951 the Orient liner *Oronsay* sailed on her maiden voyage to Australia. She was one of the fastest ships in Britain's merchant fleet after the trans-Atlantic *Queens*. She was built by Vickers Armstrong at Barrow-in-Furness and had a profile similar to her elder sister-ship *Orcades*. All the auxiliary machinery was electrically driven, electricity being supplied by four Allen 850 kW 220 volt self-contained turbo-generators. Their total generating capacity was 3,400 kW. In addition Allen emergency diesel generators were installed together with nineteen Allen motor driven pumps for various essential duties. She was one of the first ships to be built with Denny-Brown ship's stabiliser

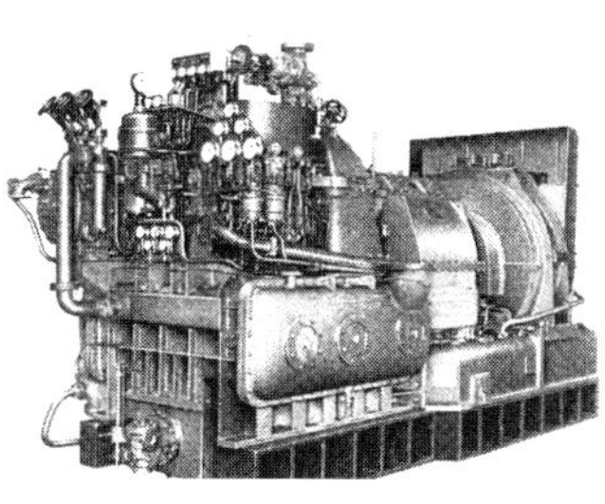
One of four Allen 1,100 kW pass-out turbo-generators installed in SS Caronia *(34,000 tons) viewed from the stern and showing the control gear.*

equipment which was operated by Allen motors of special design. Similar equipment was installed in *Orsova* which sailed on her maiden voyage in March 1954.

Six months later, the Cunard Steam Ship Company's new 22,000 ton *Saxonia* entered service on the Canadian run. During her maiden voyage she broke the previous Liverpool to St Lawrence record. Built by John Brown at Clydebank, she was similar in appearance to the larger Cunarder *Caronia* built in 1948. The electricity for heating, lighting, ventilation and other essential services throughout the ship was provided by four 570 kW 225 volt d.c. Allen turbo-generators of the pass-out type. She was the first Cunarder to be fitted with the Denny-Brown stabiliser equipment driven by Allen motors.

In the years 1956 to 1957 two 26,000 ton Canadian Pacific passenger liners were completed. The *Empress of Britain* built by the Fairfield Shipbuilding & Engineering Company was the first post-war passenger liner commissioned by Canadian Pacific for their North Atlantic service. A year later she was joined by *Empress of England* built by Vickers Armstrong at their Walker-on-Tyne yard. Each of these fine ships used Allen auxiliary machinery. Two 1,200 kW self-contained d.c. 25 volt turbo-generators and three 500 kW 2-stroke type T47 diesel engine driven d.c. generators provided the electricity for all essential power and lighting services, combined with a host of Allen pumps and electric motors. Another well-known vessel, the P & O *Uganda* was built with Allen T47 engines and d.c. generators. When she was refitted as an educational cruise ship these were supplemented by two 12VS12C engines and a.c. generators. In more recent years the vessel served as a hospital ship during the Falkland Islands conflict.

Oriana, the largest British passenger liner built for over twenty years, having a displacement of 42,000 tons, went into service in 1960. Like earlier post-war Orient Line ships she was built by Vickers Armstrong at Barrow. She had a service speed of 27½ knots and carried over 2,000 passengers on the Australasian run. She was fitted with four Allen turbo-generators, each set having a power output of 1,750 kW driving through Allen-Stoeckicht epicyclic speed reduction gearing.

Finally, reference must be made to the *Northern Star*, a splendid new passenger liner built by Vickers Armstrong for the Shaw Saville Line. Constructed on similar lines to the *Southern Cross,* and launched by the Queen Mother in 1961, these two ships were the first big passenger liners to have their engines installed aft and to have no provision for carrying cargo. Each of these vessels had three Allen 1,500 kW pass-out turbo-generators. They were amongst the first big mercantile vessels to use alternating current. In addition, as one might expect, Allen motors were used extensively to drive the various pumps and stabiliser equipment.

Throughout the post-war years a great deal of Allen-designed and built auxiliary machinery was supplied to smaller vessels of all types. They are far too numerous to mention individually by included general cargo vessels, refrigerated ships, fleet auxiliaries, tankers, ferries, dredgers and support craft of every description.

Tankers were probably built in larger numbers in British yards than any other type of vessel in the post-war years. The 67,000 ton *Serenia, Sepia* and *Solen* built for the Royal Dutch Shell Group were exceptional in many ways. They had a capacity of 8 million gallons of oil and on account of their size were unable to use the Suez Canal,

An Allen ship's propeller shaft generator undergoing tests at Queen's Engineering Works. By 1963 generators developing 300 kW at speeds of 84/124 rpm were in production.

which had in any event been closed since 1956. Their regular run to the Middle East necessitated sailing round the Cape. *Serenia* was built by Vickers Armstrong at their Walker yard, and was the largest ship ever built on the Tyne. It was also the largest ship to go into service from an United Kingdom yard since the building of the Cunard liner *Queen Elizabeth*. *Sepia* was built by Cammell Laird & Company on Merseyside and *Solen* was built by Swan Hunter & Wigham Richardson on the Tyne. The Allen machinery in each of these ships comprised two 600 kW back-pressure turbo-generators. The 440 volt, 3-phase, 60 cycle alternators were driven through double helical, side pinion, parallel shaft gearing and connected in parallel with a standby Allen alternator driven by a National diesel engine.

Two other notable tankers built in 1961 were the 47,200 ton *Tindform* built at Harland & Wolff, Belfast for a Norwegian company and the 37,200 ton *Busiris* built for the Moss Hutchinson Line by Joseph L Thompson's yard on the River Wear. Both were extensively equipped with Allen auxiliary machinery utilising alternating current. However, the day of the 'super-tanker' was dawning and most orders for these huge vessels, weighing in excess of 100,000 tons dead weight, went to shipyards in the Far East where steel prices and labour costs showed great savings. Sadly little British-built machinery went into these vessels and British shipyards were in trouble.

Shaft alternators

Marine engineers had for sometime been considering using a ship's main engines to drive electric generators. Gear, belt and chain-driven alternatives were tried with varying degrees of success, and eventually it was proposed to build a generator around the intermediate propeller shaft. Allens were commissioned to design and build such an arrangement in conjunction with the North East Marine Engineering Company. 150 kW 110 volt d.c. generators of this type were installed in the 18,500 ton motor tankers *London Majesty* and *London Victory*. The watertight generator was built as a part of the intermediate propeller shaft without any welding on the shaft, the flange at each end being integral with the shaft. The generator operated at a constant voltage over a speed range of 80 to 126 rpm.

In the mid-1960s the system was further refined by the insertion of an Allen-Stoeckicht variable-ratio epicyclic gear in the intermediate

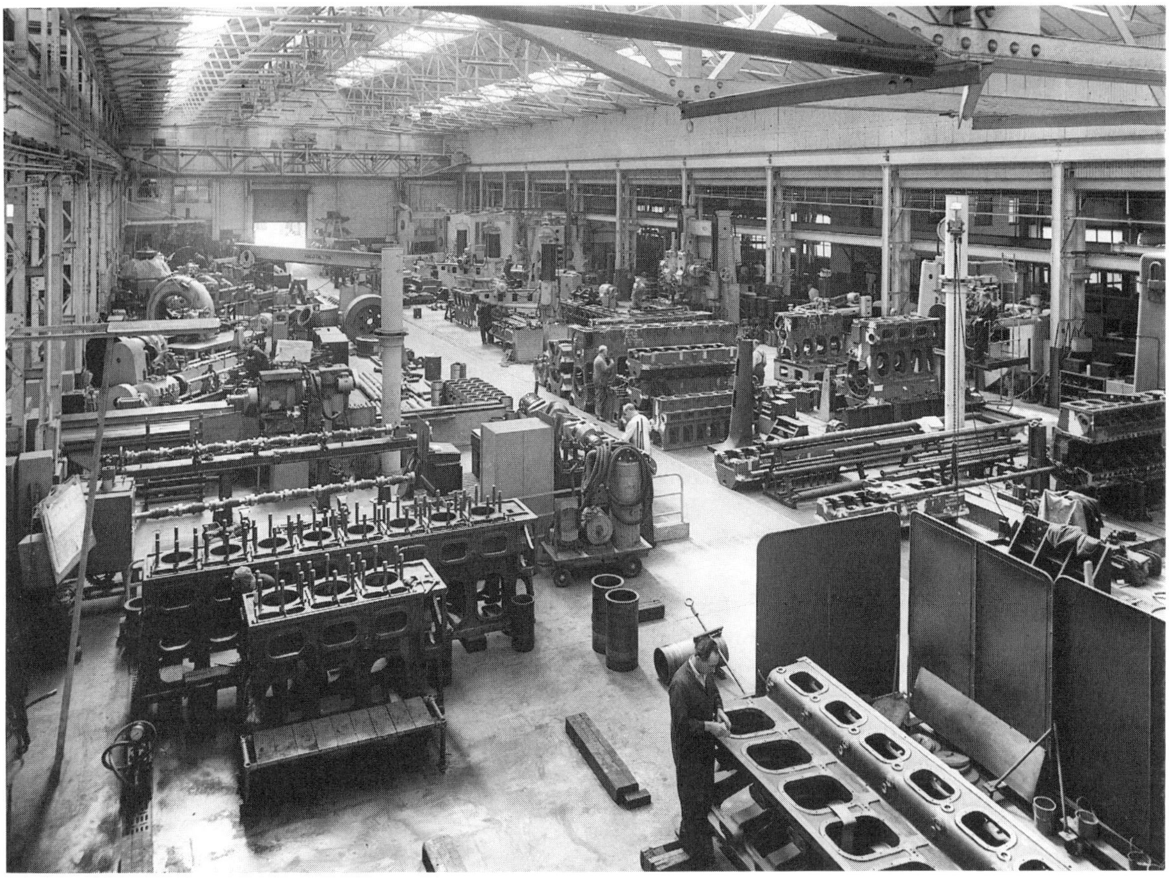

A general view of the diesel engine erecting shop in the 1960s.

propeller shaft, enabling a constant speed alternator to be driven from the ship's variable-speed propeller shaft. This eliminated one or more auxiliary generators, reduced fuel and maintenance costs and saved valuable space in the main engine room. By 1965 a 500 kW shaft alternator set with a variable ratio epicyclic gear was undergoing tests at Queen's Engineering Works.

Throughout the 1950s and 1960s Allen diesel engines underwent constant testing and development in the search for more power, greater fuel economy and improved reliability. Production of all types of engines settled down at approximately fifty-five engines per annum. The T47 2-stroke engine based on the Burmeister & Wain patents proved to be very successful for ship work and the S37 series the most popular for industrial and general duties. In 1956 pressure charging was introduced on the S12 engine; this had the dramatic effect of increasing the power output by up to 50 per cent and in a short time it was applied to all types of diesel engine. In 1962 intercooling further greatly added to an engine's power output. The challenge facing the designer had been the problem of inducing the maximum amount of the densest possible air into the cylinder prior to compression and combustion. Pressure-charging and intercooling were key factors in improving the diesel engine.

Pressure charging and intercooling introduced

The introduction of the V-form engine in 1956 augured well for the future. By 1964 a new 16-cylinder VBCS37-E V-form engine developing 3,200 bhp at 600 rpm completed its exhaustive running tests. This was the most powerful engine ever built at Queen's Engineering Works. The 4-stroke engine had cylinders with 325 mm bore × 370 mm stoke and was available with either 12 or 16 cylinders, normally aspirated or dual fuel, as well as pressure-charged

General view of the turbine room at the N.C.B.'s carbonization and chemical plant at Wingerworth, Chesterfield, showing the two Allen 5,000 kW twin-cylinder, pass-out condensing steam turbines.

A further twenty-one type S37D diesel and dual fuel engines were specified for driving Allen self-regulating alternators located in seven power stations. Motorised flow control valves on the input and output side of each station enabled the station to be by-passed by the flow of oil in an emergency, through control from the stations on either side necessitating sophisticated remote control by radio link.

At the despatching stations natural gas was available in large quantities and it was here that the dual-fuel engines were located. All the engines were naturally aspirated and used crude oil from the pipeline as fuel. Many technical problems associated with the use of the crude oil had to be solved because of its low flash point and high wax content. This necessitated special features in the engine fuel system to cater for the unusual properties in the oil.

Even while this book is being written thirty years later, the Indian authorities have recently ordered replacement engines from Queen's Engineering Works. They insist that they be identical in every respect to the 1961 engines such is their satisfaction with their reliability and performance.

Throughout the 1950s and 1960s Queen's Engineering Works undertook a significant number of important industrial contracts both at home and abroad. A few examples will illustrate the continuing and wide-ranging competence of Allen engineers and the diversity of the industries they served.

Wingerfield Carbonization Plant

Since pre-World War II days, the need for smokeless domestic fuel had been acknowledged. Engineers claimed that oven coke need not of necessity be hard and unsuitable for domestic use and that coke ovens designed and used in a proper manner could provide the answer. Following the nationalisation of the coal industry a vast carbonization plant was planned at Wingerfield, near Chesterfield. W H Allen, Sons & Co. Ltd were awarded the sub-contract for all the plant and equipment within the Power House.

The main generating plant consisted of two Allen 50,000 kW twin-cylinder, pass-out condensing turbo-alternators and a 500 kW diesel engine generating set. Allens were also responsible for the supply, erection and commissioning of two 750 kVa house transformers, a.c. and d.c. switchgear, and the d.c. battery station, together with all the pipework, valves and cabling and lighting in the Power House.

The plant was designed to carbonize 750,000 tons of solid smokeless fuel, over 5,000 million cubic feet of town gas and 6

An 85 bhp Allen back-pressure 2-crank compound reciprocating steam engine driving a George Waller exhauster installed in the E.M.G.B.'s Northampton Gas Works.

million gallons of crude benzole, plus substantial quantities of crude tar, sulphuric acid and ammonia.

The nationalised gas industry also turned to Queen's Engineering Works for plant and machinery required for its expansion and modernisation programme. In the past the efficiency of its steam turbine driven machinery had been of secondary importance owing to the large amounts of waste heat available. With the rising cost of coal it became necessary to consider using high efficiency turbo-alternators and to drive as many auxiliaries as possible by electricity. A typical example of Allen's involvement was the 500 kW geared, pass-out condensing turbo-alternator supplied to the Cheltenham works of the South Western Gas Board. This enabled the Board to turn its surplus coke economically to generate electricity for its own use and to supply the National Grid, thereby saving the transport costs of selling its surplus coke to industrial users.

Other turbo-generators were supplied to the North Thames Gas Board's Beckton Works and to the Northern Gas Board's Howdon-on-Tyne Works. The former had a capacity of 1,390 kW and the latter 530 kW, both arranged to operate in parallel with the public electricity supply.

Meeting gas industry needs

In 1961, an electrically driven high-pressure axial flow gas compressor was designed and built for the West Midlands Gas Board to operate at 25 psi. The compressor involved the latest turbine rotor blade technology and was driven through an Allen-Stoeckicht epicyclic gear with a Vulcan-Sinclair *Fluidrive* coupling. The gas handled by the compressor was considerably dirtier than air normally inhaled by a gas turbine and entirely new methods had to be devised to clean the blades while the compressor was running.

In 1965, the South Eastern Gas Board, who used a considerable amount of electricity in connection with the crude oil feedstock they took from the British Petroleum's Kent Oil Refinery, installed a new 16-cylinder VBCS37E V-form diesel engine to drive a 2,240 kW Allen-Brown-Boveri alternator. Allens had recently concluded an agreement with the famous Swiss engineering company Brown-Boveri of Baden to manufacture their alternators in the United Kingdom and to sell a wide range of their electrical products. It had become clear that d.c. machinery would be, sooner or later, replaced entirely by alternators for both land and marine applications. At this time there were eight major United Kingdom manufacturers of

5 million gallons per hour pump for the River Great Ouse Catchment Board's Welches Dam flood prevention scheme in the Cambridgeshire Fens.

Four 54/54 in. horizontal-spindle, double-suction main circulating water pumps installed at the C.E.G.B. Meaford 'B' Power Station. Duty 40,000 gallons per minute each against a head of 63 ft.

The Staffordshire Potteries Water Board Pickforton Pumping Station showing Laurene Scott variable speed motors driving Allen 2-stage horizontal spindle pumps. Duty of each pump 1040/1850 gpm at heads of 163/341 ft.

Six 100 hp Allen slip-ring motors driving suspended type pumps located in the basement at the Yeovil R.D.C. Sutton Bingham Pumping Station . Duty 666 gallons per minute, each at 332 ft. head.

alternators and serious over capacity existed in the industry. The future prospects for the Allen Electrical Department did not look good.

Cane sugar has been imported into Europe since the 16th Century. The root crop sugar beet, developed in Germany in the early part of the 19th Century to feed Napoleon's troops, was not grown in Britain in any quantity until just before World War I. A small beet factory was built at Lavenham in Suffolk as early as 1871, but sugar refining did not prosper in the United Kingdom until 1924 when the Government granted a subsidy on home-grown sugar. In 1936, the Government compulsorily amalgamated the eighteen existing factories into the British Sugar Corporation (BSC).

Meeting sugar industry needs

W H Allen, Sons & Co. Ltd had supplied plant to cane sugar refineries overseas for many years, but the advent of the British Sugar Corporation opened new avenues to them. Sugar requires steam at the rate of 0.45 tons of steam per ton of beet and electricity consumption varies between 20 and 26 kW per ton of beet.

Today, most beet sugar and cane sugar factories and refineries worldwide use back-pressure steam turbines to provide low-pressure steam and economically produced electricity, most factories operating independently of the public electricity supply. Examples of the many Allen turbines supplied in the last three or four decades are the 4,000

The largest motor-driven borehole pump in Great Britain at the Pangbourne Pumping Station. A 1,050 hp motor driving the combine borehole and force pump capable of delivering 8 million gallons of water per day.

kW back-pressure turbo-alternator at the BSC factory at Ely; the 3,500 set at Tate & Lyle's Thames Refinery in London; 3,000 kW sets at the West Indian Sugar Company's Monymusk Estate in Jamaica; and similar installations in Rhodesia, Australia and New Zealand. The sugar industry has been an extremely important source of business at Queen's Engineering Works for many years.

So much more could be written about Queen's Engineering Work's involvement in overseas projects and the benefits derived from Allen technology. Unquestionably, they have made a significant, and often unseen, contribution to the well-being of people throughout the world.

Nigerian Power Station

One final example of this is the Oji River Power Station in Nigeria. The rapid development of industrial projects and the consequent growth of towns throughout Nigeria in the 1950s resulted in the urgent need for more electricity. One such town was at Enugu in Eastern Nigeria, where the Electricity Corporation of Nigeria built a new power station. Allen supplied two 5,000 kW steam turbo-alternators and associated equipment. The cooling water was taken from the nearby Oji River through Allen pumps and the steam coal for the boilers, mined near Enugu, was transported to the power station by over head cableway.

Pumps for all manner of industrial applications continued to feature prominently in Queen's Engineering Works programme until the take-over of Fosters and Gwynnes in 1960. Their Lincoln works was already producing centrifugal pumps for water and sewage works, land drainage, docks and power stations. Increasingly the axial flow pump was beginning to replace the centrifugal and mixed-flow rotodynamic pump and for very large installations single entry

overdraft had increased three-fold to £1.7 million. During 1965 pre-tax profits had fallen by nearly 25 per cent, and the dividend was cut from 11 per cent to 6 per cent. The share price fell to a new *low* at 9s in September 1966, against a *high* the previous year of 23s 9d. A press report even mentioned the possible appointment of a liquidator which was hotly denied by the Chairman. He stressed that the Company had a healthy order book for steam turbines, diesel engines, pumps and gears. Orders to the value of £230,000 had recently been received for diesel engines.

The following year the Board was strengthened by the appointment of Sir Arnold Lindley and John H Lord, a Chartered Accountant, and the closure of the Electrical Department was announced. This was said to account for only 5 per cent of Group turnover.

Obviously a great deal went on behind the scenes during 1967. Pre-tax profits improved by £181,000 and interesting product developments took place resulting from an earlier agreement with Kühnle, Kopp and Kausch (KKK) of Frankenthal, single stage turbine manufacturers, which were of great interest to the petrochemical and oil refining industries. Allens had no suitable single stage turbine in their range and in order to avoid development costs and further increases in staff it had been arranged with KKK that Allens would purchase the smaller sizes, which could not be made economically in Bedford, and manufacture the larger sizes to their designs. Optimistic contacts had also been made with Lycoming, the American manufacturer of gas turbines, in which the Admiralty was especially interested. These offset a forecast continued decline in diesel engine and turbine production at Queen's Engineering Works.

Merger with Belliss & Morcom

In January 1968 the merger of W H Allen, Sons & Co. Ltd and Belliss & Morcom Co. Ltd of Birmingham was announced together with the formation of a new company, Amalgamated Power Engineering Ltd (APE Ltd). Each Allen £1 share would be exchanged for two 5 shilling (25p) shares in the new holding company, while each £1 share in Belliss & Morcom commanded six of the new shares. On this basis Allen shareholders received 60 per cent of the equity and Belliss & Morcom shareholders 40 per cent which was approximately in line with their respective assets. The merger provided plenty of scope for rationalisation in both companies and the news was greeted generally with satisfaction by the workforce, the shareholders and the City. Sir Kenneth Allen remained Chairman of the new company until 1971, when he commenced his well-deserved retirement. Of course, that does not mean that he became inactive. At eighty-seven he is alive and well and extremely mentally alert, the personification of three remarkable generations who have headed a truly remarkable enterprise.

CHAPTER VIII
Epilogue

THE merger between W H Allen and Belliss & Morcom took place in 1968 with the formation of Amalgamated Power Engineering Ltd.

Sir Kenneth Allen became the first Chairman with Ralph Batty of Belliss & Morcom, Deputy Chairman, and Ashley Whittall of Belliss & Morcom, Chief Executive. In the spirit of the merger equal numbers of former Allen directors and former Belliss & Morcom directors were appointed to the Board.

A survey was immediately instituted into all aspects of the combined business and assets. Among the decisions which arose was the transfer of the Allen-Gwynne pump business from Lincoln to Bedford – a decision which had been under consideration before the merger.

In 1971, Sir Kenneth Allen retired and was succeeded as Chairman by Ralph Batty, and Norman Allen became Deputy Chairman. The Allen family connection with the business was finally severed with the retirement of Norman in 1977.

The issued capital of the Company was now £3,000,000 and turnover exceeded £25 million, of which 38 per cent went in direct exports. The Group, comprising W H Allen of Bedford, Allen Gears of Pershore, Belliss & Morcom of Birmingham and their subsidiary Crossley Engines of Manchester, employed over 3,600 people. Later, in May 1979, Lee Howl & Co. Ltd of Tipton and Valtek Engineering of Pershore were added to the group. Lee Howl, an old-established family business, had been specialist pump manufacturers for over 100 years. Their main products were multi-stage borehole pumps for irrigation and water supply, light-weight petrol engine driven self-priming pumps for general industrial and agricultural applications, and the leading British-made swimming pool pump. Valtek Engineering manufactured automatic control valves under licence from the American Valtek Corporation of Utah. Their wide range of heavy-duty valves were produced mainly for the petrochemical, power and process industries and for offshore platforms. Their designs were a valuable adjunct to the Group's main activities effectively reducing noise, cavitation and vibration in control systems.

Belliss & Morcom's main areas of concentration, after nearly 100 years specialisation in the manufacture of high-quality, high-speed prime movers, were air compressors and gas boosters from $3m^3$/min to $87m^3$/min. Today this activity has been transferred to Queen's Engineering Works and their Birmingham factory closed. Belliss' subsidiary, Crossley Brothers of Openshaw, Manchester, is worthy of special mention for they had the distinction of producing the first internal combustion engine actually manufactured in the United Kingdom.

The brothers, Francis William Crossley (1839–97) and William John Crossley (1844–1911) founded their business in Manchester in 1867 as engineers and iron founders. While on honeymoon in Europe, William Crossley met Dr Nicholas Otto of Cologne and was shown the original model of his atmospheric engine. The brothers recognised the great potential of this engine and, in 1869, entered into an agreement with the German manufacturers to build it in the United Kingdom. They built no fewer than 1,400 atmospheric engines and in 1876 obtained sole rights for the Otto four-cycle gas engine. Soon the name Crossley became a household word and their subsequent development of the gas engine revolutionised the trade in small prime movers, largely supplanting the use of steam for low-power applications. The firm became Incorporated in 1882 and moved to a new location on a ten acre site in Pottery Lane, Openshaw. Francis died in 1897 and the company became publicly quoted with William as its Chairman. He was created a baronet in 1902.

In 1919, Crossley's acquired the Premier Gas Engine Company of Nottingham, manufacturers of single and tandem horizontal gas engines. Early experimental work carried out by the original owners had led to the development of the positive scavenging system, the forerunner of pressure charging, which eventually transformed the performance of the internal combustion engine. In 1936 Premier were absorbed into the Crossley organisation trading as Crossley-Premier Engines Ltd.

During the post-World War I depression Crossleys also purchased the Saunderson Tractor and Implement Co. Ltd. This firm had been one of the pioneers of the internal combustion engine agricultural tractor in the United Kingdom. It is interesting to record that during a visit to Openshaw in 1928, Henry Ford admitted to Sir Kenneth Crossley, William's eldest son, that it was an early Crossley engine which gave him the idea of using internal combustion engines in motor cars.

In the 1950s Crossleys formed an association with the French shipbuilders Chantier de l'Atlantic of St Nazaire. After the War they had invited the well-known German engineer Herr Pielstick, formerly Technical Director of Maschinenfabrik Augsburg Nurnberg A.G. (MAN) to head their new research subsidiary SEMT in Paris where the PC1 engine was developed. MAN had been the principal German U-boat diesel engine manufacturers during the war. Crossleys obtained a licence to manufacture the PC1 engine which developed 250 hp per cylinder. The PC2.2 which developed 500 hp per cylinder appeared in 1964, the PC2.5, giving 650 hp per cylinder, in 1971 and the PC2.6, giving 750 hp per cylinder, in 1981. It was claimed that the PC2-type engine was the best selling medium speed engine in service worldwide, with over 25 million horsepower installed. By 1980 over 3,500 Pielstick type PC engines had been built, many going to warship applications. Thirty-five overseas navies specified the engines which included 76 submarines, 80 patrol boats, 78 destroyers and frigates, 42 refuelling tankers and 116 miscellaneous vessels. In addition 90 mercantile vessels were fitted with Pielstick engines and many more went to land installations.

So much more could be written about both Belliss & Morcom and Crossley Brothers, but it must suffice to identify these fine old British companies in the context of Amalgamated Power Engineering Ltd. Hopefully their history will be recorded one day.

Throughout the life of Amalgamated Power Engineering Ltd, W H Allen continued to develop its range of rotodyne pumps, steam turbines and diesel engines for both land and marine applications. During the first decade of the new grouping Queen's Engineering Works supplied turbo-generators, forced-draught and ventilation fans and main circulating pumps to the Royal Navy for the aircraft carrier *Ark Royal*, *Tiger* class cruisers, *County* class destroyers, three types of frigate and the *Resolution*, *Valiant* and *Swiftsure* classes of nuclear submarine.

During this period the Ministry of Defence nominated a number of 'preferred suppliers' – Vickers for submarine work, Weirs for pumps and Allens for turbine generators. Allen acquired the industrial pump design and manufacturing business operated by Vickers Ltd. The agreement explicitly allowed Vickers to continue to manufacture their own transverse propulsion units for ships and other pumps for marine application whilst allowing Allen to manufacture and sell both Vickers and its own pumps for marine work. Allen also sought closer association with Hamworthy by proposing new designs of short-range axial-flow units. These standardised pumps were to be manufactured at Queen's Engineering Works and marketed by Hamworthy but, before the agreement could be signed, a worldwide fuel crisis occurred and the marine market collapsed. The plan was shelved and very quickly turbine driven ships became a thing of the past.

From its inception the importance of maintaining and developing the Group's export markets was understood. New overseas subsidiaries were established in major markets outside Europe – Amalgamated Power Engineering (Aust.) Ltd in Australia; Amalgamated Power Engineering in Canada, Belliss & Morcom (India) Ltd in India: APE-Uniteers Sdn. Bhd. in Malaysia; Amalgamated Power Engineering (NZ) Ltd in New Zealand; Amalgamated Power Engineering SA (Pty) Ltd in South Africa; Danway Power Engineering in the United Arab Emirates; and APE-America Inc. in the United States. In other countries many of the old-established commission agencies were renewed.

During the first decade of the Amalgamated Power Engineering Group, Queen's Engineering Works were particularly successful in increasing sales of diesel engines for electrical supply purposes throughout the Middle East, Australia, Nigeria, Uruguay, Ecuador and the Caribbean. Important orders were received also from Holland, Sweden and Canada for engines for marine applications. Other important contracts were received for diesel engines for pumping duties in oil pipelines built in India, Nigeria, Colombia and China. In 1978 the value of contracts received for Allen diesels exceeded £5.782 million or 58.5 per cent of turnover, compared with only £1.666 million for Crossley diesels. The company was awarded the Queen's Award for Industry for its export achievements.

In 1977 the ownership of Amalgamated Power Engineering passed to the north-east based Northern Engineering Industries PLC. This

PAPYRUS

LA METAMORPHOSE D'IMHOTEP

PAR DE GIETER.

PAPYRUS ET THÉTI-CHÉRI NOURRIS PAR LA DÉESSE DES ARBRES.

DUPUIS

www.papyrus.kidcomics.com

D.1998/0089/52 — R.10/2005.
ISBN 2-8001-2728-7— ISSN 0771-8969

Imprimé en Belgique.
www.dupuis.com

Depuis des millénaires, quand dans le ciel, l'étoile Sophis commence à paraître au point du jour, immuable, le Nil, solitaire et majestueux, se gonfle et envahit la terre d'Egypte.
Nourri des eaux des grands lacs africains, et de la fonte des neiges des hauts plateaux éthiopiens qui charrie les terres limoneuses, le grand fleuve fertilise le pays, avant d'éclater en sept bras; ceux qui délimitent un lac immense d'où émergent des centaines d'îlots, demeures des fellahs. C'est le delta, là où le ciel, l'eau et la terre se confondent.
C'est le temps où le fleuve apporte au pied des temples, la pierre pour les grands travaux.
C'est le temps des fêtes et des réjouissances.
Ce matin-là, non loin de Memphis, ancienne capitale du pays, une barque de papyrus cherche son chemin dans les marais.
Tu vois quelque chose, Papyrus?
Toujours rien!
Oh! Princesse, regardez!
Là, dans les hautes herbes!
DEUX AFFREUX OISEAUX!
IMHOUTEP ET PAPYRUS!
Que font-ils par ici?
DE GIETER.
1

Tu nous accompagnes dans notre promenade, Papyrus?
Non! Nous te cherchions!
Le bateau-chaland est arrivé d'Assouan avec la statue de Pharaon, cadeau des prêtres de Memphis pour son jubilé. Elle va être halée sur la rive!
Assouan: ville du sud, célèbre pour ses carrières de granit.
Tout le monde est déjà là!
Formidable! Il ne faut pas rater ça!
Oh oui! Princesse, allons-y!
Bonjour Iounis. Par Isis! Tu es toujours aussi jolie!
Hi! Hi! Hi!
Hé, les filles! Si on montrait à ces jeunes gens ce dont nous sommes capables!
Les premiers au camp de Pharaon!
Hi! Hi! Hi! Hi!
Imhoutep on y va!
Par Sebek, on va leur montrer de quelle bouse on se chauffe!
Plus vite!
Plus vite!
Je fais ce que je peux!
Mais la barque de roseau, alourdie par l'eau, ne peut rien contre une embarcation taillée pour la course, et manoeuvrée par de charmantes rameuses.
Hi! Hi! Hi! Hi!
DE GIETER.
Bah! Inutile de continuer, ce rafiot n'avance pas!
Quand soudain...
AAAAAAH
2

AU SECOURS!
En avant, Imhoutep! Il faut aller voir!
En quelques instants, ils ont rejoint la barque de la princesse
Là! Là! Un homme attaqué par un crocodile!
C'est affreux!
On ne peut rien faire! Par tous les dieux!
Déjà le monstre a happé sa victime par la jambe.
RHAAAAAA!
Trop tard!
Comme à son habitude, la crocodile entraîne sa proie dans son repaire afin de la noyer.
Le voilà! Mon glaive doit l'atteindre du premier coup, sinon le malheureux est perdu!
DE GIETER
3

Rendue furieuse par la douleur, la bête lâche sa proie et fait volte-face.
Je dois m'accrocher, ou elle me tuera!
Par de violents soubresauts, elle essaye de se débarrasser de cette guêpe qui ne la lâche pas.
En vain, le crocodile s'épuise. Les poumons près d'éclater, Papyrus suffoque, mais tient bon.
C'est le moment!
Papyrus va frapper, mais brusquement un voile rouge emplit ses yeux... tandis qu'une voix arrête son geste.
NON! NE ME TUE PAS!
Par Sebek! Si tu me laisses la vie, je jure qu'à partir d'aujourd'hui, je protégerai celui qui habite cette île!
Alors, d'un coup de queue, le monstre fait demi-tour et disparaît dans les profondeurs... Seule, flottant dans l'eau, une tache de sang crée une image fugitive.
4

Fouace : biscuit épais fait de fleur de farine.

Plus tard, rassurée, la petite troupe regagne les bateaux.
Papyrus, tu n'as rien remarqué chez le vieil homme?
Heu... non
Je ne l'ai pas bien vu, il était dans l'ombre!
Son visage. Personne n'y a fait attention, mais je l'ai regardé de près. Il ressemble trait pour trait à Pharaon, mon père!
Tu es certaine? C'est incroyable!
Nous allons arriver trop tard. La statue de Pharaon sera déjà en place!
Par Rê! C'est impossible, il faudra un demi-tour de gnomon* pour la hisser!
Tant que cela? Mais deux cents hommes sont venus pour la tracter!
C'est nécessaire, elle pèse plus de soixante tonnes!
Comment le sais-tu?
C'est Djanefer, le scribe*, qui me l'a dit!
J'ai hâte de voir cette statue!
Par Sebek! Si vous ramiez un peu au lieu de bourdonner comme des mouches, nous y serions déjà!
OH!
*Gnomon : cadran solaire égyptien. – Scribe : Fonctionnaire préposé aux écritures
Tout à coup, se reflétant dans le miroir liquide qui vient mourir à ses pieds, SAKKARAH apparaît, entourée de son enceinte blanche. La PREMIÈRE pyramide d'Egypte et son complexe funéraire, demeure éternelle du grand pharaon ZOSER*, l'HORUS NETERI-KHET, oeuvre du génial Imhotep, étend sur quinze hectares sa fabuleuse architecture.
*Zoser : IIIe Dynastie (2624-2605 AVANT J.C.)
DE GIETER.
8

Regardez! Ils ont commencé à hisser la statue de Pharaon!
Plus vite!
Du calme, on arrive!
Ho! Camarades, tirons ferme!
Pharaon nous regarde!
S'il est content, nous aurons notre récompense!
Une pleine mesure de figues ou de blé pour chacun!
Taisez-vous et gardez la cadence! Haaa...an! Haaa...an! Haaa...an! Du nerf, bande de fainéants!
...Si ce n'est pas cette canaille d'Hononi qui rafle tout!
Sans ménager leurs efforts, les hommes, transpirant et jurant, peinent sous le soleil déjà brûlant. Plus haut, entourés de la cour et des prêtres de Thèbes, Pharaon et la grande épouse royale surveillent la lente progression du colosse, qui une fois en place donnera le signal des festivités de "l'Heb-Sed", fête jubilaire du roi.
Cependant, un groupe de prêtres se tient à l'écart.
Qui est le gros, là, luisant d'huile parfumée?
C'est Chepseska, le grand prêtre de Memphis, entouré des prêtres du dieu Ptah!
Hé! Pourquoi se tiennent-ils sur le côté?

Pied par pied, tracté par plus de deux cents hommes, répartis en quatre cordées, le colosse de granit avance, glissant sur un lit de rondins de bois, recouvert d'argile, que des aidants arrosent d'eau. Tandis que les contremaîtres crient pour marquer la cadence.
Hé! Les prêtres de Memphis enragent. Ils sont jaloux de ceux de Thèbes qui aujourd'hui conseillent Pharaon!
Cette statue n'est qu'un moyen de retrouver ses faveurs!
Ils y ont mis le poids, par Horus!
Ouais! Et c'est nous qui tirons!
HAAYA! HAAYA! HAAYA!

Silance! Ou vous sentirez ma canne de jonc sur vos échines!
Ho!Ho! Ho!Ho!
Les danseuses d'Isis?...C'est pas de refus!
Du nerf! Par tous les dieux! faudra-t-il appeler les danseuses d'Isis pour vous apprendre à tirer! Ça n'avance pas!
...laissant couler un flot de sang.
DE GIETER.
n cadence! cadence!
Aussitôt son sourire se fige sur ses lèvres. Dans le visage de pierre, les yeux, soudain ont rougi ...
Tout en plaisantant, l'homme jette un coup d'oeil vers le visage du colosse.
Ho, Panefer! Vient donc prendre ma place, tu la feras bouger tout seul!
AAAAAAH
9

En un instant, une terreur superstitieuse parcourt les rangs des ouvriers.
Du sang! Du sang! La statue est maudite!
Par Horus! La malédiction des dieux est sur nous!
Nous allons tous périr!
Non! Non! N'abandonnez pas la corde. Revenez! Pleutres! Lâches! Que le feu d'Amon vous dévore tous!
La statue. ATTENTION!
Privé des centaines de bras qui le retenaient, le colosse s'est arrêté, un instant immobile.
VITE! LES PORTEURS DE LA CRÉMAILLÈRE, BLOQUEZ LA STATUE!
Mais déjà, sans guide, la masse de pierre glisse en arrière, pivotant sur elle-même
Non! Non! Il est trop tard!
Elle va nous écraser!
...pour culbuter dans un fracas épouvantable.
10

Le drame s'est déroulé en quelques secondes, sous les yeux de Pharaon qui s'est dressé, blême.
Sans un mot, il fait demi-tour et rejoint son char d'or, sous les regards du peuple qui murmure. Terrible présage pour son jubilé.
C'est un signe des dieux de Memphis!
Ils ne reconnaissent plus son pouvoir!
Le malheur est sur l'Egypte!
C'est affreux!
Il faut rejoindre Pharaon au plus vite!
Il a regagné son campement, en bordure du Nil!
Hé! Attendez! Attendez-moi! Je ne peux pas vous suivre, moi!
Bande de lâcheurs!... Voilà cette statue... Hé!? En tombant, la tête s'est brisée!...
Mais, par Horus! La tête de cette statue est creuse!? Et... OH! On dirait un... un gémissement!?
AAAAAAAAH
PAR LES DIEUX! UN NAIN! CACHÉ DANS LA TÊTE!
11

Le malheureux! Il a été écrasé par les pierres!... Il n'y a plus rien à faire!
Cependant la petite troupe, guidée par Théti-Chéri, arrive au camp du Pharaon.
Suivant une organisation militaire, le campement est délimité par une rangée de boucliers de cuir. Une allée centrale conduit vers le périmètre royal.
Ils traversent le camp et atteignent la seconde enceinte.
HALTE!
Que les dieux soient avec vous, Princesse, mais les ordres sont formels, sa Suprême Majesté Pharaon, vie, force, santé, a interdit de pénétrer dans le domaine royal. Il veut être seul!
?
Hé là, l'ami! Toi qui sors de chez le roi, dis-moi...
Mais sans répondre, l'homme fait demi-tour et s'enfuit.
Hé! Attends! Qu'est-ce qui te prend?
Par Horus! où est-il passé, celui-là?
12

Rien à faire, il a disparu !
Curieux tout de même. Pourquoi s'est-il sauvé ?
Dépité, Papyrus revient sur ses pas. Quand soudain, une voix le fait tressaillir !
J'ai suivi tes ordres, Maître ! Voici la coupe dans laquelle Pharaon a bu !...
Mon fuyard ?!
C'est bien ! Tu as bien travaillé. Tu auras ta récompense, approche !...
Que font-ils ?
Pour mieux voir, Papyrus s'est penché en avant et sursaute. Déchirant la toile, l'éclair d'un poignard a jailli.
ATTENTION !
Par tous les dieux ! Je saurai qui a fait ça !
13

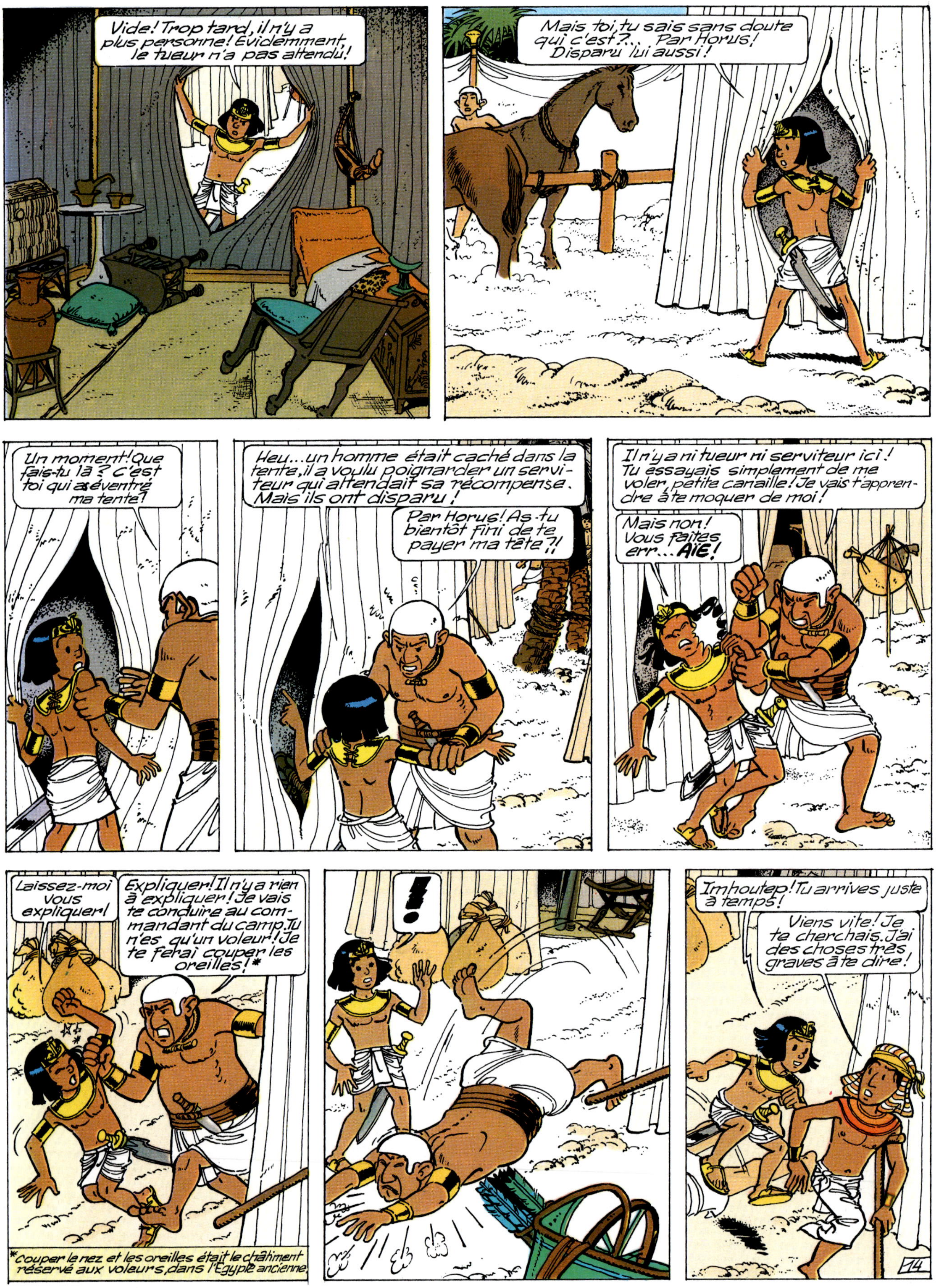
Vide! Trop tard, il n'y a plus personne! Evidemment, le tueur n'a pas attendu!
Mais toi, tu sais sans doute qui c'est?... Par Horus! Disparu lui aussi!
Un moment! Que fais-tu là? C'est toi qui as éventré ma tente?
Heu... un homme était caché dans la tente, il a voulu poignarder un serviteur qui attendait sa récompense. Mais ils ont disparu!
Par Horus! As-tu bientôt fini de te payer ma tête?!
Il n'y a ni tueur ni serviteur ici! Tu essayais simplement de me voler, petite canaille! Je vais t'apprendre à te moquer de moi!
Mais non! Vous faites err... AÏE!
Laissez-moi vous expliquer!
Expliquer! Il n'y a rien à expliquer! Je vais te conduire au commandant du camp. Tu n'es qu'un voleur! Je te ferai couper les oreilles!*
*couper le nez et les oreilles était le châtiment réservé aux voleurs, dans l'Egypte ancienne
!
Imhoutep! Tu arrives juste à temps!
Viens vite! Je te cherchais. J'ai des choses très graves à te dire!
14

Des choses graves! De quoi s'agit-il?
En quelques mots, Imhoutep raconte ce qu'il a découvert dans la statue creuse.
C'était horrible! Et dans la main, il tenait encore une outre contenant du sang!
Du sang?
Oui! Du sang animal sans doute.
Une statue creuse! Du sang que l'on fait couler, par des trous ménagés dans les yeux, au moment propice pour terrifier le peuple et jeter le doute sur la légitimité du Roi. C'est une félonie!
Allons prévenir Pharaon immédiatement. Il est en danger!
C'est impossible, personne n'oserait!
Viens!
Mais, tandis que nos deux amis se hâtent vers le périmètre royal.
MALHEUR! MALHEUR!
Pharaon, notre maître, a été empoisonné!
LE MALHEUR EST SUR NOUS!
Vas-tu cesser de crier, par Horus! Es-tu devenu fou pour semer la panique dans le campement!
Mais le roi a été empoisonné!... Empoisonné!...
Silence!
15

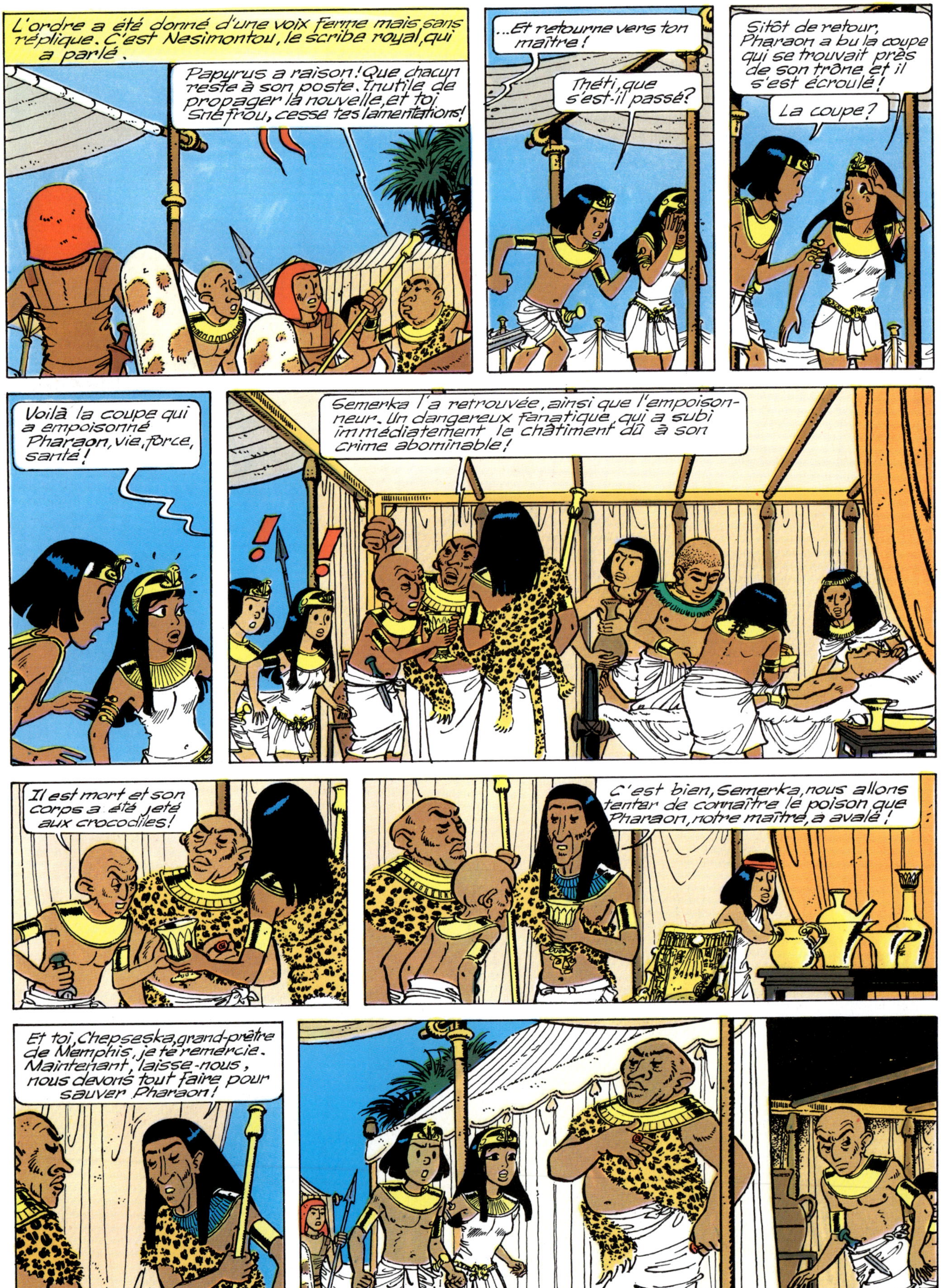

L'ordre a été donné d'une voix ferme mais sans réplique. C'est Nesimontou, le scribe royal, qui a parlé.
Papyrus a raison! Que chacun reste à son poste. Inutile de propager la nouvelle, et toi Snefrou, cesse tes lamentations!
...Et retourne vers ton maître!
Théti, que s'est-il passé?
Sitôt de retour, Pharaon a bu la coupe qui se trouvait près de son trône et il s'est écroulé!
La coupe?
Voilà la coupe qui a empoisonné Pharaon, vie, force, santé!
Semerka l'a retrouvée, ainsi que l'empoisonneur. Un dangereux fanatique qui a subi immédiatement le châtiment dû à son crime abominable!
!
!
Il est mort et son corps a été jeté aux crocodiles!
C'est bien, Semerka, nous allons tenter de connaître le poison que Pharaon, notre maître, a avalé!
Et toi, Chepseska, grand-prêtre de Memphis, je te remercie. Maintenant, laisse-nous, nous devons tout faire pour sauver Pharaon!
16

Par Ré ! C'est une abomination ! C'est un serviteur de Semerka qui a volé la coupe de Pharaon. Il n'est pas mort !... J'ai réussi à le sauver du poignard de son maître !... Ce poignard, je l'ai reconnu, il était là, à la ceinture de Semerka !
Et la statue ! Don des prêtres de Memphis, nous avons retrouvé un nain caché dans la tête. c'est lui qui faisait couler le sang des yeux du colosse. Lui est mort !... C'est un complot contre le roi, et les coupables sortent d'ici !
Calme-toi, Papyrus ! Je te connais, tu as sans doute raison. Mais que vaut ta parole face à celle du grand prêtre de Ptah, premier prophète de Memphis ?
De toute façon, il est trop tard, le complot a réussi !
Nesimontou ?!... Comment oses-tu ! Tu mérites un châtiment !
Tout doux ! Noble princesse, nous n'avons aucune preuve de la félonie de Chepseska. Je ne crois pas que Pharaon soit en danger de mort. Hélas, demain il sera incapable de présider l'Heb-Sed, la fête de son jubilé !
Il faut annuler les cérémonies !
Impossible ! La date du jubilé est sacrée et le Roi doit à cette occasion montrer qu'il est toujours capable de tenir fermement le pouvoir. Demain, devant le clergé, l'armée et le peuple rassemblés, il devra, en courant, suivre trois fois le périmètre tracé par les prêtres autour des bornes de la grande esplanade, au pied de la pyramide. Depuis le grand Pharaon Djoser, cette épreuve rituelle est immuable. Le Roi doit la réussir, sinon...
Sinon ?
Sinon il sera déclaré inapte et devra désigner un corégent. Chepseska est de filiation royale et premier prophète de Memphis. Après l'incident de la statue brisée qui a frappé le peuple de stupeur, il n'aura aucune peine à se faire introniser !
Alors tout est perdu !
17

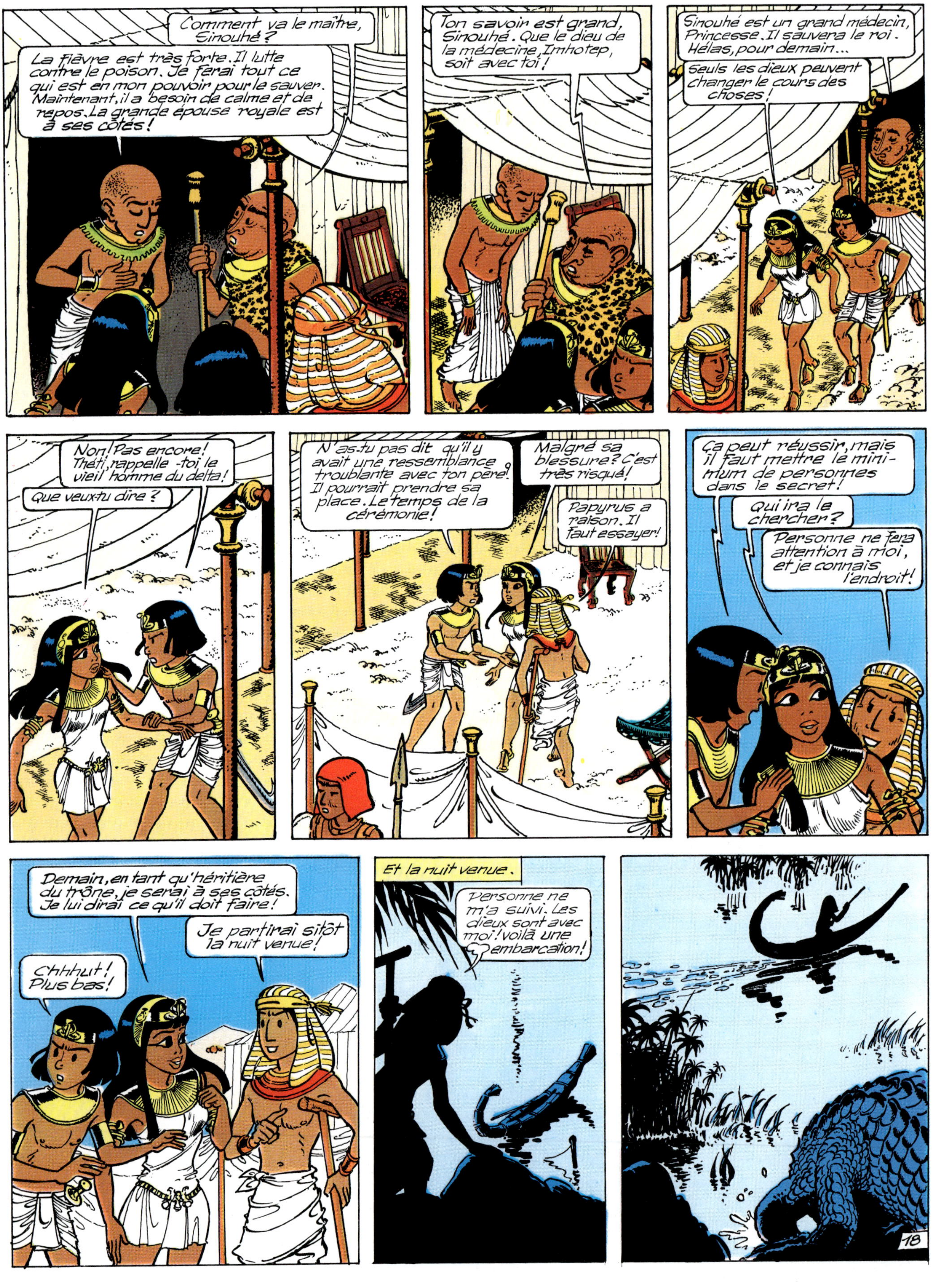
Comment va le maître, Sinouhé ?
La fièvre est très forte. Il lutte contre le poison. Je ferai tout ce qui est en mon pouvoir pour le sauver. Maintenant, il a besoin de calme et de repos. La grande épouse royale est à ses côtés !
Ton savoir est grand, Sinouhé. Que le dieu de la médecine, Imhotep, soit avec toi !
Sinouhé est un grand médecin, Princesse. Il sauvera le roi. Hélas, pour demain...
Seuls les dieux peuvent changer le cours des choses !
Non ! Pas encore ! Théti, rappelle-toi le vieil homme du delta !
Que veux-tu dire ?
N'as-tu pas dit qu'il y avait une ressemblance troublante avec ton père ? Il pourrait prendre sa place. Le temps de la cérémonie !
Malgré sa blessure ? C'est très risqué !
Papyrus a raison. Il faut essayer !
Ça peut réussir, mais il faut mettre le minimum de personnes dans le secret !
Qui ira le chercher ?
Personne ne fera attention à moi, et je connais l'endroit !
Demain, en tant qu'héritière du trône, je serai à ses côtés. Je lui dirai ce qu'il doit faire !
Je partirai sitôt la nuit venue !
Chhhut ! Plus bas !
Et la nuit venue.
Personne ne m'a suivi. Les dieux sont avec moi ! voilà une embarcation !
18

Quand dans l'aube "la brillante"* illumine d'un ruissellement doré la pyramide de Djoser, un long cortège se dirige vers le camp du Pharaon.
* Les Egyptiens divisaient le jour comme la nuit en douze heures. Chaque heure avait un nom. La première heure de la nuit s'appelait: "La déconfiture des ennemis de Ré". La première heure du jour s'appelait "La brillante".
Tout est en place, Seigneur, nos espions ont répandu les bruits les plus suspects sur l'incapacité de Pharaon. Le peuple a été frappé par l'accident tragique du colosse, il murmure et est prêt à nous suivre!
C'est bien! Mais il faut respecter les règles!
Tenant en main le sceptre "Khérep" symbole d'autorité, Chepseska s'avance, sûr de lui.
Halte! Personne ne pénètre dans l'enceinte royale!
Par Ptah, dieu de Memphis, moi, premier prophète et la procession des prêtres, nous sommes au bon vouloir de Pharaon, vie, force, santé. Les dieux d'Egypte attendent l'hommage du Roi, afin que débute l'Heb-Sed, suivant le rituel sacré!
Hé! Hé! Hé!
19

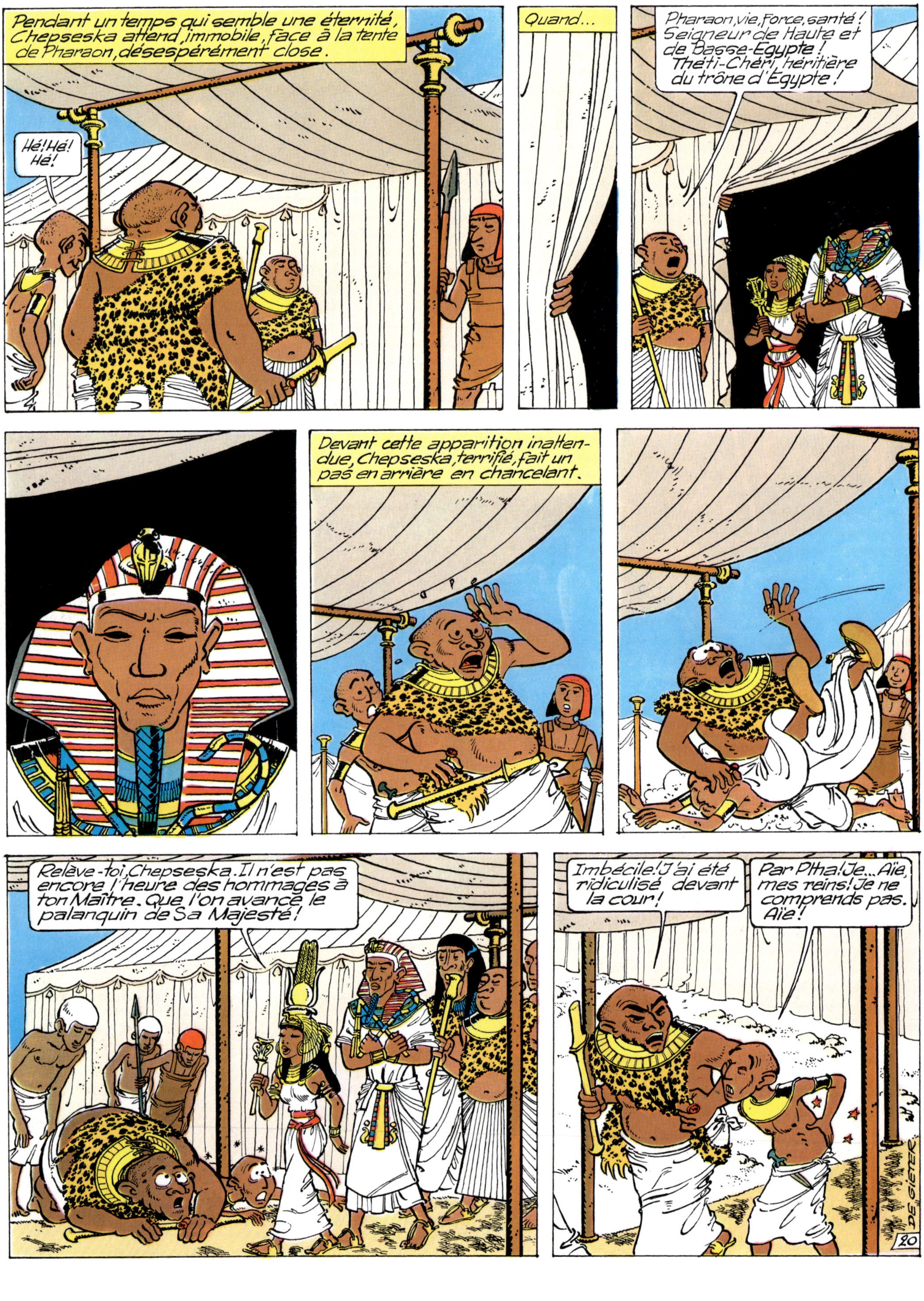

Pendant un temps qui semble une éternité, Chepseska attend, immobile, face à la tente de Pharaon, désespérément close.
Hé! Hé! Hé!
Quand...
Pharaon, vie, Force, santé! Seigneur de Haute et de Basse-Egypte! Théti-Chéri, héritière du trône d'Egypte!
Devant cette apparition inattendue, Chepseska, terrifié, fait un pas en arrière en chancelant.
Relève-toi, Chepseska. Il n'est pas encore l'heure des hommages à ton Maître. Que l'on avance le palanquin de Sa Majesté!
Imbécile! J'ai été ridiculisé devant la cour!
Par Ptha! Je... Aïe, mes reins! Je ne comprends pas. Aïe!
DE GIETER
20

Voilà une diversion qui est venue à point. Personne n'a remarqué votre difficulté à marcher!
Hélas! La fièvre n'a pas quitté mon père de la nuit et Sinouhé ne peut rien!
Ayez confiance, Princesse, j'ai passé toute ma vie dans les marais du delta. Si votre ami trouve la vieille Nimââth, elle connaît les herbes qui guérissent les fièvres!
Trouver la vieille Nimââth! Trouver la vieille Nimââth! C'est vite dit. Par Horus! Dans ce dédale de canaux et de fourrés!...
Tu vois quelque chose, Papyrus? C'est pourtant l'endroit qu'il nous a renseigné!
Rien! Pas la moindre habitation en vue!
?
Papyrus! Au secours!
Mais déjà, jaillissant des fourrés...
Par tous les dieux!...
Attends! Nous ne sommes pas des ennemis!
27

Un instant, la brute semble déconcertée.
Puis soudain furieuse, elle se jette sur Papyrus, mains nues.
Instinctivement, Papyrus se protège de son glaive magique, qui foudroie le colosse.
AAAAAAAH!
AAAAH!
Toi... magi... magicien! Pas... tuer... Aya!... magicien... comme... Nimââth!
Nimââth!... Tu as dit Nimââth! Tu la connais?... Conduis-nous à elle. Je ne te ferai pas de mal!
Nimââth! Nimââth!
Imhoutep, tu entends? Nous allons...
IMHOUTEP!
Imhoutep! Ça va?
Ça va!
22

Plus tard...
Toujours rien! Pourtant c'est la direction qu'il a indiquée!
Peut-être pour nous perdre!
En tout cas, il connaît Nimââth!
Tu me cherches, Papyrus?
Tu viens chercher les herbes qui pourront sauver Pharaon!
Ma...gi...cien!
Le murmure du vent parcourt le domaine d'Osiris* et apporte les nouvelles du monde, mieux que le bavardage des humains!
* LES MARAIS DU DELTA.
Vous êtes Nimââth? Com... comment savez-vous?
Alors vous connaissez aussi les herbes qui sauveront le roi. Vous allez nous aider!
Je n'ai rien à refuser à celui qui porte le glaive de Sébek, le dieu crocodile. Mais les prêtres de Memphis sont puissants, et les herbes des marais ne peuvent rien contre leur magie!
Alors tout est perdu?
Hélas! Seule l'herbe aux crocodiles peut guérir du mal qui ronge Pharaon!
L'herbe aux crocodiles?! Où peut-on la trouver?...
Personne ne le sait. Elle naît au hasard, au fond de l'eau, du sang du crocodile!
...Du sang de crocodile?!...
ALORS JE SAIS OÙ LA TROUVER!!
?
23

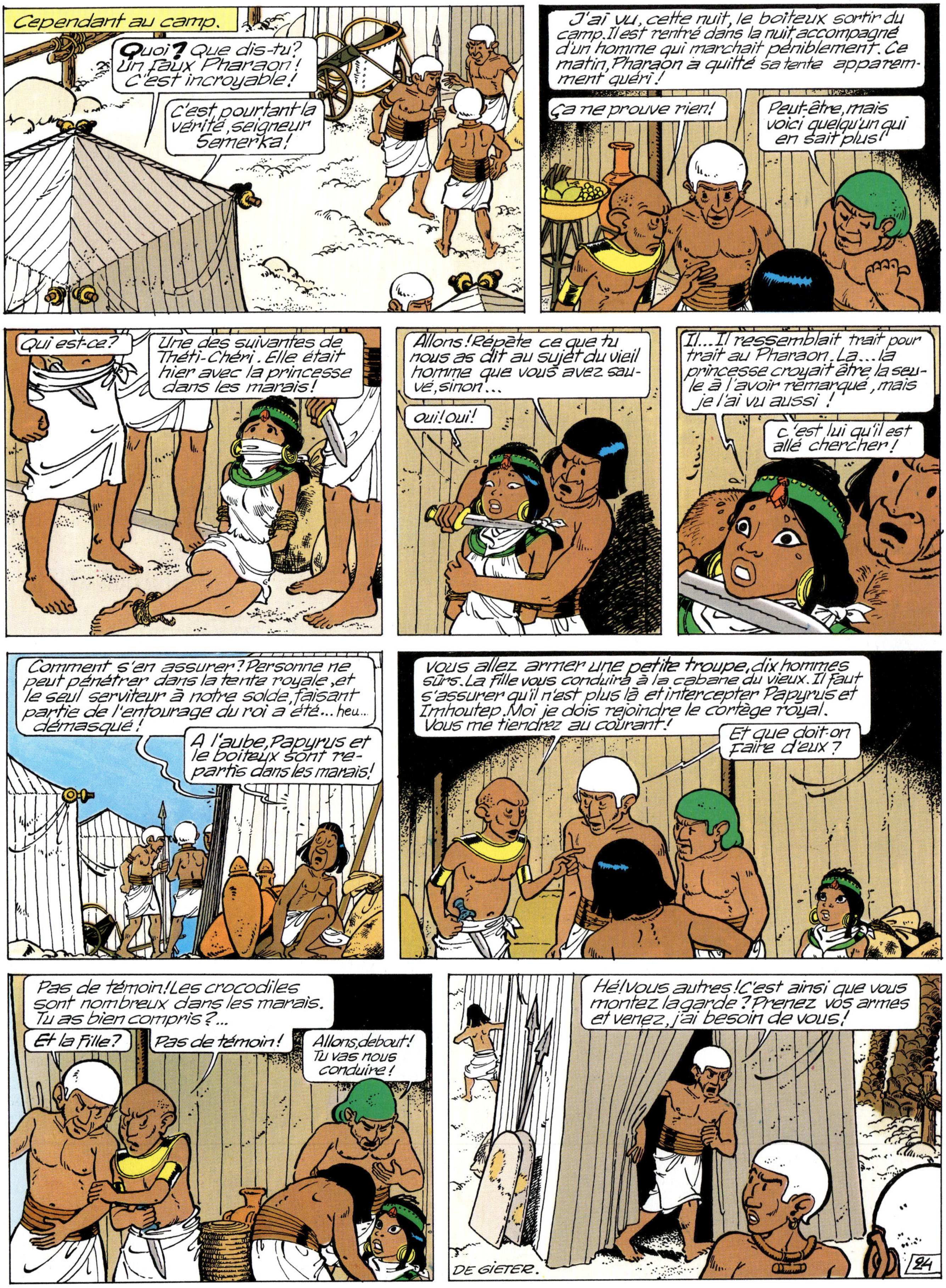
Cependant au camp.
Quoi? Que dis-tu? Un faux Pharaon! C'est incroyable!
C'est pourtant la vérité, seigneur Semerka!
J'ai vu, cette nuit, le boiteux sortir du camp. Il est rentré dans la nuit accompagné d'un homme qui marchait péniblement. Ce matin, Pharaon a quitté sa tente apparemment guéri!
Ça ne prouve rien!
Peut-être, mais voici quelqu'un qui en sait plus!
Qui est-ce?
Une des suivantes de Théti-Chéri. Elle était hier avec la princesse dans les marais!
Allons! Répète ce que tu nous as dit au sujet du vieil homme que vous avez sauvé, sinon...
Oui! Oui!
Il... Il ressemblait trait pour trait au Pharaon. La... la princesse croyait être la seule à l'avoir remarqué, mais je l'ai vu aussi!
C'est lui qu'il est allé chercher!
Comment s'en assurer? Personne ne peut pénétrer dans la tente royale, et le seul serviteur à notre solde, faisant partie de l'entourage du roi a été... heu... démasqué!
A l'aube, Papyrus et le boiteux sont repartis dans les marais!
Vous allez armer une petite troupe, dix hommes sûrs. La fille vous conduira à la cabane du vieux. Il faut s'assurer qu'il n'est plus là et intercepter Papyrus et Imhoutep. Moi je dois rejoindre le cortège royal. Vous me tiendrez au courant!
Et que doit-on faire d'eux?
Pas de témoin! Les crocodiles sont nombreux dans les marais. Tu as bien compris?...
Et la fille?
Pas de témoin!
Allons, debout! Tu vas nous conduire!
Hé! Vous autres! C'est ainsi que vous montez la garde? Prenez vos armes et venez, j'ai besoin de vous!
DE GIETER.
24

Pendant ce temps...
Toujours rien! Pourtant c'est bien ici que je me suis battu avec le crocodile!
C'est bien la vingtième fois que je plonge!
Toujours rien! Je continue!
Non, Papyrus! Ne restons plus ici! Viens! Viens! Allons-nous-en au plus vite!
?
Imhoutep! Mais qu'est-ce qui te prend ?
Regarde! Ils sont là. Ils nous épient depuis un moment. Ils viennent venger leur congénère!
Les crocodiles!
Il faut fuir!
DE GIETER
Trop tard! Nous sommes encerclés!
25

Soudain, les oiseaux des marais se sont tus, le cercle des crocodiles se resserre, tandis que Papyrus et Imhoutep restent immobiles.
Je ne comprends pas ! Ils se sont arrêtés !... Ils semblent obéir à un ordre !
Lentement, la barque de roseaux dérive.
Ils vont se jeter sur nous, tous ensemble !
Mais NON, Imhoutep ! Nous n'avons rien à craindre ! J'AI COMPRIS ! Ils nous ont poussés vers les herbes magiques !
Tu es fou !
PAPYRUS, NON !! Tu vas te faire dévorer !
L'herbe rouge !
DE GIETER

Par tous les dieux! Papyrus, c'est formidable! Comment as-tu compris qu'ils nous montraient l'endroit ?
Héhé!...
Les dieux sont avec nous! Dans quelques heures Pharaon sera sauvé!
Attention, les voilà!
Laissez-les approcher, il ne faut pas les rater!
Je les veux morts de votre première flèche!
Encore un peu...
FUYEZ! FUYEZ!
Ils vous attendent derrière les fourrés! Ils vont vous tuer!
!
!
Qu'est-ce que..?! D'où sort celui-là?... Par Anubis! C'est le serviteur de Pharaon!
27

Là! Je les vois!!
Vite! Demi-tour! Demi-tour!
Fuyez!...AAAAAAH!!
Le malheureux! Il faut l'aider!
Non!... Sauvez-vous!... Pour moi, il...il est trop tard!... Que Pharaon me...par...donne!
Abattez-les! Abattez-les!
Plus vite! Dans ce labyrinthe de canaux, nous avons une chance de leur échapper!
DE GIETER.
Dépêchez-vous! Ils vont disparaître dans les hautes herbes!
Par Horus! Imhoutep, nous n'avançons plus! La barque est enlisée dans les papyrus!
28

* AU NORD-EST DE LA PYRAMIDE DE SAKKARAH S'ÉTEND UN CIMETIÈRE SOUTERRAIN SUR PLUSIEURS DIZAINES D'HECTARES.

A cet instant, le cortège précédé des hérauts royaux, pénètre dans l'enceinte de la pyramide par l'unique porte qui, après un étroit passage, débouche sur une longue colonnade...
Pharaon et Théti-Chéri, princesse héréditaire, sont suivis de SEKHAT-HOR*, déesse vache portée par les prêtres de Memphis, et de tous les dignitaires du pays.
* SEKHAT-HOR (HATHOR) est la déesse nourrice d'Horus et des Pharaons.
Personne ! Tout va bien. Pharaon sera bientôt sauvé !
Hé ! Imhoutep ! Tu viens ? C'est pas le moment de lambiner !
Par Horus ! J'arrive !
AAAAH !
PAPYRUS !
!
Imhoutep ?!
Mais emporté par son élan, Papyrus glisse sur le sable qui se dérobe sous ses pas.
Hééée !
30

Ça va?
Où sommes-nous?
Je n'en sais rien. Sans doute dans le puits de ventilation d'un ancien mastaba*. La région en est truffée!
*TOMBEAU SOUTERRAIN.
Du sable! Rien que du sable! Impossible de remonter par là!
Tout ça, c'est ta faute! Tu nous as mis dans de beaux draps. Tu pourrais regarder où tu marches avec ta béquille!
Je sais, j'ai perdu l'équilibre, Excuse-moi!
Imhoutep, c'est ridicule, pardonne-moi, mais tous nos efforts anéantis si près du but! J'ai eu un mouvement de découragement.
Tout n'est pas perdu! Regarde, le couloir descend dans la terre! On y va?
On y va!
Par Horus! La voûte s'est écroulée!
Tu vois quelque chose?
Le couloir s'élargit, on dirait... Il y a de la lumière!
Mais soudain.
PAPYRUS!
DE GIETER.
31

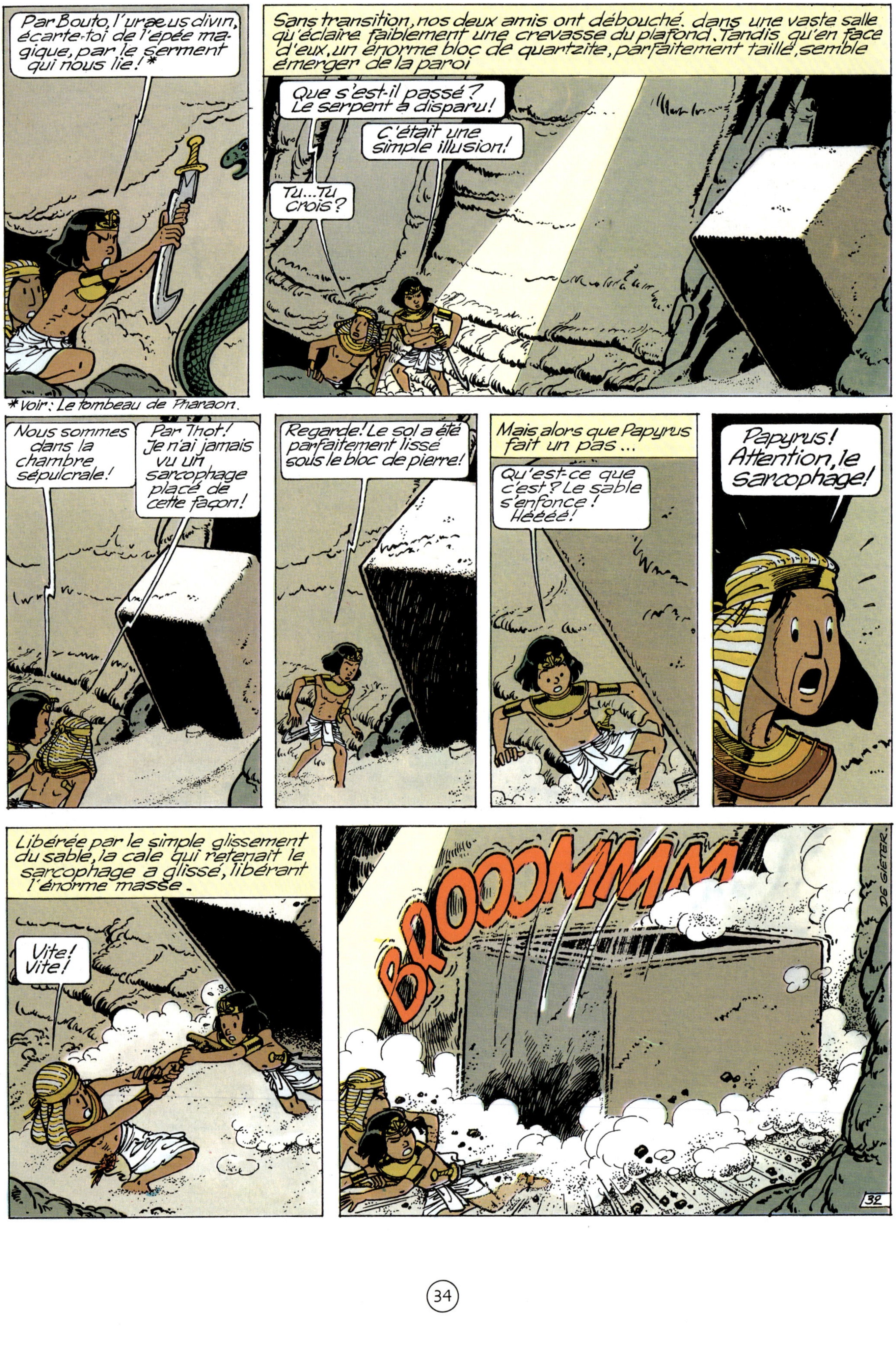
Par Bouto, l'uraeus divin, écarte-toi de l'épée magique, par le serment qui nous lie! *
Sans transition, nos deux amis ont débouché dans une vaste salle qu'éclaire faiblement une crevasse du plafond. Tandis qu'en face d'eux, un énorme bloc de quartzite, parfaitement taillé, semble émerger de la paroi
Que s'est-il passé? Le serpent a disparu!
C'était une simple illusion!
Tu... Tu crois?
* Voir: Le tombeau de Pharaon.
Nous sommes dans la chambre sépulcrale!
Par Thot! Je n'ai jamais vu un sarcophage placé de cette façon!
Regarde! Le sol a été parfaitement lissé sous le bloc de pierre!
Mais alors que Papyrus fait un pas ...
Qu'est-ce que c'est? Le sable s'enfonce! Hééé!
Papyrus! Attention, le sarcophage!
Libérée par le simple glissement du sable, la cale qui retenait le sarcophage a glissé, libérant l'énorme masse.
Vite! Vite!
BROOOMMMM
DE GIETER
32

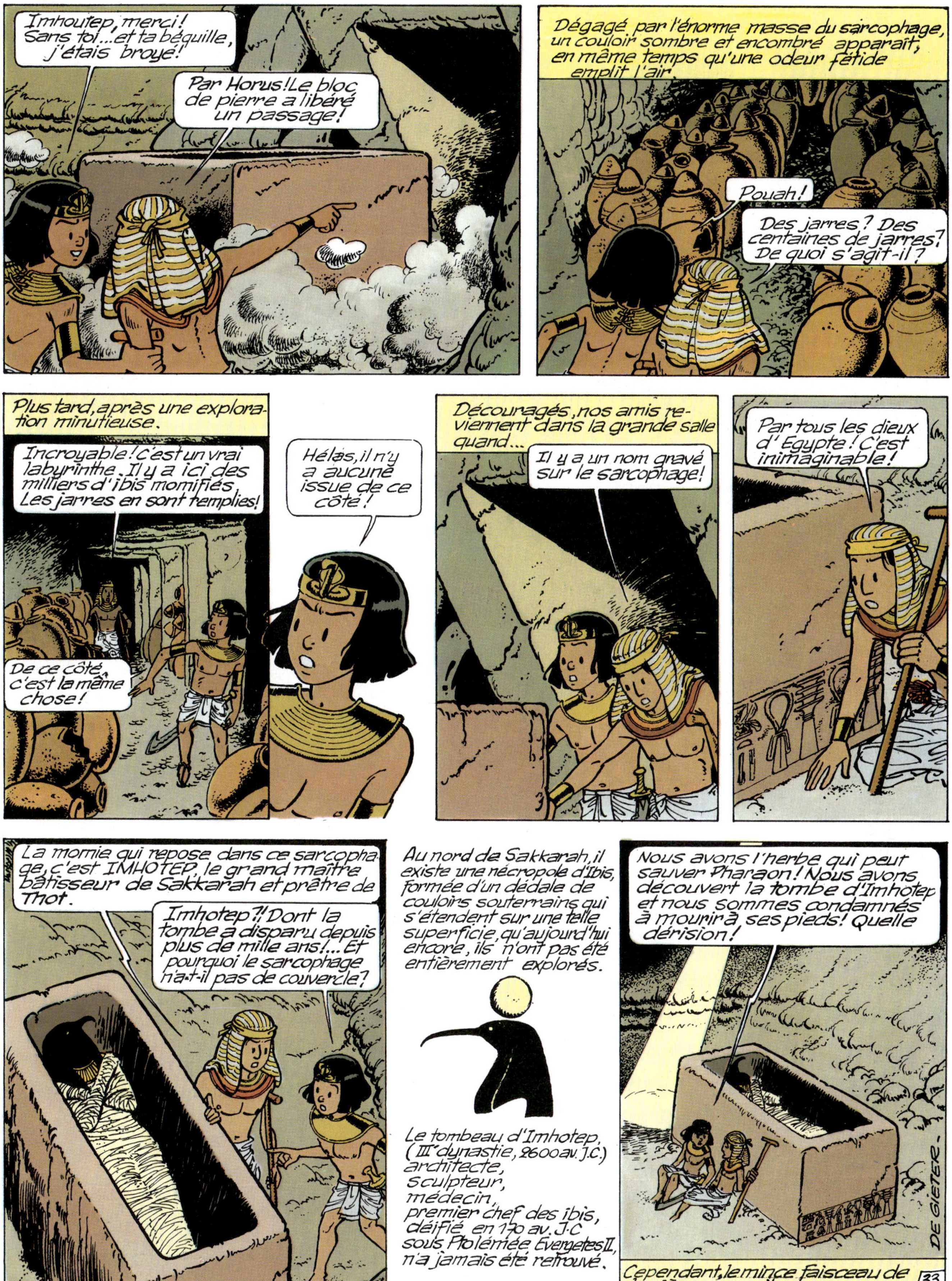
Imhoutep, merci! Sans toi... et ta béquille, j'étais broyé!
Par Horus! Le bloc de pierre a libéré un passage!
Dégagé par l'énorme masse du sarcophage, un couloir sombre et encombré apparaît, en même temps qu'une odeur fétide emplit l'air.
Pouah!
Des jarres? Des centaines de jarres? De quoi s'agit-il?
Plus tard, après une exploration minutieuse.
Incroyable! C'est un vrai labyrinthe. Il y a ici des milliers d'ibis momifiés. Les jarres en sont remplies!
De ce côté, c'est la même chose!
Hélas, il n'y a aucune issue de ce côté!
Découragés, nos amis reviennent dans la grande salle quand...
Il y a un nom gravé sur le sarcophage!
Par tous les dieux d'Egypte! C'est inimaginable!
La momie qui repose dans ce sarcophage, c'est IMHOTEP, le grand maître bâtisseur de Sakkarah et prêtre de Thot.
Imhotep?! Dont la tombe a disparu depuis plus de mille ans!... Et pourquoi le sarcophage n'a-t-il pas de couvercle?
Au nord de Sakkarah, il existe une nécropole d'Ibis, formée d'un dédale de couloirs souterrains qui s'étendent sur une telle superficie qu'aujourd'hui encore, ils n'ont pas été entièrement explorés.
Le tombeau d'Imhotep, (IIIe dynastie, 2600 av. J.C.) architecte, sculpteur, médecin, premier chef des ibis, déifié en 170 av. J.C sous Ptolémée Evergetes II, n'a jamais été retrouvé.
Nous avons l'herbe qui peut sauver Pharaon! Nous avons découvert la tombe d'Imhotep et nous sommes condamnés à mourir à ses pieds! Quelle dérision!
DE GIETER
Cependant, le mince faisceau de lumière poursuit sa course.
33

Et pour la première fois, les rayons solaires viennent réchauffer la momie millénaire.
Alors, tel un gigantesque cocon, la momie-chrysalide commence son incroyable métamorphose, et du fond des âges, IMHOTEP, le dieu bâtisseur, l'homme-ibis renait pour l'éternité...
34

Ecrasés par cette apparition fantastique, Papyrus et Imhoutep tombent à genoux.
Relevez-vous, mortels!
Depuis mille ans, mon corps momifié attend les rayons de Râ* pour renaître à l'éternité. Vous êtes la main du destin. Que vos noms soient vivants à jamais. Adieu!
* LE DIEU SOLEIL.
NON!
Divin bâtisseur de Sakkarah, en ce moment, ton temple est profané par les intrigues des prêtres de Memphis. Pharaon est en dange de mort!
En un instant, l'homme-ibis semble frémir de fureur.
Par les dieux! Cela ne sera pas!
LA VENGEANCE DE L'IBIS LES PLONGERA DANS L'ÉPOUVANTE!
Et tout à coup, du fond du tombeau au million d'ibis, un grondement sourd ébranle la terre.
Alors, telle une ruche bourdonnante à l'appel du maître, du fond des âges, les ibis brisent les alvéoles qui les retenaient...
35

...Et s'élancent, ailes contre ailes, à la suite de leur dieu.
Papyrus, attention! La voûte s'écroule!
Précédant l'envol des oiseaux-momies, l'homme-ibis pulvérise le bouchon rocheux de la grande chambre funéraire.
Et la voix d'Imhotep résonne pour la dernière fois.
REJOIGNEZ PHARAON!
Oui, mais comment sortir d'ici?
Rien de plus simple!
36

Hé! Hé! Il suffit de grimper sur les éboulis!
Attends, j'arrive!

Papyrus, nous sommes libres!
Allons rejoindre Pharaon!

Pendant ce temps à Sakkarah, le cortège royal a traversé l'immense esplanade qui s'étend au pied de la pyramide et a pénétré dans la cour de l'Heb. Sed où Pharaon et Théti, installés sur l'estrade de maçonnerie, reçoivent l'hommage des grands du royaume.
Il était temps que nous arrivions, ma jambe me fait atrocement souffrir!
Courage!

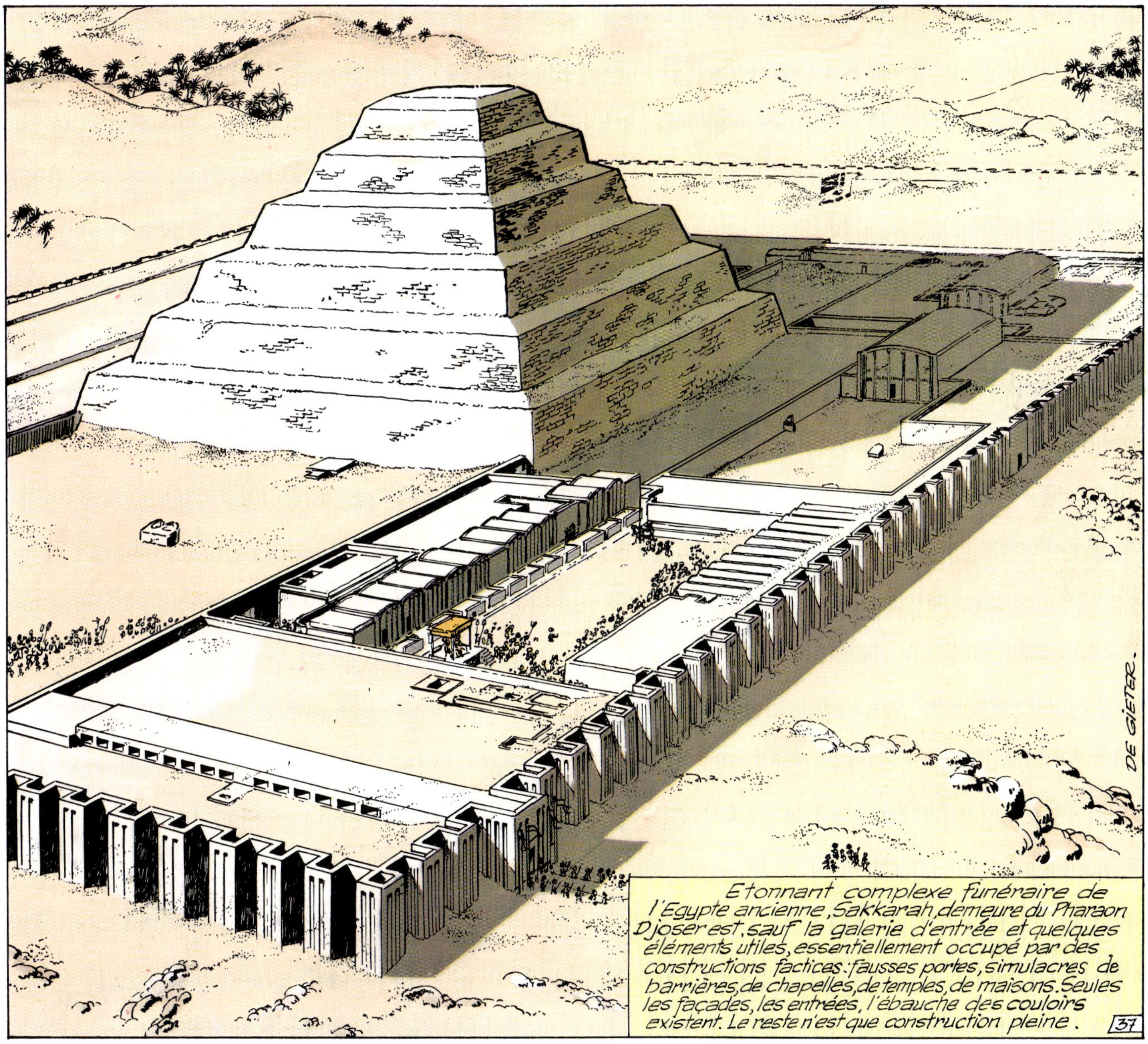
DE GIETER.
Etonnant complexe funéraire de l'Egypte ancienne, Sakkarah, demeure du Pharaon Djoser est, sauf la galerie d'entrée et quelques éléments utiles, essentiellement occupé par des constructions factices: fausses portes, simulacres de barrières, de chapelles, de temples, de maisons. Seules les façades, les entrées, l'ébauche des couloirs existent. Le reste n'est que construction pleine.
37

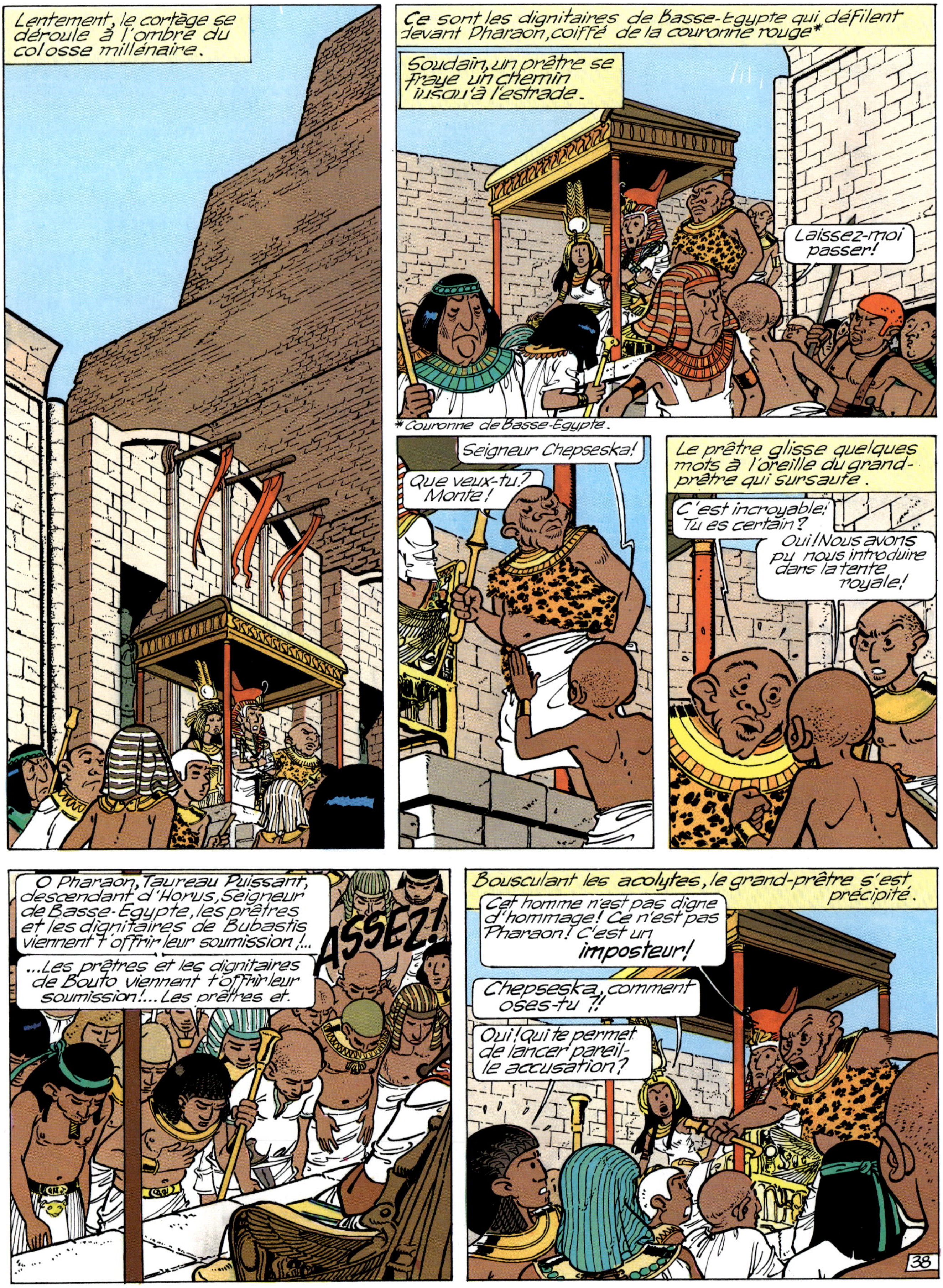

Lentement, le cortège se déroule à l'ombre du colosse millénaire.
Ce sont les dignitaires de Basse-Egypte qui défilent devant Pharaon, coiffé de la couronne rouge*
Soudain, un prêtre se fraye un chemin jusqu'à l'estrade.
Laissez-moi passer!
* Couronne de Basse-Egypte.
Seigneur Chepseska!
Que veux-tu? Monte!
Le prêtre glisse quelques mots à l'oreille du grand-prêtre qui sursaute.
C'est incroyable! Tu es certain?
Oui! Nous avons pu nous introduire dans la tente royale!
O Pharaon, Taureau Puissant, descendant d'Horus, Seigneur de Basse-Egypte, les prêtres et les dignitaires de Bubastis viennent t'offrir leur soumission!...
...Les prêtres et les dignitaires de Bouto viennent t'offrir leur soumission!... Les prêtres et
ASSEZ!
Bousculant les acolytes, le grand-prêtre s'est précipité.
Cet homme n'est pas digne d'hommage! Ce n'est pas Pharaon! C'est un imposteur!
Chepseska, comment oses-tu?!
Oui! Qui te permet de lancer pareille accusation?
38

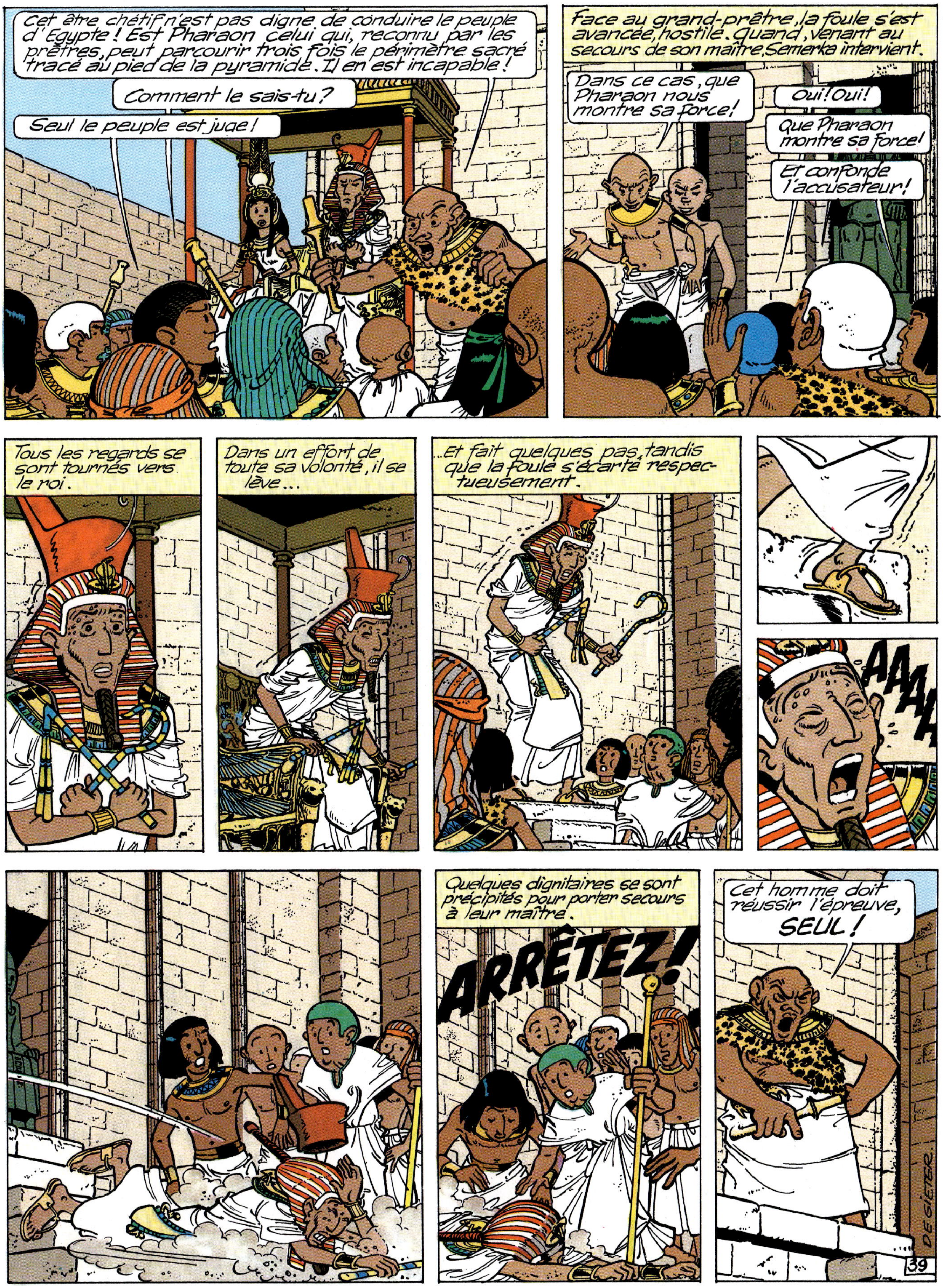

Cet être chétif n'est pas digne de conduire le peuple d'Egypte ! Est Pharaon celui qui, reconnu par les prêtres, peut parcourir trois fois le périmètre sacré tracé au pied de la pyramide. Il en est incapable !
Comment le sais-tu ?
Seul le peuple est juge !
Face au grand-prêtre, la foule s'est avancée, hostile. Quand, venant au secours de son maître, Semerka intervient.
Dans ce cas, que Pharaon nous montre sa force !
Oui ! Oui !
Que Pharaon montre sa force !
Et confonde l'accusateur !
Tous les regards se sont tournés vers le roi.
Dans un effort de toute sa volonté, il se lève...
...Et fait quelques pas, tandis que la foule s'écarte respectueusement.
AAAA
Quelques dignitaires se sont précipités pour porter secours à leur maître.
ARRÊTEZ !
Cet homme doit réussir l'épreuve, SEUL !
DE GIETER
39

TOUT SEUL !
Par... pardonnez-moi, Princesse, je... je ne peux plus bouger... je ne peux pas remplir la mission que Pharaon m'a donnée...
Peuple d'Egypte, écoute-moi ! Je suis Chepseska, celui qu'Horus a appelé pour confondre le faux Pharaon ! Pharaon est mort ! La princesse Théti-Chéri ne peut régner ! Nous ne voulons pas d'une nouvelle Hatchepsout *
Non !
Non !
HATCHEPSOUT : fille de Thoutmosis I, fut la seule femme Pharaon. (1490-1468 Av. J.c)
Tandis que l'assemblée reste frappée de stupeur, habilement placés parmi la foule, les partisans du grand-prêtre réagissent.
Gloire à toi, Chepseska !
Premier prophète de Ptah ! Béni des dieux !
Taureau puissant ! Descendant d'Horus !
Sois notre Pharaon !
La cérémonie sacrée ne peut être interrompue. Que l'on m'apporte l'Imyt-per * Par ma course rituelle, je montrerai au peuple que je suis digne de porter la double couronne.
* Rouleau que le Pharaon tient en main, et qui représente le titre de propriété de la terre d'Egypte.
Tu n'as pas le droit ! Les dieux ne le permettront pas !
Alors, qu'ils m'en empêchent ! Ha ! Ha ! Ha !
Mais soudain...
40

Un sourd grondement, pareil à la colère de Seth, dieu de l'orage, monte de derrière la pyramide à degrés...
?
Conduits par Imhotep, les millions d'ibis, ailes déployées, emplissent le ciel.
Alors, les ténèbres envahissent la terre, plongeant les hommes dans une terreur sacrée.
Attendez ! Non! Non! Revenez !
41

Et brusquement, le voile noir se déchire. Une clarté éblouissante fait irruption dans l'enceinte du temple.
Vêtu du pagne divin, et de la couronne blanche, orné de la barbe royale, le **flagellum** (qui dissipe les énergies négatives et condense les positives) dans la main droite, l'**imyt-per** dans la gauche, le vrai Pharaon apparaît.
PHARAON !
Et c'est devant une foule prosternée que Pharaon s'élance pour parcourir, selon le rite ancestral, la course symbolique qui fera de lui le maître incontesté de l'Egypte.
Il traverse la cour "Heb-Sed", et quelques instants plus tard, débouche dans l'immense esplanade qui s'étend au pied de la face sud de la pyramide à degrés. Trois fois il va parcourir le périmètre qui entoure les deux bornes de pierre, symbole des deux Egyptes.
42

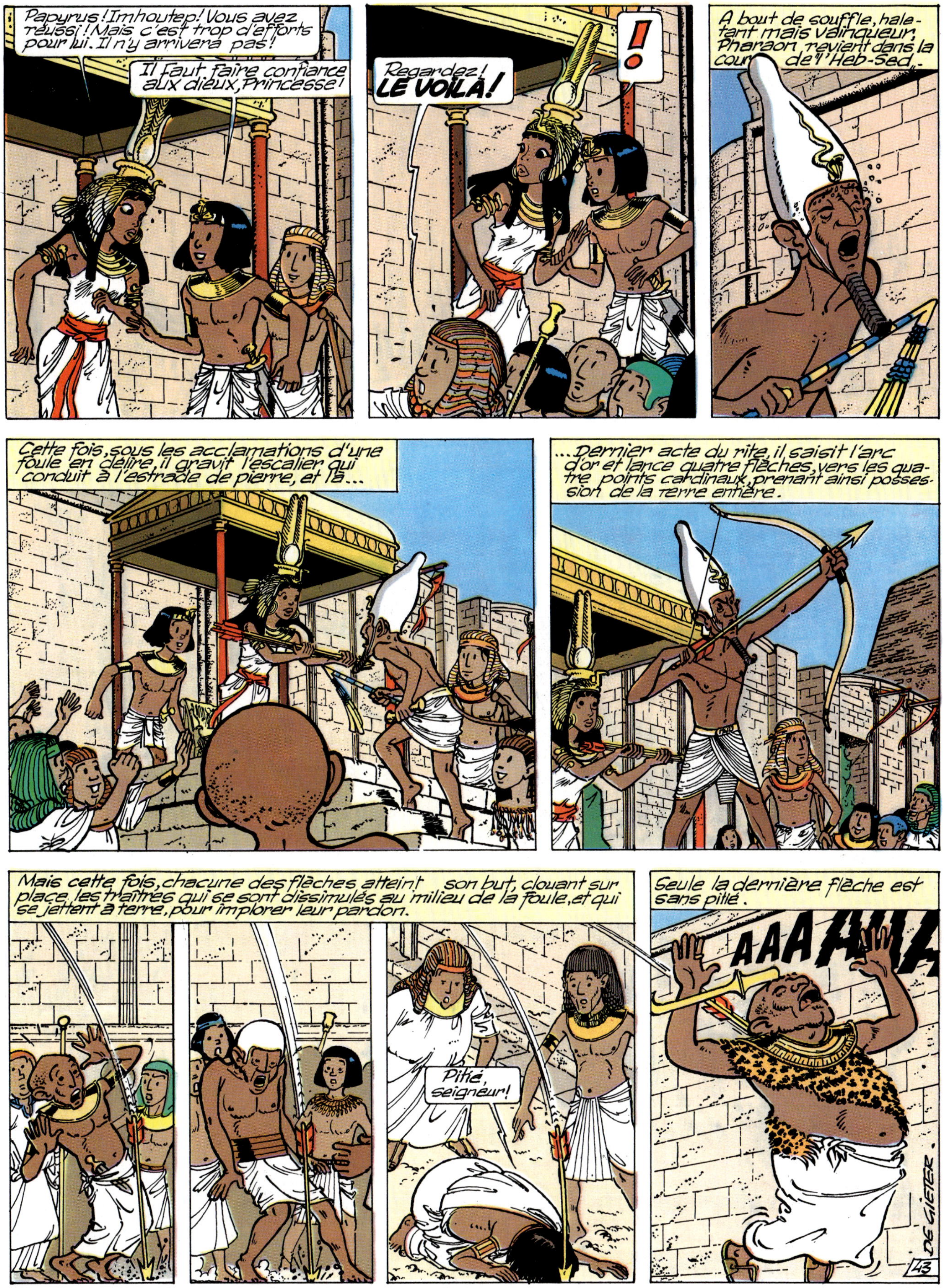
Papyrus! Imhoutep! Vous avez réussi! Mais c'est trop d'efforts pour lui. Il n'y arrivera pas!
Il faut faire confiance aux dieux, Princesse!
Regardez! LE VOILÀ!
!
A bout de souffle, haletant mais vainqueur, Pharaon revient dans la cour de l'Heb-Sed...
Cette fois, sous les acclamations d'une foule en délire, il gravit l'escalier qui conduit à l'estrade de pierre, et là...
...Dernier acte du rite, il saisit l'arc d'or et lance quatre flèches, vers les quatre points cardinaux, prenant ainsi possession de la terre entière.
Mais cette fois, chacune des flèches atteint son but, clouant sur place, les traîtres qui se sont dissimulés au milieu de la foule, et qui se jettent à terre, pour implorer leur pardon.
Pitié, seigneur!
Seule la dernière flèche est sans pitié.
AAAAAA
DE GIETER
43

MORT AUX PRÊTRES DE MEMPHIS!!
SILENCE!
VENGEANCE!
PUNISSONS LES TRAÎTRES!
Les dieux ont fait justice! Nous ne voulons pas que la haine profane notre jubilé. Mais nous voulons accomplir un geste...
...Relève-toi, homme du delta, aujourd'hui, ta place est à nos côtés. Que tous rendent hommage à ceux qui ont aidé Pharaon à conserver son trône et la paix d'Egypte!
AUJOURD'HUI, IL Y A DEUX PHARAONS!
HOURRA!
LONGUE VIE À PHARAON ET À LA PRINCESSE THÉTI-CHÉRI!!
HOMMAGE À TOI, TAUREAU PUISSANT!
Vive Papyrus et Imhoutep!
Aujourd'hui, il reste de Sakkarah : la pyramide à degrés, quelques vestiges du grand mur d'enceinte, l'entrée, le mur des cobras, la cour Heb-Sed...
On découvre encore, prisonnières des sables, des statues brisées, témoins silencieux de bien des aventures. Certaines aussi étranges que
LA MÉTAMORPHOSE D'IMHOTEP.
fin.
scénario et dessins : L. DE GIETER.
couleurs : COLETTE DE GIETER.
44